CARL GROSE: PLAYS ONE

Carl Grose

PLAYS ONE

Superstition Mountain

Grand Guignol

Horse Piss For Blood

49 Donkeys Hanged

The Kneebone Cadillac

OBERON BOOKS
LONDON

WWW.OBERONBOOKS.COM

For Mandy and Arthur Ray

This collection first published in 2019 by Oberon Books Ltd
521 Caledonian Road, London N7 9RH
Tel: +44 (0) 20 7607 3637 / Fax: +44 (0) 20 7607 3629
e-mail: info@oberonbooks.com
www.oberonbooks.com

A catalogue record for this book is available from the British Library.

PB ISBN: 9781786825674
E ISBN: 9781786825681

10 9 8 7 6 5 4 3 2 1

Contents

Introduction

He begins with a proposition – a sting:

Mark Gunwallow, filthy, haggard, bloodied:

> *"Welcome to the Lost Dutchman's Gold Mine… I'm Mark Gunwallow and I think… I'm about… to… die"*

Or...

A torch flashing in the darkness. A shadowy form, terrified. A voice-over:

> *"'Twas said that the mere sight of the fiend was a sign that terrible things were to befall the world…"*

Or…

Stanley Bray stands alone before us with a noose dangling from a branch:

> *"So. You wanna knaw 'ow to 'ang a donkey?"*

Carl is a deconstructivist – deconstruction in the architectural or filmic sense, nodding to the Coen brothers, Charlie Kaufman and Quentin Tarantino, mixing the romance of American myth-making with a backstory of Cornish not-so-rugged idiosyncrasy.

But first he anchors us in a reality – a time and a place, offers an interruptive event, builds the circumstance, characters and backstory.

It's intriguing, promising, entertaining. We're hooked. We are in the safe hands of a master storyteller, we feel, settling lower into our seats, balancing our metaphorical popcorn on our knees. We will happily suspend our disbelief. Big mistake. Huge.

Carl's first interest is in storytelling. He's good at it. None better.

And our collective rehearsal task has been to find his world, its reaches, its limits – the detail, the plotting, who can live in this world, who can't. 'Never underestimate the effort it takes to tell a story', we say to actors. 'Always know which story you're telling at any one time', we say – and that can be a lot harder than you'd think. He often employs a frame narrative – frame, yes, or frames, a succession of Chinese boxes. Carl's commitment to storytelling can be deceptively tough on our actors (and directors, designers and stage management) and can certainly make your head hurt. But for audiences, it's a delight and seems simplicity itself.

The *Grand Guignol* company specialises in macabre horror stories, delivered with heightened style, but they don't do winking-at-the-audience, look-at-me-doing-melodrama acting. No, they are good actors, of course; a successful, brilliant company, and we must be drawn into their style and believe in their story. Maybe the whole play will be like this. Who knows? *Grand Guignol*'s story begins with 'what sort of a madhouse is this?' The *Guignol* actors' objective is to build controlled dramatic tension and put over their story so vividly that it creates terror and mayhem in their audience. Difficult, but doable. 'Our' actors' objective is to make their own characters' stories so sufficiently vital and engaging that a stylistic contract begins to be agreed between the performers and 'our' audience. A second ball to keep in the air. And then, in the outside world, there's a different kind of mayhem – there's horror, there's a community creating the horror and now there's horror disrupting the community… and a detective story. My head hurts.

That supposedly agreed contract becomes important. Carl's enquiry is often about observation and knowledge itself. Who has it? What to believe? Who to believe? Is this meant to be true? Or are they kidding? The cat of theatrical invention, as in Schrödinger's sardonic experiment, really can exist in some superposition zombie state of being both true and false at the same time. And Carl likes zombies.

And he likes much else - the collective childhood memory stored in our cultural larder. Outlaws, aliens, gumshoes, villains, heroes, superheroes, Mafiosi, murderers, monsters. They're exciting. They're fun. He likes fun.

He begins with real places, real people, real events, real myths, real legends, real truths, real lies, real lives – just as we all do.

For him realities are important and they lay down the framework of the story. What we've said and what we've done, our hopes for the future and our fears make up our identity, our ambitions, who we are. For example, *Le Théâtre du Grand-Guignol* was an enormously successful fringe theatre, which opened in 1897 in the Pigalle district of Paris and specialised in horror plays written by André de Lorde and starring Paula Maxa, whose characters were murdered more than 10,000 times in her illustrious career.

Sarin and VX agents were actually produced at Nancekuke (where *Horse Piss For Blood* is set) as an outpost of the Chemical Defense Establishment at Porton Down, and an underground Control and Reporting Post is still there.

You can still have a great day out at the United Downs Raceway in St Day, where the events of *The Kneebone Cadillac* unfold.

The Lost Dutchman State Park is to be found on the west side of *Superstition Mountain* in Arizona, USA.

You can find Cornwall just across the Tamar.

The plays are rooted in a community – or, more usually, a warring family scratching their heads and living on the fringes of a community – surviving through scrap-metal dealing or double-glazing, farming or theatre. In Cornwall these are the people Carl knows and remembers. Further abroad, the plays maybe become classified as enjoyably idiosyncratic, Cornish absurd. In the US they would simply be screwball English comedy. When they open in the new theatre in Mars Central, as they surely will once Elon Musk gets his shit together, they'll be advertised as earthling or, possibly, tellurian, I daresay.

A sense of community and identity varies by distance and observation as quantum physics had it, just like the harmless electron, surfing a Cornish wave, baffled to hear that they think he's a particle.

But the realities are not narrow, earnest or constrained. His characters can be determinedly dogged, certainly, but also wild, passionate, euphoric, anguished - their situations desperate, sometimes desperately absurd. Their reality is absurd. Absurdity, these days, is our reality.

And the absurdity is heightened by the demands of a rapidly changing society. His stories are laced through with very current themes.

- Masculinity in crisis: in a changing world, the desperation of young men claiming the pre-eminence of ancestral male tradition to counteract a feeling of modern chaos, incompetence and powerlessness. (*Superstition Mountain, The Kneebone Cadillac*)
- A resourceful young woman determined, in a world of male advantage, not to be marginalised or distracted from her objectives (*The Kneebone Cadillac*. Note - *The Kneebone Cadillac* is a reconstructed retelling - almost a parallel universe spin-off - of *Superstition Mountain*, in which three desperate Cornish brothers seek mythic gold in America. In *The Kneebone Cadillac*, the macguffins are still rooted in Americana, but the youngest sibling (and our now revised and emergent hero) is Maddy, a young woman. The plays begin with numerous similarities, but the elements are re-conceived to deliver something very different.)
- The environment exploited by the mendacity of ruthless capitalism. The powerlessness of the 'little man' against corporate wilfulness (*Horse Piss For Blood, 49 Donkeys Hanged*)
- Who controls our communal narratives? Fake news, propaganda and public menace. The creation and manipulation of fear in the community. (*Grand Guignol, Horse Piss For Blood, 49 Donkeys Hanged*)

And with the theme in play, our world established, the hopes and fears suggested… then starts the deconstruction.

He's several steps ahead of the audience all the time, his route map sometimes hiding in plain sight. He wastes nothing. A comic fancy once enjoyed and then dismissed can end up as a pivotal plot twist. He's cunning, he's detailed, he's sly.

Our world will suddenly collide with a seemingly incompatible other. We thought we had set the boundaries to our universe. It turns out not. We thought we had secured the promised contract as to where we were and how it worked. We hadn't read the small print.

You think you're hearing one story, but really he's telling you another. He can start at the end and work backwards or start in the middle and work fore and aft simultaneously. And, as in Schrödinger's tale, one story can simultaneously mean different things.

Like the script, production is invisibly high style. Tarantino sets the bar, or Sergio Leone. Movement is spare, concentrated and studied. A scene may seem to be aimlessly domesticated, but it has a ruthless purpose. Dialogue is spoken and heard – no domestic TV mumbling here. The story must be told, information supplied. Actors use the entire bandwidth of their range with accuracy in the service of the story. Changes are seamless or have a rhythmical purpose. We play with theatrical conventions, shifting the rules of the contract. What kind of a play is this? we ask. We create a world, we mine its depths, we deconstruct it.

Like the White Queen, Carl believes we should be able to believe six impossible things before breakfast. And under his spell, we can.

Enjoy these plays. I do.

Simon Stokes
Director

SUPERSTITION MOUNTAIN

Superstition Mountain was first performed by o-region on 9th September, 2009 at The Drum Theatre, Plymouth.

CAST

Slim Gunwallow	Simon Harvey
Dwayne Gunwallow	Dan Harvey
Mark Gunwallow	Brett Harvey

CREATIVE TEAM

Director	Carl Grose
Producer	Simon Harvey
Set Designer	Laura McKenzie
Costume Designer	Tracey Dawn Stevens
Sound and Music	Wayne Chudley
Lighting Designer	Alex Wardle
Film	Mark Jenkin
Set Construction	Alex Rogers
Publicity / Photography	Olly Berry
Stage Manager / Operator	John Crooks & Simon Ramsden
Production Assistant	Ben Carlin
Programme Design	Natalie Grose
Additional voices	Helen Tiplady & Mark Jenkin
Loan of cowboy boots, Bowie knife & Hank LPs	Ian Grose

Part One

In the darkness, handheld camcorder footage:

An extreme close-up of a young man, MARK GUNWALLOW; filthy, haggard, bloodied, surrounded by darkness.

MARK: *(To camera.)* So. Welcome to Supersition Mountain... and the Lost Dutchman's Gold Mine... That's Slim. E's unconscious. Again. Dwayne's done a runner... Behind me is Elias Bolt, a treasure hunter… e's dead… there's the gold… and there – I dunno if you can see? – are some deadly poisonous rattlesnakes… say 'ello snakes…

Rattlesnakes rattle.

MARK: *(Turning camera on himself.)* And I'm Mark Gunwallow… and I think… I am about… to die –

The image cuts out.

Sound of thunder and continuous rain.

An old granite-built house in St. Day, Cornwall.

The living room is gloomy, sparse, tidy. A small dining table with three chairs. On the table is a biscuit tin, and a jar with a slit made in the lid. There's a few coins in it. At the back is the entrance to the kitchen and the outside world. A few coats hang nearby.

There's another doorway leading upstairs. On the back wall, an old framed sepia photograph of two men standing either side of the entrance to a mine in a harsh desert landscape. Elsewhere, an old cabinet record player, with a stack of country & western records sat proudly on display.

SLIM (30) holds a letter. He studies it with deep concern. SLIM hears someone coming through the kitchen. He slips the letter in his wallet.

Enter MARK (20) from outside, wearing a bright yellow raincoat. He's soaked.

MARK: Sorry I'm late.

SLIM: 'fuck you bin?

MARK: Seth kept me on to clean the pumps.

SLIM: Didn' you tell 'im you ad to go?

MARK: Yeh but you know Seth – e's a twat.

SLIM: Thass yer uncle yer talkin about there.

MARK takes his coat off, flaps the rain off it, hangs it up next to the others, goes to biscuit tin, finds crumbs.

MARK: E's gone downhill, then?

SLIM: See for yourself. Or did ya just pop round for a fuckin biscuit?

Enter DWAYNE (25) from upstairs.

DWAYNE: 'fuck you bin?

SLIM: E's bin workin, Dwayne, leave'm alone.

DWAYNE: Fuckin 'workin'.

SLIM rattles the swear jar in front of DWAYNE.

DWAYNE: Whassis?

SLIM: Swear Jar. Father dun't want no cussin whilst e passes. I said no swearin. Us? You gotta be fuckin jokin. But e was adamant so cough up.

DWAYNE: *(Fishes for a coin, inserts it. To MARK:)* You get my Chinese?

MARK: Didn't 'ave time.

DWAYNE: What the fuck?

The swear jar rattles. DWAYNE fishes, inserts.

DWAYNE: You know I kent be seen on the fuckin streets of St. Day!

Swear jar rattles.

MARK: Oh yeh. I forget. You're a 'wanted man'.

DWAYNE: Pork balls, Mark, thass all I ask for but no you stride past The 'appy Dragon just to fuckin spite me!

Swear jar rattles.

DWAYNE: *(To SLIM.)* I'm fuckin skint!

SLIM: Christ, whassamatter with this family? Daddy's up there dyin. You turn up late and all you'n think about's your empty stomach!

(To MARK.) You better get up there. Say yer farewells.

MARK lingers. SLIM watches him. MARK eventually exits upstairs.

DWAYNE: *(Opens the biscuit tin.)* Fucksake! Never any biscuits in this fuckin house!

DWAYNE goes to the records, sorts through 'em.

SLIM: Whaddid e say to ya?

DWAYNE: Not a lot.

SLIM: No final last words?

DWAYNE: E wants 'ank Williams on.

SLIM: Ere. I'll choose the track.

DWAYNE: E ast me to do it, Slim.

SLIM: Yeh but you dunno.

DWAYNE: I dun't know what?

SLIM: What 'is favorite track is.

DWAYNE: 'course I do now get off –

SLIM: Gimme that 'ank Williams –

DWAYNE: I'm puttin it on.

SLIM: Stop bein so childish.

DWAYNE: Fuck off, you knob-shank!

MARK enters from upstairs, ashen.

SLIM: Let me do it, Dwayne!

MARK: Slim…

DWAYNE: No!

SLIM: I shall hit you in a minute.

MARK: Slim!

The brothers look to MARK.

MARK: E's dead.

The needle on the record player drops. 'You'll Never Get Outta This World Alive' by Hank Williams plays. SLIM comes to, rips the needle off the record.

SLIM: Nice one Dwayne, that was 'ighly appropriate!

DWAYNE: E didn't even get to fuckin hear it!

SLIM: Cus you're a stubborn prick, thass why!

DWAYNE: E wanted me to choose a track! Me! 'is last request!

Beat.

No wonder people keep pissin off round ere.

SLIM: Eh?

DWAYNE: They gotta move to Cardiff or die to get away from you!

SLIM: You apologise for that Dwayne, or there'll be two dead Gunwallows wheeled out of ere tonight!

DWAYNE: Sorry.

SLIM: Can't hear ya!

DWAYNE: I'm sorry, Slim.

SLIM: You better be.

Beat.

Rude!

MARK: Whadda we do now?

SLIM motions for them to go upstairs. One by one, they go.

Father's bedroom.

They gather around the (unseen) body, awkwardly, and speak in hushed tones.

SLIM: Strange seein im like this, so still and quiet –

DWAYNE's mobile goes off.

DWAYNE: *(Turns it off.)* Sorry.

Reverence is regained.

SLIM: Tis like e ain't real. Tis like e's made outta…

DWAYNE: Rubber?

SLIM: Wax. Dwayne. I was gonna say. Like e's made outta wax. Did e say anythin to you, Mark?

MARK: E was gone before I got ere.

DWAYNE: So you coulda got my Chinese?

MARK gives him a look.

MARK: Did e say anythin to you before e…?

SLIM: No. No. Not really. No. E… no.

The doorbell rings, makes 'em all jump.

MARK: Thass the ambulance.

SLIM: Best say our goodbyes.

Beat.

(To MARK.) Gib'm a kiss.

MARK: Eh?

SLIM: This is the last time you'll see 'im in this house. You wun't get another chance. Now kiss your father farewell. *Kiss* 'im.

MARK leans down and kisses father.

DWAYNE: Ugh.

MARK: What?

DWAYNE: Not on the lips, you perv!

Bell rings again.

SLIM: Let em in.

MARK exits the bedroom, heads downstairs to the kitchen. DWAYNE's mobile goes off again.

DWAYNE: Shit!

SLIM: Just answer the thing, will ya?

DWAYNE exits the bedroom.

DWAYNE: *(Answers it, quiet.)* O'right Deaks howzit goin mate? Yeh sorry, tonight's bin a bit mad. Me dad's just died. Deacon mate, chillax. I'll find it – ello? Deaks? Fuck.

SLIM: We're on our own now brother. We're on our own.

Living room. Later.

DWAYNE sits smoking, watching 'True Grit' in the dark.

MARK enters from the kitchen with a cup of tea.

MARK: 'True Grit'?

DWAYNE: Put it on for Dad outta respect.

MARK: How many times have we seen this?

MARK & DWAYNE: 'This is a rat writ writ for a rat…'

(Mimes firing a gun.) Phoff!

MARK: That was clever, bringin up Cardiff.

DWAYNE: I like pushin 'is buttons.

MARK: Thought e was gonna knock you through the wall.

DWAYNE: As if. 'sides, e 'its like a fanny anyhow.

DWAYNE turns off TV with a remote.

DWAYNE: Fuckin endless rain… Right. I'm goin yard.

MARK: It's two in the mornin.

DWAYNE: Deacon phoned. I gotta find the drugs I lost or re-pay the money by tomorra.

MARK: Scoured the place once already.

DWAYNE: I know, but if I dun't find 'em the Manchester Crew'll come down and serve me my bodger on a silver plate. Hence the late night treasure hunt. I'm takin your coat. Wish me luck.

Exit DWAYNE in MARK's yellow raincoat.

MARK: Good luck. You'll fuckin need it.

He fishes and puts a coin in the jar, and exits upstairs.

Next morning.

Hank Williams plays on the record player. SLIM enters from the kitchen in a dressing gown and pants, mug of tea in his hand. He sorts through the post. One of is an ominous-looking brown envelope – the kind you get from the Inland Revenue. He opens it. Squints. Finds his glasses, and reads.

SLIM: Aw fuck. Fuck. Aww, fuckin 'ell. No. You fuckin –

SLIM grabs his mobile and furiously dials a number on the revenue letter.

SLIM: Fuckers. Fuckin. Fuck.

(Cannot contain it.) Fuck you!!!

SLIM smashes his mobile phone on the table til it breaks. Enter MARK from upstairs with an old suit case. SLIM sees MARK, turns the music off, hides the letter in the record player.

MARK: O'right?

SLIM: O'right?

MARK: What was all that?

SLIM: Altercation with the Inland Revenue. Nuthin for you to worry about.

MARK: Wanna talk about it?

SLIM: No I fuckin don't. Gotta quid?

MARK fishes one out, hands it him. SLIM puts it in the jar.

SLIM: Fuck.

MARK: Trawled through Dad's stuff like you ast. Amazin whass ere. Old letters, school photos, 'is Bowie knife –

MARK produces items from the case – one of which is a strange clay shape with a triangular hole in the centre, and what appears to be Native American markings (hereafter known as 'the Peralta Stone')... and a small leather-bound book brimming with faded pages packed with etchings... (hereafter known as 'The Diary')... an old tobacco tin which rattles when SLIM shakes it. SLIM picks up the Peralta Stone.

SLIM: Hey. 'member this?

MARK: No.

SLIM gives him a look, and leafs through the diary.

MARK: Check this, look.

MARK pulls out a coat from the case – a big worn leather jacket.

SLIM: Thass 'is horse-ridin coat.

MARK: Dad didn' ride 'orses.

SLIM: E wore it watchin John Wayne on the telly ride 'em. Thass as close to 'orse as e'd like to get.

SLIM takes off his dressing gown, and puts it on. MARK takes a battered cowboy hat from the box, frisbees it to SLIM.

SLIM: E ad all the gear, o'right.

SLIM dons the hat. Enter DWAYNE, wired and looking like shit.

DWAYNE: Dad?!

SLIM turns.

DWAYNE: Fuck me, I thought e was back.

MARK: Find the missin drugs?

DWAYNE: Stashed 'em in one of the scrap skips. Kent remember which one.

SLIM: Taffy's put the scrap through the crusher.

DWAYNE: What? But e should only crush skip metal come the end of the week!

SLIM: Taffy can crush what e pissin well likes. There's no rhyme nor reason to Taffy. What e crush and when e crush is Taffy's business.

DWAYNE: Yeh well Taffy's a fuckin prick-ass. E's just signed my death warrant.

MARK and SLIM laugh at him.

DWAYNE: This is serious shit, Slim!

SLIM: There's nuthin more serious than arrangin Daddy's burial day so siddown and shuddap. I gotta phone Webb the undertaker. Give us yer mobile.

DWAYNE: I ab'm got it on me.

DWAYNE's mobile goes off.

SLIM: You pratt. Give it ere.

MARK: Borrow mine.

MARK gives SLIM his mobile. DWAYNE takes out his mobile, and looks at it.

DWAYNE: *(Genuine fear.)* Shit. Deacon.

He sits on it.

SLIM: Thought e was yer mate.

DWAYNE: Deacon? E is. E's a good man.

MARK: Izze fuck. Anyone oo sells 'orse tranquiliser to the Brownies ain't a good man.

SLIM: Funeral's Thursday. If you wanna make yourself useful phone around, let everyone know.

DWAYNE: What am I gonna do?

SLIM: If the old man was in his grave e'd be… in it… turnin.

SLIM exits to kitchen.

DWAYNE: Whass all this shit?

MARK: Dad's personal effects.

DWAYNE: Can we sell any of it?

MARK: Sentimental value only.

DWAYNE: *(An epiphany.)* Wait. The Will. E woulda left us the yard in The Will, right?

SLIM: *(Off.)* Fuck!

Enter SLIM with MARK's mobile – in his other hand is the tobacco tin that rattles.

SLIM: Six 'undred quid headstone cost. I told'n to piss off.

MARK: So we ain't gonna 'ave one?

SLIM: 'course we're gonna 'ave one! E's only dead once. It's oo's gonna pay for it's the fucker.

DWAYNE: Kent the business pay for it?

SLIM: I dunno if you noticed but it ain't exactly Mercedes-fuckin-Benz out there.

DWAYNE: Just suggestin Slim. We're all of us strapped so I thought the business or The Will maybe…

SLIM: The Will what maybe?

MARK: God's sake Dwayne e only died last night.

DWAYNE: I'm des'prate. What e think, Slim? See what the old man left us?

SLIM: I'll talk to the solicitors tomorra.

The mobile in SLIM's hand rings. Without thinking, he answers it.

SLIM: Ello? Aw. Uh. No. 'ang on.

(To MARK.) Tina.

MARK: I'll take it outside.

MARK takes the phone.

MARK: You seen my yellow coat?

DWAYNE: No.

MARK: You –

SLIM: Ere.

SLIM takes off the riding coat and throws it to MARK.

MARK: Cheers.

SLIM: Hey, I'm uh. I'm cookin a chicken tonight. Be ere for seb'm sharp.

MARK and DWAYNE catch eyes.

MARK: *(To phone, cute.)* 'elloooo.

Exit MARK.

SLIM: You phone around yet?

DWAYNE: I'm doin it now! Christsake.

SLIM: Dwayne. Taffy'd stack the weeks' crusher blocks by the wheel loader. You could check whass there, crack the bastards open maybe find what yer lookin for?

DWAYNE exits to kitchen with phone. SLIM pulls the tax demand out of the record player, flattens it, reads it again. Slumps.

SLIM: *(To record player.)* Why didn' you tell me, Daddy? Why didn't you tell me you never paid no tax? I'da never sent the year's receipts in.

Beat.

It is a lot, yeh! Thirty years' back payment thank you very much. Fuckers. 'scuse my language, Daddy, but we're in the shit. I dunno. I dunno what to do about it. I dunno what to do 'bout Dwayne. I dunno what to do about yer headstone. And I dunno how to tell Mark, Daddy. I just dunno. I'm gettin a chicken in tonight so we'll see how things turn out...

SLIM's attention falls to the tobacco tin. He shakes it, rattles it, opens it carefully. Inside, something glimmers.

SLIM: Well, would ya look at that.

Living room. That night.

MARK has the diary and flicks through it. Enter SLIM from kitchen in a bright, flowery apron.

SLIM: That diary was Great Grandma Julia's. It's all in there.

MARK: What is?

SLIM: How to get to Superstition Mountain –

MARK: *(With a laugh.)* Aww God.

SLIM: And locate The Lost Dutchman's Gold Mine.

MARK: How many times did we hafto hear that story?

SLIM: Everything you need to know.

MARK: What, like how to climb Weaver's Needle? And what to do with the Peralta Stone when you finally get to the top?

SLIM: Just like the old man usta tell us. Where's Dwayne?

MARK: Out there takin them scrap blocks apart. Shall I go fetch 'im?

SLIM: Don't bother. E's keepin a low profile.

MARK: But if we're havin chicken –

SLIM: They was all outta chicken. But you like pizza, don't ya Mark?

Exit SLIM.

SLIM: *(Off.)* Fuck.

Enter SLIM with a smouldering pizza on a baking tray.

SLIM: Bit burnt.

He snaps the pizza in two and chucks each half on a plate. They attempt to eat. After a while:

SLIM: Not quite the same is it?

MARK: What, now that Dad's gone?

SLIM: Pizza insteada chicken.

MARK: No. It ain't quite the same.

MARK: Slim?

SLIM: Mm?

MARK: Tell us about Superstition Mountain? Tell us the story like Dad usta?

SLIM: *(Taken aback, after a while.)* O'right.

He stands, dons the cowboy hat, looks to the photograph on the wall.

SLIM: You see this ere photograph?

MARK: Like Dad, yeh.

SLIM: There's two men ere either side the entrance to a mine. One on the right is Jacob Waltz. The man on the left is Tobias Gunwallow, our great grandfather! Tobias Gunwallow was a miner. Left for America round 1897. E braved yellow fever and the freezin winters of Wisconsin before runnin into Waltz in Arizona. Jacob Waltz was a connivin Dutchman born privy to knowledge of a motherlode in the Superstition Mountains, but e couldn' work it alone. They became equal partners. Waltz ad a small amount of money to kick-start the dig but Tobias ad the skill and knowhow required to mine it. The first batch of ore they brung up –

SLIM & MARK: Weighed in at a thousand dollars a ton!

SLIM: They'd hit bonanza! But had to keep their newfound fortune a secret for fear of word gettin out. They hid the pure gold ore there in the mine itself.

MARK: Then they met Great Grandma Julia!

SLIM: 'ass right, Mark. Julia Thomas owned a chicken farm in Phoenix. The story goes both men fell for 'er in an instant! The woman had to choose, and she chose to marry Tobias Gunwallow.

MARK: Big mistake.

SLIM: She fast bore him a son –

MARK: Grandpa Raymond.

SLIM: With Jacob spurned, a wedge was driven between the two men. The partnership turned sour. Julia told em: Settle your differences or never come back. The boys disappeared into The Superstitions but neither was heard from again. There all knowledge of the mine woulda bin lost forever but for Julia! She wrote down every scrap of information, every hint of a direction, every clue to the secret whereabouts of the lost mine, and she put it all down in this diary. Years later, after Julia passed away, Granddad Raymond returned from America and brung the precious book with 'im. Along with trinkets and memories, and this very photograph.

The photograph returns to normal.

MARK: That was like Dad, o'right.

MARK crunches into a carbonized pizza. SLIM stiffens, looks to the record player, slowly opens his wallet, extracts the letter and offers it to MARK.

SLIM: *(Hand trembling.)* Mark.

MARK: What is it?

SLIM: Take it.

MARK reaches for it. SLIM recoils. SLIM offers it. MARK tries again. SLIM recoils, and puts the letter back in his wallet.

SLIM: I kent.

MARK: Why?

SLIM: No chicken.

MARK: What is it?

SLIM: S'fer another time.

SLIM exits to kitchen.

MARK: Slim?

Follows him out.

Slim?

The next day.

DWAYNE is at the table with a big block of crushed metal. He frantically chips away at it with a screwdriver. Enter MARK with a camcorder.

MARK: And ere we find a sorry sight. The last act of a desperate man. Hangin by 'is fingernails, above the bottomless abyss.

DWAYNE: Get fucked.

MARK: Found yer drugs?

DWAYNE swipes at the camera.

MARK: Careful! T'idn mine!

Beat.

Hey, you know when Slim says I'll get a chicken in, and your ass clenches cus you know e's gonna announce summin big?

DWAYNE: Yeh, like when e and Carole was gonna get married, e got a chicken in. And when Carole told us she was pregnant wi' Maddy, they got a chicken in.

MARK: Yeh. Well, e never announced nuthin. It was like… e was gonna… but e didn't.

DWAYNE: Well, whaddaya expect wi' pizza? It's gotta be chicken or nuthin if an announcement's to be made.

(Re: metal block.) Oh, this is fuckin useless!

Enter SLIM from outside in stetson and riding coat.

SLIM: I spoke to Sandy Sutton the solicitors.

DWAYNE: And?

SLIM: Father ad strict instructions regardin 'is send-off. E wants to be laid out in the Caddilac, in his ridin jacket and stetson, surrounded by 'is 'ank Williams collection… and then put through the crusher.

They all look to the metal block.

DWAYNE: I got no problem wi' that. What about the yard? Did e leave us the yard, Slim?

MARK: *I* gotta problem with Dad going through the crusher.

SLIM: It was the man's final wish, Mark.

MARK: It's illegal surely. 'sides Taffy would never –

SLIM: E spoke to Taffy. Taffy's 'appy to 'it the button.

DWAYNE: Slim? The yard? Did e leave it to us?

SLIM: Sorted the damn headstone out now an' all.

MARK: We kent scrap the Caddy. S'worth a bob or two.

SLIM: I know. I was conceived in that car.

DWAYNE: Cus if e split the yard between us then I wanna sell my share to you and Mark, pay off the Manchester Crew –

SLIM: There is no yard!

DWAYNE: Eh?

SLIM: E left it to us three ways but –

Beat.

I balls'd it up.

DWAYNE: What e talkin about?

SLIM: I discovered the other day Dad never paid a penny of tax in 'is life. He was off all records 'til I took over the office. I did the accounts for the first time ever. Sent 'em off. They's fed into some computer up Bradford and set alarm bells ringin.

MARK: 'ow much do we owe?

SLIM: Eighty one thousand seven 'undred and fifty two pound… n'forty nine pence.

Stunned silence.

DWAYNE: We ain't got that kinda money.

SLIM: So what'll they take instead?

DWAYNE: *(Realising.)* Fuck. But I need my share of the business! I'm countin on that to sell to you and Mark! Aw, nice one, Slim.

SLIM: Yeh, blame me! It's all my fault!

MARK: Ain't your fault, Slim, it's Dad's.

SLIM: What did you say?

MARK: You did what was right. It's 'is negligence we're havin to deal with.

SLIM: How dare you.

MARK: Well, is it any wonder that Mum –

SLIM whacks MARK.

SLIM: *(To MARK.)* You keep your mouth shut on things you know nuthin about. I'm to blame for this mess, not Daddy. Got it?

SLIM exits outside. MARK exits upstairs with camcorder. DWAYNE takes up the screw-driver and starts to frantically chip away again.

DWAYNE: I am so dead.

Funeral Service.

SLIM addresses the congregation. DWAYNE and MARK, in black jackets, stand on either side.

SLIM: *(To congregation.)* I thought it best I say a few words bein as now I am head a the family.

(Produces a speech on a scrap of paper.) The Gunwallows 'ave always stood strong in the face of adversity. Great Grandfather Tobias did it diggin gold in Arizona. Granddad Raymond did it too, with copper, but perhaps none more… did it more… than Abel Gunwallow and his United Downs Scrap Metal Empire. With it, e eked an honest livin, providin for his family when times got 'ard. And 'ard they did get… times. But e kept on whistlin 'is favorite 'ank Williams tune, and e kept on fuckin smilin!

MARK winces.

SLIM: E was a man of high principle. E operated above the law and e bowed to no one. Rest assured, his sons will carry on that family tradition. We 'ave lost a great St. Day man this week. Abel Gunwallow. Father. Legend. Hero… Let us honour 'is memory in song.

Organ music plays.

BROTHERS: *(Sing, badly.)*
Dust to dust, the mortal dies,
Both the foolish and the wise

None forever can remain,
Each must leave his horded gain.
Yet within their heart they say
That their houses are for aye,
That their dwelling places grand
Shall for generations stand…

MARK: *(Under his breath.)* Well that was lovely.

Church yard.

They tremble and shake as the coffin is lowered into the ground.

DWAYNE: Jesus Christ!

SLIM: Stop fuckin swearin!

MARK: E's heavy!

DWAYNE: It's all them 'ank Williams records.

MARK: Maybe we shoulda put 'im through the crusher!

DWAYNE: Too late now!

SLIM: Take the tension!

DWAYNE: Keep it even, Mark!

MARK: Why's my end shorter'n everyone else?

DWAYNE: Lower im down, ya prick!

MARK: I can't! There's no more strap!

SLIM: Dun't let go e's only two foot down!

MARK: I can't – I – *fuck* – I'm goin in. I'm goin in –

MARK is pulled headfirst into the open grave.

DWAYNE: *(Cracks up.)* Weak.

Pub.

SLIM and DWAYNE stand with pints while a Hank Williams songs play quietly throughout: 'Thy Burdens Are Greater Than Mine', 'My Son Calls Another Man Daddy' and 'I Won't Be Home No More'.

DWAYNE: Good turnout.

SLIM: It's a shit turnout. You phone around like I ast?

DWAYNE: Yeh.

SLIM: Did ya?

DWAYNE: Yes.

SLIM: So why's no one ere?

DWAYNE: Taffy's come. Auntie Joy's turned up. Cousin Clyde. Phyllis and the boys come all the way from Bude. No one from mother's side.

SLIM: I wadn't expectin them.

DWAYNE: Terry Duff's showed 'is face.

SLIM: Terry's only ere cus there's free cocktail pasties. Terry dun't count. Terry's a sneaky, slimy bastard.

SLIM & DWAYNE: *(Raising glasses.)* O'right Terr?

DWAYNE: I was gonna ring Carole about the funeral…

SLIM: What the 'ell for?

DWAYNE: She thought the world of Dad.

SLIM: Fuh!

DWAYNE: I can call 'er if ya want? Let 'er know whass happened?

SLIM: No. I dun't 'want'.

DWAYNE: Thought you'd want me tellin her for yer daughter's sake?

SLIM: Maddy is two, Dwayne. All she knows is nappy and boob! She won't remember oo father is. She prob'ly dun't remember oo I fuckin am.

DWAYNE: 'course she does.

Beat.

So you *dun't* want me to call 'er?

SLIM: Get it through your thick head. I *dun't* want ya to phone Carole. That bitch made 'er choice.

SLIM slopes off.

DWAYNE: Furry muff.

Enter MARK with a plaster on his forehead.

MARK: Auntie Joy's well pissed.

DWAYNE: Auntie Joy's a dickhead.

MARK: Why are we even ere? Dad hated this place.

DWAYNE: S'generous of Uncle Seth to let us come back.

(Calling down the bar, glass raised.) Cheers Uncle Seth!

MARK: *(Staring at Uncle Seth.)* Dad put up with his brother but e never liked im.

DWAYNE: I can relate to that.

MARK: I never liked 'im either. E's always gimme the creeps. Uncle Seth.

DWAYNE: E's bendin Slim's ear about summin.

MARK: Rather Slim thun me.

DWAYNE: *(Sees someone.)* Fuck.

MARK: What?

DWAYNE: Deacon. You ab'm seen me, right?

DWAYNE ducks and exits. SLIM, getting pissed now, joins MARK.

SLIM: *(Arm around MARK.)* Is this all father amounted to? Is this the tribute e deserves?

MARK: I'm glad we thought twice 'bout puttin 'im through the crusher.

SLIM: It was 'is last wish and we completely ignored it.

MARK: It wadn't right, Slim.

SLIM: E loved that car. Wanted to merge with it. Flesh and metal. Dashboard and bone. But we put 'im in the ground to rot.

MARK: You can't always get what you want.

SLIM looks at him sternly, holds out the letter.

SLIM: *(Hand trembling.)* Mark.

MARK: Not this again?

SLIM: Yeh.

MARK goes to take it. SLIM recoils. He offers it again. MARK goes to take it. Recoils.

SLIM: Maybe another time, eh?

MARK: I'm gonna go talk to uhh… yeh.

MARK wanders off.

SLIM: Yeeeeeh.

SLIM knocks back his drink, catches eyes with someone.

SLIM: O'right Terry?

Living room.

Three hours later. In the dark, DWAYNE lays on the kitchen table, his nose pouring blood. Enter MARK from outside.

MARK: Dwayne?

DWAYNE: What?

MARK: It's Slim. E kicked off at kickin out time.

DWAYNE: Oo'd e kick off on?

MARK: Terry Duff. Give us a hand? E's fucked.

Enter SLIM staggering in behind MARK.

SLIM: I'm fine.

MARK switches the light on to reveal both DWAYNE and SLIM bruised, torn and bloody.

MARK: Christ. Not you as well?

DWAYNE: Manchester Crew caught up wimme.

SLIM: Bastards.

DWAYNE: Whaddid Terry do to provoke ya?

MARK: E made the mistake of askin after Carole.

MARK exits to kitchen.

SLIM: It suddenly became clear. Terry Duff was the one ad the scene wi' Carole.

DWAYNE: Yeh?

SLIM: I said 'You the bloke ad the affair wi' my wife?' Terry said no so I went for 'im.

DWAYNE: Didn't e protest?

Enter MARK with tea towels, bowl of water.

MARK: Hard to when you got no teeth.

He darts around dabbing their wounds, wipes the blood away.

DWAYNE: Serves Terry right, shaggin Carole.

SLIM: Precisely, brother. Serves 'im right! To commit the sin of adultery!

DWAYNE: Unforgivable.

SLIM: Ha. Finally sussed oo the fucker was wrecked my marriage! Niggled me for months that 'as.

DWAYNE: Terry Duff. Brought to justice. Thass great, bro. Wish I'd bin there to see it.

MARK: It was not 'great'. The bloke's face was hangin off.

SLIM: I got it out me system. I'm fine now.

MARK: Tell that to the judge.

SLIM: And you?

DWAYNE: Got jumped outside the pub. Six or seven of 'em. I put up a good fuckin fight though, Slim!

SLIM: You've ad yer beating. You've learnt yer lesson now.

DWAYNE: I still gotta find the money.

SLIM: Eh?

DWAYNE: This is a gentle warnin. Next time, you'll hafta scrape me out the bottom of Wheal Maid or drag my bloated body outta Wellington Dam.

SLIM: Wellington Dam's three foot deep, y'fairy.

DWAYNE: A full-sized man can drown in a teaspoon of water, Slim!

SLIM: They're serious then, these Mancunians?

MARK: How much you owe?

DWAYNE: Sixteen.

MARK: 'undred?

DWAYNE shakes his head.

SLIM: You stoopid bleddy sod.

DWAYNE: Oo's the stoopid one? If you adn' fucked the yard up with the tax-man I wouldn't be in this mess!

SLIM goes for him.

DWAYNE: Sorry, Slim!

DWAYNE sits at the table, gets out his bag of grass and starts to roll a joint.

SLIM: Thass it! Roll a-bleddy-nother one!

DWAYNE: It relieves the burdens of everyday existence.

SLIM: Fuck you know about burdens?

MARK: How long you got to find the money?

DWAYNE: Three days.

SLIM: Eighty-one grand to the revenue. Plus sixteen to the drug lords. Thass almost 'undred K.

MARK: Nice goin, boys.

DWAYNE: Oh fuck you, you Goody-fuckin-Two-Shoes! You bin taken care of all yer life! You've never known shit like this!

SLIM: Dwayne.

DWAYNE: Well!

MARK: Thass cus I dun't try'n earn a livin dealin drugs thass why.

DWAYNE: *(Squaring up.)* How proud you must be. Daddy's fuckin fav'rite.

They start to fight –

SLIM: Thass enuff!

MARK: I'm goin bed.

DWAYNE goes for MARK again.

SLIM: Wait! Wait!

(Breaking them up.) Look at us, cowerin and squabblin in our own 'ouse. Father wouldn't stand for this. No Gunwallow would.

DWAYNE: It ain't like the good old days, Slim.

SLIM: But the good old days could 'elp us out Dwayne. Look, I bin thinkin… I've ad this… daft idea. Hear me out, boys… Siddown. What would ya think to headin out to Arizona, find this gold mine? The Lost Dutchman's. Superstition Mountain. Locate that hidden fortune stashed away by Great-Granddad Tobias. Pay back our debts. Live happy lives. What d'ya reckon?

MARK: Superstition Mountain?

SLIM: Yeh.

MARK: Go to Superstition Mountain?

SLIM: Yeh.

MARK: In Arizona?

SLIM: Yep.

MARK: To find this lost gold mine?

SLIM: Yeh.

MARK: You're off your head.

SLIM: Dwayne?

DWAYNE: I'll go. Sounds brilliant.

MARK: But it dun't exist.

SLIM: Yes it does.

MARK: It's just one of Dad's stories.

SLIM: It ain't. It's real. And the proof's right ere in front of us! Thass Tobias Gunwallow standin outside the damn mine! Great Grandma Julia's diary holds the key. Information. Clues. Directions. It's all in this old diary, and in the stories father told us! Our heads are full of it!

MARK: Dad was full of it.

SLIM: Hey.

MARK: If e knew the secret location to a gold mine 'ow come e never went after it?

SLIM: Guess we'll never know. But e spoke to me about it on 'is damn deathbed!

MARK: Did e?

SLIM: This is the answer to our prayers! It's out there. All we gotta do is find it.

MARK: But there idn gonna be any –

SLIM: Gold?

MARK: No.

SLIM: No?

SLIM produces the old tobacco tin.

SLIM: I found this in 'is possessions. A gift from Grandpa Raymond. Feast yer eyes, brothers! Feast yer eyes!

He opens it. SLIM picks it up between finger and thumb.

DWAYNE: Looka that! Gold!

MARK: It's a speck!

SLIM: Thass just a taster! So. Oo's wimme?

DWAYNE: Let's do it! Let's find the gold!

SLIM: Good, Dwayne. Baby Sister?

MARK: No.

SLIM: Eh?

MARK: I kent just up-sticks and go to Arizona. I got things to take care of ere.

SLIM: Like what?

MARK: Like… Tina.

DWAYNE: Tina? Polkinghorne?

SLIM: She'll still be ere when you get back.

MARK: She needs my 'elp.

SLIM: Whass wrong with 'er?

DWAYNE: Whass right with 'er?

MARK: Shut yer trap.

DWAYNE: Why she need 'elp?

MARK: Because.

SLIM: Because what?

MARK: S'personal, Slim.

SLIM: Out with it.

MARK: She's pregnant.

SLIM: Aw.

DWAYNE: My.

SLIM: God!

MARK: I'm warnin you, Dwayne.

DWAYNE: *(Pissing himself.)* You poked Polkinghorne?

SLIM: This is not good.

DWAYNE: You pumped pongy Polkingwhore?

SLIM: Just drops it into conversation –

MARK: Well how'd ya want me to tell ya?

SLIM: Do it properly, son, like father taught ya! Get a chicken in!

MARK: I never wanted to tell ya in the first place.

SLIM: Yer comin to Arizona!

MARK: I'm not.

SLIM: You'll need money to support the child!

DWAYNE: You parked yer pleasure pole in 'er pork-port?

MARK: Yeh well, least I dun't drive the women I sleep with gay.

DWAYNE freezes.

DWAYNE: Say that again?

MARK: You heard.

DWAYNE: Nah. Please repeat.

MARK: At least I don't drive the women I sleep with gay.

DWAYNE: Grow up.

MARK: Hit a nerve, have I?

DWAYNE: S'bullshit.

MARK: Yeh?

DWAYNE: Yeh.

MARK: That last one you ad –

DWAYNE: Michelle.

MARK: One night wi' you and she was battin for the other team, I heard.

DWAYNE: She shacked up with a lesbo. That dun't necessarily make 'er a lesbo, do it?

MARK: I dunno. Does it?

DWAYNE: No. It dun't. Now get outta my face, you Pampers-buyin prick.

MARK: But Dwayne, mate. First time's a fluke. It's just… outta the past three women you bin with, this is the third one gone gay on ya.

SLIM: Dwayne? Is this true?

MARK raises his eyebrows: well?

DWAYNE: You little fuckin shit.

DWAYNE flies at MARK who darts out the way. SLIM separates 'em.

DWAYNE: I'm glad e ain't goin Arizona! Means we can split the gold 'alf 'alf. I'm goin bed. Prick-ass.

Exit DWAYNE upstairs.

SLIM: Now look what ya done!

MARK: E started it!

SLIM: Right. Get yer shit together. Tomorra you'll tell Tina you're goin to Arizona.

MARK: No!

SLIM: Yer goin!

MARK: I'm not goin.

Photo booth.

SLIM sits. The flash goes off four times.

Living room.

MARK: *(On mobile.)* Sorry Uncle Seth, I'm on my way.

(Hangs up.) Cock.

(Shouting upstairs.) You got that fiver you owe me?

DWAYNE: *(From upstairs.)* I'm not talkin to you.

MARK: You dun't hafta talk to me, Dwayne, you just hafta pay me back.

Silence.

MARK: Dwayne? I need bus fare. I'm late for work.

DWAYNE: You'll get nuthin outta me.

MARK: You kent stay in a sulk forever.

DWAYNE: I fuckin can.

MARK makes to go, sees the Swear Jar, checks it for money, thinks about breaking it open, thinks better of it. MARK heads for the door. SLIM appears from nowhere, barring his way.

SLIM: Look. I respect your decision to wanna stay ere and if you dun't wanna go, thass fine – but you are goin.

MARK: I'm not goin.

SLIM: E told me on 'is damned deathbed.

MARK: Told you what?

SLIM: To go! 'Go,' e said (with his last breath). 'Go. Take the trip, Slim. Take the boys. Find that gold whass so rightfully ours.' The gold I bin talkin about all me life!'

MARK: E said all that?

SLIM: I dunno about you but I kent ignore the last wish of a dyin man.

MARK: I'm late.

SLIM: You're goin.

MARK: I'm not goin.

Exit MARK, in a rush.

SLIM: *(To record player.)* I'm tryin, Daddy. I'm tryin. But e's s'damn stubborn.

A mobile rings. SLIM finds it on the record player. He dashes to the door.

SLIM: Mark?

(He weighs the phone in his hand, brews an idea, answers the phone.) 'lo Tina. Mark's brother Slim ere. O'right? It appears e left it at 'ome. Mm. Pregnant, then? Listen. Sounds to me like you ab'm told my little brother the full story. Yes I know. 'course I know. I'm a Gunwallow. E's workin at the pub. You'd best tell 'im today. Or I will. There, there, dear.

(Hangs up, to record player.) That oughta do it, Daddy.

(Shouts.) Dwayne?

Enter DWAYNE from upstairs.

DWAYNE: What?

SLIM: Post office. Pronto!

Photo booth.

DWAYNE sits, poses. The flash fires three times. DWAYNE moves. A fourth flash catches him out.

Living room.

Hours later. DWAYNE eats a packet of Quavers. SLIM paces. His ears prick up when he hears MARK enter. MARK looks gutted.

SLIM: O'right?

MARK: Not really, no.

SLIM: Why? Whass happened?

MARK: Me and Tina're finished.

SLIM: Oh?

MARK: Just found out the baby ain't mine.

DWAYNE: Aw.

(Offers the packet.) Quaver?

SLIM: She say oo the daddy was?

MARK: I dun't wanna talk about it.

MARK goes upstairs. SLIM watches him go. He looks at DWAYNE. DWAYNE solemnly nods. SLIM follows MARK up.

MARK's bedroom.

MARK's curled up in bed. SLIM's face appears in a crack of light.

SLIM: Mark? You asleep?

MARK: Yes.

Pause.

SLIM: Yer goin.

Pause.

Yer goin.

Pause.

Yer go–

MARK: O'right. I'm goin.

SLIM smiles, retreats into shadow.

Downstairs, DWAYNE smiles, and eats a Quaver.

Photo booth.

MARK plonks himself down, miserable. FLASH!!! (x4)

Living room.

Days later. Items for packing everywhere, rucksacks, etc. Enter MARK from upstairs.

MARK: We got our plane fare!

SLIM: You sold the Cadillac?

MARK: Ebay.

SLIM: Thass that then. We're off! Oo bought it?

MARK: Some goth rocker called Glen.

SLIM: Christ.

MARK: E's gonna convert it into a mobile discotheque.

SLIM: Thank God Daddy's dead. E'd shit kittens if e knew we'd gone against 'is will. Sellin 'is beloved Cadillac. Family heirloom that is. I was conceived in that car!

MARK: Only rottin in the garridge.

SLIM: So whass the plan?

MARK: Drive to Mether Tydvil. Deliver the Caddy to goth rocker Glen. E'll pay us in cash. Then we get train to Newport, Gwent.

SLIM: Wha' for?

MARK: None of us 'ave passports.

SLIM: No.

MARK: It takes four to six weeks to process 'em by post.

SLIM: Oh for fuc –

MARK: Or we head to our nearest branch office and fast-track 'em there and then.

SLIM: Which is Newport, Gwent.

MARK: It is.

SLIM: Wales.

MARK: Yes.

SLIM: I might run into Carole…

MARK: Chances are slim, Slim.

SLIM: Wales. Why does it hafto be Wales? It's almost like the old man's testin me…

MARK: Ya know, it wouldn't be 'ard to stop off and see Maddy if ya wanted?

SLIM: I couldn't just turn up.

MARK: No. You'd hafto ring Carole first.

SLIM: Ring Carole? Are you outta your fuckin –

MARK: Slim. As yer brother and fellow traveller I just wanna say… you gotta reign yer temper in.

SLIM: What?!

MARK: We can't go to another country or be in a confined space such as an airplane with you bein so… hot-headed.

SLIM: *'ot-'eaded?* And how do you propose I control the rage within me?

MARK: Yoga?

SLIM stares at him.

MARK: Or count back from ten, or take a deep breath, say a little rhyme, anything. You can't kick someone's face in just cus they mention Carole.

SLIM: I'll see what I can do.

SLIM clips a bum-bag round his waist, and transfers the contents of his wallet in it, including (we see) the letter. MARK has the camcorder out and does a test shoot on SLIM.

MARK: Where'd ya get yer bum-bag?

SLIM: These're de rigueur in the States. Plus I saw on telly there's a lotta muggers out there. It wun't be like St. Day, boy.

MARK: I bloody hope not.

SLIM: *(Sees he's being filmed.)* Hey, what ya doin?

MARK: I'm gonna document the journey for my end of term project. A cultural study of a modern Cornish family in financial dire straits.

SLIM: You'n film us findin the gold.

MARK: *(Packing camcorder away in bag.)* Yeeeh. Maybe.

Enter DWAYNE, breathless, with MARK's yellow raincoat.

DWAYNE: Let's get the fuck out of ere!

Beat.

Nice bum-bag.

SLIM: Where's your fuckin bags?

DWAYNE: I travel light.

SLIM: Since when?

DWAYNE: Since the Manchester Crew burnt me caravan down.

MARK: What?

DWAYNE: They're closin in. Let's go.

SLIM: You gotta take summin to Arizona. Kent just ruck up in jeans and t-shirt!

MARK: Guide book says it's cold in the desert at night.

DWAYNE: I got me coat.

MARK: Which is mine.

MARK takes it back off him and puts it on.

DWAYNE: C'on. Let's piss off.

SLIM: We got everything?

DWAYNE: Dun't forget the plane tickets.

MARK: We ain't got 'em yet. We gotta sell the Caddy first.

DWAYNE: Oo we sellin the Caddy to?

SLIM: Some goth rocker called Glen.

DWAYNE: You kent sell that car to someone called Glen! Thass a 1953 Cadillac Eldorado. Dad's pride and joy. Took 'im years to restore. Plus, it's a family heirloom. I was conceived in that car!

SLIM: That was me, ya pratt.

DWAYNE: Was it?

SLIM: You was Redruth Cinema, remember?

DWAYNE shrugs.

SLIM: Wait. Before we go...

SLIM drags Daddy's suitcase out, opens it.

SLIM: Father would want us to take these with us. Gather round.

(To DWAYNE.) To you e bequeaths his ring.

DWAYNE: What ring?

SLIM: 'is Masonic ring.

SLIM hands it to DWAYNE.

DWAYNE: Wicked.

SLIM: It has great sentimental value.

DWAYNE: It's got fuck-all value. E wadn't even in the pissin Masons!

SLIM: It gets ya free parkin up Truro so like it or lump it.

DWAYNE: Whadda you get?

SLIM produces a large ornamental knife from the case, and adopts a masculine stance.

SLIM: I got 'is knife. 'is huntin knife. 'is Bowie knife.

DWAYNE: How come you get summin cool like a knife and I get a useless fuckin ring?

SLIM: I'm 'avin the knife.

DWAYNE: Whass e get?

SLIM: Mark gets Great Grandma Julia's diary. Guard it with yer life.

DWAYNE: I'll look after that. You'n have the ring.

MARK: Brilliant.

SLIM: Yeeeeeeee-haaaaaaaa! Saddle up, brothers.

MARK and DWAYNE share a look. SLIM hoists his rucksack on his back. MARK loads himself up with gear (Huge racksack, camcorder bag, one-man tent, etc.). As they leave the house:

MARK: Oo's drivin to Wales?

DWAYNE: Thought we was goin Arizona?

SLIM: Arizona via Wales, Dwayne.

DWAYNE: The scenic route.

MARK: It'll be a miracle if we make it outta St. Day.

DWAYNE and MARK exit. SLIM lingers. Looks about the house one last time.

SLIM: We're off now, Daddy. I promise I'll do what you asked. I just kent do it ere. Wish me luck.

SLIM listens to the silence, turns off the light, and exits. The record player gives off an eerie golden glow…

Interval.

Part Two

Rotten timber cracks, gives way with a deafening crash. Three brothers tumble down a 49ft shaft of an abandoned mine. A little light seeps in from above. Dust swirls, settles. Eventually:

MARK: Fuck!

DWAYNE: O'right, Mark?

MARK: Me fuckin arm!

DWAYNE: Lemme look.

MARK: Is it bad? It feels bad.

DWAYNE: It's *real* bad.

MARK: Where's Slim?

DWAYNE trips over SLIM's head.

DWAYNE: E's ere.

MARK: Is e conscious?

DWAYNE: Slim?

SLIM: Guhh…

DWAYNE: Alive. Thank God.

MARK: I did say, didn't I?

DWAYNE: Whaddid you say, Baby Sister?

MARK: That this trip was destined for nuthin but disaster.

TANNOY ANNOUNCEMENT: Will passengers Slim, Dwayne and Mark Gunwallow please make their way to boarding gate twelve immediately.

Aeroplane.

The engines roar as the brothers buckle themselves into their seats, breathless.

DWAYNE: I kent wait to see the desert, can you? Sit on the very edge of the Grand Canyon off my face on weed.

MARK: You be careful. Guide book says you get the electric chair for just breathin in some states.

DWAYNE: Dwayne dun't buy. Dwayne brings 'is own.

MARK: Dun't tell me you smuggled drugs onto this plane?

DWAYNE: Nope. But you did.

MARK: How'd e mean?

DWAYNE: I forgot I left me stash in your coat pocket.

MARK pales as DWAYNE reaches over and pulls out a bag of grass from the pocket of his raincoat.

MARK: You fuckin *dick*, Dwayne!

DWAYNE: We in the business refer to people like you as 'mules'.

MARK: I coulda gone to jail, you wanker!

DWAYNE: Chillax, dude.

MARK: Dun't tell me to fuckin chillax!

DWAYNE calmly pockets it.

MARK: *(To SLIM.)* You see that?

SLIM: *(Reads the diary.)* Dun't talk to me.

MARK: How come?

DWAYNE: You o'right, Slim?

SLIM: Never bin on a plane before. I am absolutely shittin meself. When do we take off?

PILOT ANNOUNCEMENT: Cabin crew, prepare for take off –

The engines roar.

SLIM: Ahhhhhhhhhhhhhhhhhh!!!

Later. Somewhere over the Atlantic Ocean. Engines drone. DWAYNE's asleep. MARK reads the guide book, circles and underlines important passages with a marker pen. SLIM sits tense in his seat.

SLIM: And then what?

MARK: We take a bus from Phoenix airport to Apache Junction. I've booked us a family room at the Gold Canyon Motel. Dad'd be proud of us, eh? Thirty thousand feet up and on our way to Arizona.

SLIM: Mm.

MARK: *(Re: DWAYNE.)* Look at that prat. Teach 'im to smuggle drugs.

MARK writes 'TWAT' on DWAYNE's forehead. DWAYNE wakes.

MARK: *(Expertly picking the conversation.)* So when we arrive at the motel –

SLIM: Yeh.

MARK: One of us needs to be in charge of telling reception of our whereabouts.

SLIM: Right.

MARK: Guide book says always inform *the front desk* of where you're goin and for how long cus it's a big desert and folk d'get lost all the time. It's called Traveller's Safety Policy. O'right Dwayne?

DWAYNE: Aren't I part of this family?

MARK: Sadly, yeh.

DWAYNE: Then include me in all discussions please?

SLIM: You was asleep!

DWAYNE: Gimme summin to do.

SLIM: No way.

DWAYNE: Why not?

MARK: It's a big job, man. Our lives depend on it.

DWAYNE: I can manage to tell the front desk of the motel where we're goin and for how long. Fucksake. Sometimes you treat me like I'm some sorta –

SLIM & MARK: Twat?

SLIM and MARK giggle as the plane makes its descent.

PILOT ANNOUNCEMENT: Ladies and gentlemen, we're now preparing to make our descent into Phoenix –

SLIM: Ahhhhhhhhhhhhhh!!!

Mine.

DWAYNE: Wadn't a complete disaster. We found it! We found The Lost Dutchman's!

MARK: Then where's the gold?

DWAYNE: I kent see fuck-all. Prolly back there somewhere…

MARK: There ain't gonna be any!

DWAYNE: Reckon?

MARK: Dwayne. I bin tellin you this since the first night we got ere!

A sign flickers to life: AL DORADO'S.

A bar in Apache Junction.

Country music. SLIM and DWAYNE sit at a table with bottles of beer. DWAYNE reads the diary with disinterest.

DWAYNE: Tequila?

MARK storms up and dumps a load of tourist leaflets on the table.

MARK: How did I let you convince me to come here?

SLIM: Whass up wi' you?

MARK: Seen this?

(Holds a leaflet up.) 'Follow The Lost Dutchman's Trail!'

(And another.) 'Visit Superstition Mountain Golf Course!'

(And another.) 'Excursions to find the legendary gold mine!' This place idn' a secret! It's a tourist attraction!

DWAYNE: Like Flambards?

SLIM: Yer drawin attention to yerself. Siddown.

MARK: Guess how many people go lookin for the Lost Dutchman's Gold Mine per year?

DWAYNE: How many?

MARK: Guess.

DWAYNE: I dunno.

MARK: You gotta guess!

DWAYNE: I dunno! One?

MARK: Approximately eight thousand people a year.

DWAYNE: Piss off!

MARK: You said Jacob Waltz and Great-Granddad made the claim in –

SLIM: 1897.

MARK: *(Writes it on a napkin.)* So approximately eight thousand people for… one undred and thirteen years is… 904,000 treasure hunters!

DWAYNE: What?

SLIM: Thass a rough estimate.

MARK: This paper napkin has more of a chance of finding the mine than we do!

SLIM: These vultures, they dunno nuthin. We know the facts. The true whereabouts.

MARK: Slim. It's just a story. There is. No gold.

They all look to SLIM.

SLIM: You'll see.

MARK headbutts the table.

DWAYNE: Tequila?

SLIM: Big day tomorra.

DWAYNE: I know but I'm gettin the glad eye from that girl by the jukebox. Dun't look.

They all look.

SLIM: Stay focused, Dwayne.

DWAYNE: I'm just gonna buy 'er a drink is all.

DWAYNE dashes to the bar. SLIM picks some leaflets and peruses them.

SLIM: Yeh. None of this is on the right track. Tis all guess work.

(He pockets one.) Fluff. Crap.

MARK sits up.

SLIM: Come on, Mark. Yer ere now. Put some fuckin effort in.

MARK: Dad's dead, Slim. E's dead and there's so much I never got to ask 'im.

SLIM: *(Taken aback.)* Well… what e mean?

MARK: Wish I ad the chance to ask what happened between 'im and Mum.

SLIM: E didn't like to talk about it.

MARK: I know e didn't. E never talked. We never talk unless there's a fuckin chicken nearby, but as 'is sons, dun't you think we gotta right to know what happened between Mum and –

SLIM: Ere's Dwayne wi' the drinkies!

DWAYNE returns with five tequilas.

DWAYNE: Wish me luck.

He grooms himself, necks one, and heads off with two shots.

SLIM: *(Calling after him.)* Mind you dun't turn 'er gay!

SLIM downs his tequila.

MARK: Ab'm you ever wondered what happened between 'em, Slim? It dun't ad up. It never 'as.

SLIM downs MARK's tequila.

SLIM: Where's bogs to?

MARK: Behind that big plastic Indian.

SLIM goes off. DWAYNE comes strutting back.

DWAYNE: How long 'ave I ad 'twat' on me head?

MARK: Since the day you was born.

DWAYNE: 'er name is Bobby Jo. She works at the motel we're stayin at. Guess where? The front desk. I said, I need to inform you of my movements tomorra. She says why wait til tomorra? Says my accent is 'awesome'. And check this: apparently in America an ass ain't called an ass, it's called 'fanny!'

MARK: Good to see you're bridgin the cultural divide there, Dwayne.

MARK has whipped his camcorder out and starts to film DWAYNE.

DWAYNE: Dun't you get it? Slim ain't wearin a bum-bag. E's wearin a 'fanny-pack.'

MARK: Thass brilliant!

DWAYNE: Not 'brilliant', Mark. 'Awesome'. I'm gettin 'er another drink. Want one?

SLIM comes back. All eyes (and camcorder) to the 'fanny-pack' – which SLIM unzips and checks the contents of.

MARK: O'right?

SLIM: Just sortin me bum-bag out.

They snort.

SLIM: What?

DWAYNE: Nuthin. Tequila?

SLIM: I thought we was only havin a few beers tonight?

DWAYNE: Totally. Thass all we want. Just a few sweet beers.

Mine.

MARK: 'Thass all we want. Just a few sweet beers...'

DWAYNE: Well.

Al Dorado's.

MARK films SLIM as he knocks back a tequila and has a little dance. DWAYNE approaches.

DWAYNE: Trouble, boys. Trouble.

SLIM: Eh?

DWAYNE: I just spoke to the dude with the cowboy boots...

MARK: They all got cowboy boots.

DWAYNE: The old leathery fucker at the bar, eyepatch, looks like John Wayne in 'True Grit'. Dun't look.

They all look.

MARK: Fuckin ell...

MARK's camera droops and we see a shaky camcorder image of a man's snake-skin cowboy boots at the bar.

DWAYNE: His name is Elias Bolt.

SLIM: What e say?

DWAYNE: E said you boys after girls or gold cus life's too short to chase both.

MARK: What did you say?

DWAYNE: I said girls tonight, Mr Bolt, gold tomorra! E said get in line. E said e bin seekin that lost treasure trove all his life and e's never found it yet.

MARK: See?

SLIM: Whaddid you say?

DWAYNE: I told 'im our chances were better than most seein as our great grandfather was the bugger sunk that shaft in the first place.

(Produces the diary from his back pocket.) I showed 'im Julia Thomas's diary to prove we was legit, the bastard's face dropped. I said, me and me two brothers come to claim whass rightfully ours!

MARK: E's lookin over, Dwayne.

DWAYNE: E said Tobias Gunwallow was a nasty bastard died with blood on 'is hands. Said e murdered Jacob Waltz to get all the gold 'isself.

SLIM: E said that did e? This Elias Bolt?

MARK: Keep a lid on it, Slim.

DWAYNE: But that kent be right, can it? Lyin? Cheatin? Violent? Thass not like the great man father told us about at all, is it Slim? Slim? Slim?

SLIM stands on the table.

SLIM: *(To the bar.)* Oi!

The music stops dead.

SLIM: You in the eyepatch! Tobias Gunwallow never killed Jacob Waltz! The Gunwallows ain't no killers! And I'll fuckin stab anyone oo begs to differ!

He draws his Bowie Knife. A brawl ensues. Chairs fly. Glass is smashed. Punches are thrown. MARK films as the place is turned upside down.

Mine.

MARK: *(Winces with pain.)* I know we bin through this Dwayne but… the Traveller's Safety Policy –

DWAYNE: Jesus.

MARK: I just need to know.

DWAYNE: For the last time, I told 'er! I told Bobby Jo! She'll have a search party out for us. Fact, we're prolly 'bout to be rescued any minute now!

They look to the light high above, in hope.

DWAYNE: Any minute now…

Outside Motel.

MARK is loaded with gear, his head in the guide book. DWAYNE is in vest and shades. SLIM presents the hire car.

SLIM: Brothers! I give you The Daihatsu Rocky. The classic American desert vehicle. She's a little roughed-up, but she'll get you from A to B. And you can throw that guide book away, Mark. We got Sat Nav.

MARK: Well thass o'right then.

DWAYNE: *(To MARK.)* Got enuff fuckin gear with ya?

MARK: Guide book says be prepared.

DWAYNE: We're only goin for a couple hours.

MARK: Guide book says not to underestimate nature.

SLIM: What happened to you after the scrap last night?

DWAYNE: The King of Dwayne Island got lucky.

MARK: You get yer end away? The girl on the front desk?

DWAYNE: The girl on the front desk… under the desk… on top of the desk… in the office… on the photocopier… Bobby Jo.

MARK: Beast.

DWAYNE: Ah?

MARK: And now she's gay.

DWAYNE: She *ain't* gay now so that proves it!

SLIM: Did you tell 'er?

DWAYNE: What that I turn women gay?

SLIM: No, ya plum. Did you tell 'er we was off today?

MARK: Traveller's Safety Policy.

DWAYNE: Traveller's Safety Policy. Yes.

SLIM: Then we're all set. Come brothers! Let us follow in Great-Grandfather Gunwallow's footsteps!

MARK: Yeh, by drivin there.

SAT NAV: Your final destination stop is approaching.

Daihatsu.

SAT NAV: Prepare to take the second turning on your left… in 200 meters… 100 meters…

DWAYNE: Kent we shut that fuckin thing up?

MARK: Guide book says the Visitor's Spot is the ideal place to take in the exquisite desert panoramas.

SLIM: Fuck the guide book. Let's go off-road.

SLIM jerks the wheel. They come off the road and onto bumpy track.

SAT NAV: You are going the wrong way! You are going the wrong –

SLIM punches the Sat Nav out cold.

SLIM: Sounds like me ex-missis.

Wheels skid to a halt. Doors slam. The brothers gaze out over the blistering expanse of desert.

SLIM: There she is, boys. Dead ahead. Superstition Mountain!

DWAYNE: Beautiful.

MARK: I think *that's* Superstition Mountain there.

SLIM: *(Re-adjusts.)* There she is, boys. Superstition Mountain.

DWAYNE: Beautiful. Beautiful.

MARK: *(Reading.)* 'To the West stands the geological oddity known as 'Weaver's Needle'. This is the last recognisable marker before 60 inhospitable miles of desert wilderness… But superseding all, the eerie jagged peaks of the mighty mountain 'erself…'

MARK films the vista with his camcorder.

MARK: Any words, boys?

SLIM: *(Profoundly moved.)* Specktackaler.

Beat.

Let's start!

DWAYNE: Start what?

SLIM: Let's check out Weaver's Needle.

MARK: Thought this was just a recce?

SLIM: Why waste time? There's a riddle to the Needle has to be cracked in Julia Thomas's diary… Oo ad it last?

DWAYNE: You did.

MARK: You ad it in the bar last night.

DWAYNE: I never!

MARK: You showed it to Elias Bolt!

DWAYNE pulls it out of his back pocket. SLIM snatches it.

SLIM: I'll look after that.

MARK: *(To DWAYNE.)* Ring piece.

DWAYNE: Can I 'ave the Bowie knife?

SLIM: No.

Diahatsu.

SLIM: *(Leafs through the dairy.)* 'And you shall see through the eye of a needle, you shall hear the call of the mountain's mouth, and you shall know as if it by heart!'

DWAYNE: *(Pointing ahead.)* Thass the needle e means, surely? Weaver's Needle!

MARK: And the Eye? Stands to reason that'd be at the very top!

SLIM: What if Tobias Gunwallow did not risk settin the directions down on any map made of paper, but made a map out of the very landscape itself?

DWAYNE: We gotta climb up the Needle to figure out where to go next?

SLIM: Good, Dwayne! Good!

Brakes. Doors slam. They observe the Needle.

MARK: That? We kent climb up that!

DWAYNE: Thass helluva height, Slim.

SLIM: Let's take a closer look.

They forge on. And climb. Eventually they reach –

The top of Weaver's Needle.

Fierce sun. MARK and DWAYNE catch their breath. SLIM appears from below, red-faced and wheezing.

MARK: Ere e comes. Indiana fuckin Jones.

SLIM: Now…

(Examines dairy.) Julia Thomas speaks of a mysterious Secret Ledge somewhere below ere…

MARK: A 'Secret Ledge'?

DWAYNE: *(Points off, below.)* Maybe thass The Secret Ledge there?

SLIM: Beauty, Dwayne!

MARK: Thass 'ardly a Secret Ledge.

DWAYNE: How'd e mean?

MARK: Didn't take us long to find.

SLIM: Others mighta bin ere before us, but they never ad this sweet baby!

SLIM holds up the strange, clay-made, heart-shaped talisman with holes and lines cut into it that we saw in Act One.

DWAYNE: What is it?

SLIM: The wotsit. The macguffin. The Peralta Stone.

MARK: Thass from Dad's box of stuff.

SLIM: Hand-made by Apache Indians, this was.

DWAYNE: Whassit do?

SLIM: Diary suggests The Secret Ledge is some kinda viewin platform. Once there, hold up the Peralta Stone before you. Insert yer nose through the hole – only a Gunwallow nose'll do! No other nose will fit its precise dimensions –

MARK: And then what?

SLIM: It dun't say. The diary stops dead. Like the last few pages 'ave bin torn out.

(To DWAYNE.) Let your eyes scour the desert floor. Let the Peralta Stone guide ya. You will see where the next leg leads us from down there!

DWAYNE: Why you tellin me?

SLIM: Cus you're goin over.

DWAYNE: Me?

SLIM: *(To MARK.)* 'elp me lower 'im down.

DWAYNE: I aren't goin. Make 'im go!

SLIM: E got weak arms.

MARK: Yeh!

SLIM positions DWAYNE and forces him down.

DWAYNE: It's helluva drop, Slim.

SLIM: It's only a coupla feet, ya prick! Don the Peralta Stone.

SLIM forces the Peralta Stone onto DWAYNE's nose.

DWAYNE: I kent see piss all!

SLIM: Quit wingin' and get over there! Secret ledge. Peralta Stone. Gunwallow nose. Easy!

SLIM prises DWAYNE's grip from the edge. DWAYNE drops with a yell. Desert wind blows. MARK reads the guide book. SLIM slowly unzips his bum-bag, produces the letter.

SLIM: *(Hand trembling.)* Mark.

MARK turns, sees it, ignores it.

MARK: You broke your promise last night.

SLIM: Did I?

MARK: You said you would reign yer temper in.

SLIM: Elias Bolt insulted our family.

MARK: Promise is a promise.

SLIM: Yer tellin me.

SLIM puts the letter away.

SLIM: *(Calling over.)* How e doin, Dwayne?

DWAYNE: *(From below.)* Pretty good, yeh. I can see the a cactus shaped like a cock! Reckon we should head for that!

Mine.

MARK: *(Switching on torch.)* Forgot I ad this.

DWAYNE: Let's find the gold!

DWAYNE takes the torch and stumbles about.

MARK: Can't ya use it to find a way out first?

DWAYNE: Entrance is 50ft up. There's nuthin to climb. The walls are sheer. All this wood is rotten…

MARK: Great. Then what are we gonna do? Where's this rescue party? Why's it takin so long to find us?

DWAYNE: Ya know, even if we do die down ere, you kent deny we've ad some damn good times, eh?

Desert. 'Day Two'.

DWAYNE sits in the Diahatsu Rocky. Turns the key. It won't start.

DWAYNE: S'fucked.

MARK: Can we 'itch back?

SLIM: I say let's forge on!

MARK: You are jokin?

SLIM: We're 'alf way there! Why turn back?

MARK: It's 60 miles across that desert.

SLIM: Do it in a day!

MARK: It's near noon. We'll fry.

DWAYNE: Let's head back to the motel get some dinner.

SLIM: Gyah, yer just thinkin wi' yer dick!

DWAYNE: I dun't eat dinner wimme dick.

MARK: Dwayne's right. We ain't prepared for another day out ere. No food, no water –

SLIM: We're goin.

MARK: Aw, look out.

SLIM: *(Draws his knife.)* We're goin.

MARK and DWAYNE crack up.

SLIM: *(Furious.)* We're goin!

Mine.

MARK stares blankly into the darkness.

DWAYNE: Good times… Hey. What was the name of that great game I invented?

Desert.

The three of them plod in the searing heat.

DWAYNE: *(Points.)* Lizard!

(Plods… points.) Lizard!

(Plods… points.) Lizard!

(Plods… points.) Lizard!

(Plods… points.) Lizard!

Mine.

MARK: 'Lizard'?

DWAYNE: That was it! 'Lizard!' That was a good game.

MARK: Remember when you needed a poo?

DWAYNE: No.

Desert.

DWAYNE: I need a poo.

SLIM: Go then.

DWAYNE: *(To MARK.)* You bring any toilet paper?

MARK: Quilted or Soft and Long?

DWAYNE: Sarky fuck.

SLIM: Ere, use one a these tourist leaflets.

DWAYNE: They're too glossy. They dun't absorb nuthin!

SLIM: Suit yerself, pard.

MARK: Hey, Dwayne. I got the Andrex puppy in me rucksack, you can wipe yer ass on that if ya like?

Mine.

DWAYNE: I thought thass what you did in the wild. Wiped yer ass on a leaf.

MARK: Yeh but not on deadly poisonous spit weed.

Desert.

DWAYNE, in agony, has his ass out. His brothers stare at it in horror.

DWAYNE: *Pleeeeeeze?*

MARK: No.

DWAYNE: I'm beggin ya!

SLIM: I kent do it.

DWAYNE: One of ya, suck the poison out?!

SLIM: *(Gravely.)* You're on yer own, brother.

DWAYNE: *Suck it out!!!*

A helicopter flies overhead. DWAYNE tries to grab its attention, but it's already gone.

DWAYNE: 'elp me!

MARK: Came from Superstition Mountain.

SLIM: Keep walkin.

They walk through the dusk. Night falls.

Rocky alcove.

The brothers huddle around a very small fire. DWAYNE *is on all fours, his bare ass to the cool night breeze. His trousers are slung nearby.* MARK, *reading his guide book, offers him something blackened on the end of a stick.*

MARK: Lizard?

DWAYNE: Fuck off.

SLIM: S'gettin cold.

DWAYNE: The breeze is good.

SLIM: Need more shit for the fire. No more leaflets.

DWAYNE: Burn 'is prissy little guide book.

SLIM: I'll burn you in a minute, you fuckin shower! Cock-shaped cactus, my ass!

DWAYNE: Sorry Slim. I swear, it looked like one!

MARK: And in tryin to find it we are now completely lost.

SLIM: Where's yer trousers?

MARK: If you'd read this guide book you'd know all about how not to wipe your ass with certain desert flora.

SLIM *goes through* DWAYNE's *trousers, finds a bag of something, opens it, sniffs it, dumps the contents in the fire.*

DWAYNE: Whass that?

SLIM: Teach you to see cock-shaped cacti when ya shouldn't!

DWAYNE: Not me weed!

SLIM: Damn drug addict!

DWAYNE: Aww, thass me weed for when I'm at the Grand Canyon, Slim! Aww, me *weeeeeed!*

DWAYNE *crawls to the fire, puts his face over the flames and inhales deeply.*

SLIM: Pathetic.

DWAYNE: S'nice… eases the pain…

MARK sniffs the smoke too.

MARK: *(Offering it.)* Slim?

SLIM: No way.

MARK: Chills you out.

SLIM: Does it?

SLIM has a quick sniff.

SLIM: We're close to the gold. I can feel it.

DWAYNE: How?

SLIM: Metal. Us Gunwallows 'ave always dealt in the stuff. We 'ave an affinity with it. Tobias mined the earth. Knew where to look. Tis in our blood.

MARK: Good to know we're still upholdin the family tradition. A bunch of losers scrabblin round in the dark on the promise of metal.

SLIM: We're takin the same journey our ancestors took, Mark!

MARK: Yeh, only we got less of a clue!

MARK starts to assemble his one-man tent. DWAYNE catches SLIM's eye, tuts, shakes his head.

SLIM: What you tuttin at?

DWAYNE: Mark. *E's* a loser.

SLIM: If anyone's a loser in this family, Dwayne, it's you. Wi' yer big-shot ways!

DWAYNE: You're the one oo's 5,000 miles away from your only daughter on her third birthday!

MARK: Is it Maddy's birthday?

SLIM: It is.

DWAYNE: Well then, whadda you doin ere Slim?! Why aren't you with 'er? We was in Wales, droppin off the Caddy, you didn't even try to see 'er! Loser? Me? Whaddabout you, Slim? Whaddabout you?

Silence.

DWAYNE: That was out of order. It's me ass. I'm in agony. I'm tired and teasy. I'm sorry, Slim. I'm –

SLIM: Dwayne. There's summin I bin wantin to say to you since we was small. Promise me. Promise me that when you speak out loud these unthought-through comments of yours, that you not apologise immediately after. The things you do, the things you don't do, the general fuck-ups in life you make on a day-to-day basis (and I'm talkin about you specifically ere)… do 'em, and live with 'em. Dun't do 'em, and say sorry for 'em. Even if you shit out the world's biggest turd and are forced to, I dunno, stash it in some kiddy's lunch-box… dun't shrug it off as some filthy accident. Take responsibility for it. Live with it. Cus if I hear you apologise one more time, I swear to Christ I'll…

DWAYNE: I hear ya, Slim.

SLIM: I made a promise to Mark to keep me temper in check. Now I ask the same of you. So promise. Promise me. No more apologisin.

DWAYNE: OK, I promise.

SLIM nods, exhausted but satisfied.

SLIM: And for the record, I phoned Carole before we left for Wales.

DWAYNE: Did ya?

SLIM: She didn't want me to come round. But at least we spoke.

MARK: Thass great, Slim.

SLIM: Look at those stars… Ya know it's times like this I wish I could sing.

DWAYNE: You can sing, Slim. You gotta lovely voice.

SLIM: Maybe… Maybe…

(Quietly breaks into song.) 'And I… I… I… I… I… will always love you… ooo-ahh… I will always love yoooooooooooooou…'

Somewhere in the desert, a creature howls.

MARK: Well. I gonna turn in.

DWAYNE: Yeh me too.

SLIM: I could murder an 'obnob. Anyone gotta biscuit?

MARK: I wish. Night.

MARK heads into his now fully rigged tent.

DWAYNE: Oi. How'd you expect us all to fit into that?

MARK: I dun't. It's a one-man tent.

DWAYNE: Well where we spus to sleep?

MARK: In your one-man tent?

DWAYNE: I didn't bring a one-man tent.

MARK: Aw well…

MARK slips into the one-man tent. SLIM and DWAYNE watch him. The desert wind blows cold. DWAYNE waddles over to the tent and crawls in. The tent bends and bulges and then falls still. MARK crawls out, annoyed. Eyes SLIM, pulls out a secret stash of Hobnobs and slips away. SLIM sits and stares at the fire.

SLIM: I ab'm forget what you asked of me on your deathbed, Daddy. Still got the letter. I keep waiting for the right moment to do it but it never comes… I feel like we gotta keep goin… But if we keep goin, we'll die. And Julia's directions in the diary, they just stop. No more pages. What should I do, Daddy?

SLIM finds a half-singed Superstition Mountain leaflet in the ashes.

SLIM: Can I trust in yer stories? Or is Mark right? Is this crusade just a loada tourist leaflets and dodgy gold-mine themed motels?

SLIM reads the leaflet… a hole burnt through… he holds it up against the sky. SLIM freezes. Sees something on the horizon.

SLIM: Mark? Dwayne? Look at this! There's a man on horseback. Silhouetted against the moon. E looks like… e *is*, e's… it's Daddy! Come to lead the way!

(SLIM looks back, his face drops.) Don't go, Daddy! Don't go!

He tries re-creating the vision by looking through the leaflet again. Nothing. But his focus adjusts to the leaflet…

DWAYNE: *(Head out of tent.)* You o'right, Slim?

MARK returns.

SLIM: Yes. Fuckin *yes!* S'right under me nose! Starin me in the face! Thank you, Daddy. I know what I gotta do now!

(Shouting back but reading the leaflet.) Come on, boys! Shake a leg! Daddy's showed us the way! Let's find this gold!

Through blazing sun, an obsessed and frantic SLIM leads DWAYNE and MARK on and on into the desert, over, under, down, up, always keeping ahead. He snatches glances at a tourist leaflet. Eventually, he finds the boarded up entrance to a mine, and prises up the planks beneath them.

SLIM: Boys! We found it!

There is a tremendous creaking and crashing of rotted timber, and the sound of three brothers falling down a mine shaft –

Mine.

DWAYNE: You ad Hobnobs?

MARK: Emergency supply.

DWAYNE: Greedy fucker. Eat 'em all?

MARK: I did, yeh. I'm greedy. You're a loser. And Slim?

DWAYNE: Slim's lost it. For definite.

SLIM: Lost it 'ave I?!

The flashlight finds SLIM glowering in the darkness.

SLIM: Dun't you trust in your big brother, boys? You want gold? Ere's yer fuckin gold!

SLIM grabs the torch, heads into the bowels of the mine, kicks aside pieces of rotted timber, then throws off ancient tarpaulins. Beneath, buckets and buckets of ore. He tips them over (one, two, three) spilling the contents into the light. It glitters and gleams.

DWAYNE: It is! It's gold!

SLIM: What did you expect from the Lost Dutchman's Gold Mine?

DWAYNE: We found it! We did it!

SLIM: With a little 'elp from the family.

DWAYNE: Yeeeeee-hooooooooo!

SLIM: *(To MARK.)* Believe me now?

MARK: *(Beaten.)* I'm passed tryin to make sense of it. I'm just gonna accept it. I take it all back, Slim.

(Examining it.) Is it…?

SLIM: Ore. Near 'nuff pure by the looks.

DWAYNE: We're rich. We're rich! Fuck you Manchester Crew! And fuck you, Inland Revenue! Fuck you all! We're fuckin sorted!

MARK: What do we do with it?

SLIM: Take it. It's ours. 8,000 people a year? They wadn't countin on the Gunwallow boys!

MARK: No, I mean how we gonna shift it?

SLIM: Eh?

MARK: We kent get ourselves up. How we spus'd to haul ten tons of gold out?

SLIM: Look, me and Dwayne are tryin to enjoy this!

MARK: I dun't mean to spoil the moment but as I keep tryin to tell ya, I am almost empty of blood.

SLIM: 'ow many days we bin travellin?

MARK: Lost count.

SLIM: Three days. And what did the guide book say we absolutely ad to do before leavin to find the gold? It said to always tell the front desk –

DWAYNE: Bobby Jo.

SLIM: And Dwayne saw to that, didn't you Dwayne?

DWAYNE: Yes.

SLIM: E told 'er all the requisite information. Told 'er precisely how long we would be gone –

DWAYNE: One day.

SLIM: And if we ain't back by then to come look for us.

MARK: You really think they're gonna find us down the bottom of a lost gold mine?

SLIM: Damn right! We left such a trail of shit behind, they wun't fail to! There's the Daihatsu Rocky out by Weaver's Needle. The fires we made –

DWAYNE: My poo!

SLIM: Dwayne's poo! A seasoned desert ranger will sniff 'is way into Superstition Mountain –

DWAYNE: Show some sense of optimism, Mark.

SLIM: It kent end ere.

DWAYNE: Be a cruel fate to 'ave us come a cropper now we finally laid our 'ands on the fortune!

SLIM: We seen helicopters buzzin round.

DWAYNE: The rescue party is up there.

SLIM: Find us any minute now.

DWAYNE: Traveller's Safety Policy.

SLIM: Damn right. So calm down. Help is on it's way, brother.

They all look up the shaft, hopeful. Long pause.

DWAYNE: I didn't tell 'er.

Pause.

I didn't tell Bobby Jo.

SLIM: Say that again, Dwayne?

DWAYNE: We never ad sex that night. She wadn't interested. Turns out she was a lesbian. I ad nuthin to do wi' it! We just talked all night.

MARK: So you *didn't* mention the Traveller's Safety Policy?

DWAYNE: I thought we'd only be gone a day. Didn't think it would matter.

SLIM: So… no one. Knows. We're ere?

DWAYNE shakes his head.

MARK: 'kay.

(Screaming up the shaft.) 'ELP ME SOMEBODY!!! I'M TRAPPED DOWN ERE WITH MY BROTHER!!! WHO!!! IS!!! A!!! TWWWWWAAAAAAATTTTTTT!!!!

'Twat' echoes through the mine.

DWAYNE: You'll notice I'm stickin to the promise I made Slim and ain't apologisin.

MARK: All this time and you was just lyin?

DWAYNE: Once I started I couldn't stop. I ad to pretend I got me end away otherwise you'da both ribbed me.

MARK: Ribbed ya? Better a ribbin than bein starved to death, surely, Dwayne, you... fuckin... *EGG.*

From the surrounding darkness, an ominous rattling stops them all dead.

SLIM: What was that?

DWAYNE: Somebody's down ere.

MARK: Wait. Stay in the light.

MARK throws a handful of gold ore into the darkness. More rattling, more agitated now.

SLIM: What the fuck is it?

MARK: *(Shines a light.)* Says in me guide book we might run into 'em. Rattlesnakes. Fuck-off great nest of 'em.

DWAYNE: Rattlesnake? Like the one at the end of 'True Grit'?

MARK: I doubt it's the same one Dwayne but yeh. There look.

DWAYNE: Oooh, oooh bloody Christ!

SLIM: Stay in close, Mark.

(Unsheaths his Bowie.) They're slitherin this way.

DWAYNE: *(Shouting up the shaft.)* 'elp! Somebody! We're trapped down ere wi' a loada killer snakes!

MARK: There's more than just snakes wanna kill ya down ere, Dwayne.

DWAYNE: O'right, Mark. Simple mistake.

SLIM: You're the simple mistake, you fuckin tit! I knew we couldn't rely on you! I knew it!

MARK: *(Wandering the mine.)* I shouldna come ere. I shoulda bin strong. I shoulda fought for her!

SLIM: 'er oo?

MARK: Tina Polkinghorne. I shoulda told 'er I loved 'er! Cus I do! I love Tina fuckin Polkinghorne!

SLIM: But you called it off. There's no goin back from that.

MARK moans in horror and wanders the mine.

DWAYNE: There is if Mark swaggers back to St. Day loaded. She'll crawl back then, 'specially if she gotta baby in tow.

SLIM: The baby ain't Mark's though is it?

MARK moans, wanders.

DWAYNE: Innit?

SLIM: Mark thought it was 'is, but it wadn't, was it?

MARK moans.

SLIM: Dun't you listen?

DWAYNE: So oo 'is the real daddy then?

SLIM: Fucksake. Keep up, Dwayne. It's Uncle Seth's innit.

MARK turns to SLIM. SLIM realises his error.

SLIM: Innit?

DWAYNE: Seth's?

MARK: Yes. The baby is Uncle Seth's. How did you know?

SLIM: Uhh…

DWAYNE: Seth got Tina Polkinghorne pregnant?

MARK: *(To SLIM.)* How the fuck did you know?

DWAYNE: But e's old enuff to be 'er –

MARK: Grandfather. Yes, Dwayne. *Slim?*

SLIM: Seth mentioned it at the funeral.

MARK: And you never thought to ask me about it?

SLIM: It's family matters. Private. And Seth, e dun't know you know. E dun't know you love Tina. Tina was stringin you along. Both of ya.

MARK: No she wadn't.

SLIM: She was. Thass why I told 'er to tell ya oo the real dad is…

MARK: You told 'er to tell me? Of course, to get me to come… *ere!*

SLIM: I blame Tina. You and Seth, yer just innocent parties! Sure, Seth 'as an eye for the younger ladies but e's o'right –

MARK: Stop it, Slim! Stop defendin your family for the shit things they do!

SLIM: What e mean by that?

MARK: Tobias Gunwallow cheated and killed 'is partner to make his fortune. Uncle Seth serves under-agers, pays under the fuckin minimum wage and 'as got a young girl pregnant. Dad ran a firm with lawless methods, drove his poor wife to suicide whilst e fixed up a Cadillac Eldorado e never even drove so e wouldn't hafto speak to 'is three dippy sons! And dun't even get me started on them!

The snakes rattle.

SLIM: Steady, brother. You got no idea what yer talkin about.

MARK: Oh, dunt I?

SLIM: No idea whatsoever.

MARK: Thass right cus I'm Baby Sister. Whaddo I know?

SLIM: You dun't know nuthin.

MARK: No? I know enuff to know this Masonic ring is nuthin but worthless scrap!

MARK yanks it from his finger and pitches it into the darkness of the mine. SLIM flinches at its loss.

DWAYNE: That was *bang* out of order, Mark.

SLIM: Shut up, Dwayne.

DWAYNE: Just puttin 'im straight. That was a family heirloom!

SLIM: I said shut up.

DWAYNE: What ya turnin on me for?

SLIM: Cus I know what yer doin! Yer doin what you always do which is side with the strongest and attack the weaker.

MARK: I am *not* the weaker!

SLIM: Yes you are. You know Dwayne? I'm gonna side with Mark right now.

MARK: I dun't want ya to!

SLIM: I'm gonna side with 'im just to spite ya, because e's right. We are a waste of space. And you're the worst. You're an embarrassment. You act all cool, think yer so clever, like a hero, like yer John bloody Wayne –

(Sudden, loud.) WELL JOHN WAYNE NEVER DEALT DRUGS!

Rattlesnakes rattle.

SLIM: E was a man of true grit. Like father.

MARK: Uh!

SLIM: Dwayne Gunwallow. Whadda big man.

DWAYNE: I *am* a man.

SLIM: Are ya? Are ya really? I bet the women you sleep with (those you can get to sleep with ya) would beg to differ!

DWAYNE: Ere we go again. Same old tired shit.

SLIM: I just wanna get to the bottom of it.

DWAYNE: Bottom of what?

SLIM: I wanna know why every woman you shag goes gay.

MARK: Great. And now you're pickin on 'im.

SLIM: Shut up.

DWAYNE: It's not *every* woman –

SLIM: Whadda you do in the sack that turns 'em so?

DWAYNE: I dun't *do* anythin.

SLIM: Maybe thass yer problem?

DWAYNE: Maybe you're my problem.

SLIM: Maybe you're, y'know –

DWAYNE: No. What.

SLIM: A gay boy.

DWAYNE: A gay boy?

SLIM: Wouldn't matter if ya were.

(Nose to nose.) Yeh! Gay Boy Gunwallow. Gay Dwayne. Gay Dwayne Strikes Again.

Tense silence, then… they all piss themselves laughing.

MARK: *(Relieved.)* Buncha pricks.

DWAYNE: *(To SLIM.)* Ya know, I could get you so badly right now.

SLIM: Yeh?

DWAYNE: You are this close…

SLIM: Go on. Go on. Do it.

DWAYNE: I've got such a doozy.

SLIM: Is it a peach?

DWAYNE: It's me secret weapon.

SLIM: 'it me with it.

DWAYNE: Every time you gimme grief, I hafto bite me tongue on this one.

SLIM: Come on then, bro.

DWAYNE: Shall I?

SLIM: Do it.

DWAYNE: *(Prepares himself.)* O'right. This is for all the shit you've given me all these years.

SLIM: Payback time!

DWAYNE: Oh yeh.

SLIM: Go on. I need a good laff.

DWAYNE: Gyah, I kent.

SLIM: Whassamatter?

DWAYNE: You'll go fuckin ape-shit.

SLIM: I wun't. I made a promise.

DWAYNE: You'll take it all in good humour?

SLIM: I shall take it on the chin. Cus there is nuthin you can dish out mate that I can't handle.

DWAYNE: *(Primes himself.)* You want proof not every woman I shag goes gay?

SLIM: *YEH!*

DWAYNE: Ask yer wife.

SLIM: Eh?

DWAYNE: Ask Carole.

SLIM: What e mean?

DWAYNE: What e mean, what I mean? I shagged Carole. And to the best a my knowledge she ain't gone gay.

SLIM: Yer pullin my leg.

DWAYNE: Am I?

Silence.

SLIM: O'right. When?

DWAYNE: 'member last Christmas? Dad got sick after dinner, you took 'im hospital? While you was gone, she came on to me. Came on strong. Said gimme a kiss under the mistletoe? I was 'ammered. So I did. And it happened.

SLIM: Right.

DWAYNE: So there.

SLIM: And?

DWAYNE: And it was pretty good, yeh.

SLIM: I dun't mean 'and' 'ow was it, I mean – and?

DWAYNE: And what?

SLIM: You slept with my wife.

DWAYNE: Yep.

SLIM: Now thass bad.

DWAYNE: I spus.

SLIM: I can try to forgive you as long as…?

DWAYNE: As long as…?

MARK: For fuck's sake Dwayne say yer *SORRY.*

DWAYNE: Oh.

SLIM: You've let me down. Betrayed me. Destroyed my life. But you are family. Just say yer sorry and let's be done with it.

DWAYNE: *(Considers this.)* Nah.

SLIM: Say yer sorry Dwayne.

DWAYNE: I made a promise to you. I intend on stickin to it.

SLIM: But that was before you confessed to bein the cause of my marriage break-up and reason for my current mental breakdown…

DWAYNE: I take full responsibility.

SLIM: I know what we said but –

DWAYNE: I aren't apologisin for what I done.

SLIM: *(Softly.)* But see, I need you to say the words otherwise I'm gonna lose me temper…

MARK: Fuck.

DWAYNE: Good.

SLIM: You want that?

DWAYNE: Teach me to go shaggin me brother's wife behind 'is back. Forgettin the Traveller's Safety Policy. Drug dealin. Yer right. I'm a twat. I deserve a good kickin.

SLIM: Poor Dennis Tilly. I broke 'is jaw for no good reason. Nigel Lame, e near 'nuff lost an eye.

DWAYNE: Terry Duff.

SLIM: I damn near killed Terry. And it was you all along.

DWAYNE: What a twist.

SLIM: Did you love 'er?

DWAYNE: Nah. Just shaggin.

SLIM: It makes sense now. The way she left without sayin goodbye.

DWAYNE: She said goodbye to me.

MARK: Dwayne, Jesus Christ…

SLIM: You saw 'er that day, before she left?

DWAYNE: She came by the caravan. With Maddy.

SLIM: All that shit I went through and you just sat and watched.

DWAYNE: I'm glad I got it out in the open. Feels like a weight's been lifted…

SLIM: Oh, I'm so pleased…

Beat.

You know, for all this, I actually respect ya Dwayne for not apologisin. For keepin the promise you made to yourself. But… I'm afraid I gonna hafta go back on mine.

SLIM brings the Bowie knife into the light.

DWAYNE: I understand that, bro. Kent be 'elped.

MARK: Remember yer promise –

DWAYNE: Shuddup, Mark.

MARK: Apologise, Dwayne. Now.

DWAYNE: It's too late for that.

SLIM: Way too late. Yer gonna get what's comin to ya.

DWAYNE: Get it all out, brother.

MARK: Whass this gonna achieve?

SLIM: It'll make me feel better.

MARK: Put it down, Slim.

DWAYNE: Let im do it, Mark.

MARK: E'll kill ya!

DWAYNE: Good.

SLIM: I will. I'll kill ya!

MARK: *(Standing in front of DWAYNE.)* Then you'll hafto kill me first.

SLIM: Dun't tempt me, sunshine!

DWAYNE: Out the way, Mark!

MARK: Just look at yerself! What would Dad say if e saw you two now?

SLIM: *(Trying to get to DWAYNE.)* You got no right to bring 'im into this!

MARK: I got as much right as anyone ere!

SLIM: That ain't strickly true, I'm afraid! Guess what, Baby Sister? Abel Gunwallow ain't yer dad!

MARK: Oh, yeh right! So oo is me Dad then, Slim? Uncle Seth?

SLIM: YES.

In the stunned silence, snakes rattle.

MARK: E ain't my dad.

SLIM: Yes. E is.

MARK: E ain't my fuckin dad!

SLIM: Just let me kill Dwayne and then we can talk about this.

MARK, overflowing with emotion, flies at SLIM. A brutal, messy fight ensues. MARK gets slammed by SLIM. DWAYNE is caught. DWAYNE holds off the knife blade with all of his might but it edges closer and closer to his throat… DWAYNE is about to lose when –

MARK: Slim!

SLIM turns and – BLAM! – MARK renders SLIM unconscious with an empty bucket.

Suddenly, darkness. Confusion. A hideous scream from above: 'Geronimo!' The whip-crack sound of a rope twanged taut. The light returns to reveal a new scene. MARK and DWAYNE stand on either side of the mine, lagged in sweat and dust and blood. SLIM is on the floor unconscious. Hanging in the middle of the chamber below the shaft is a dead man (though we only need see his boots). The rope creaks. The boots slowly revolve. MARK is in a crumpled heap, staring into the darkness.

DWAYNE: Elias Bolt. Poor bastard's hanged 'isself. Spent 'is whole life lookin for this gold. Guess e gave up at the last minute. We beat ya to it, Mr Bolt! Sorry bout that. Ah well.

DWAYNE fills his pockets with gold.

MARK: What you doin?

DWAYNE: E's kindly provided an escape route in case you adn noticed?

MARK: Yer goin?

DWAYNE: Well Slim clearly ain't up to it and you kent climb wi' that arm. I'll shimmy up chap ere and fetch 'elp.

MARK: Leave the gold.

DWAYNE: Eh?

MARK: It'll just weigh ya down.

DWAYNE: I ain't makin off with the lot. I just gotta couple a handfuls to prove we found the mine but… if you dun't trust me?

MARK: Take it. Ya might need it.

DWAYNE: Nice one, bruv.

MARK: It's true, idn't it? What Slim said?

DWAYNE: Dun't ask me, Mark. No one tells me fuck all in this family. Yes. I reckon it's true. Gizza bunk-up.

MARK gives DWAYNE a painful bunk-up. DWAYNE somehow manages to climb up the body –

DWAYNE: Scuse me, Mr. Bolt.

And up the rope. As he does:

DWAYNE: Hey Mark. E got summin in 'is pocket.

MARK: What?

DWAYNE: Newspaper. Musta read some pretty bad news!

DWAYNE drops down a tightly rolled-up newspaper. MARK catches it.

DWAYNE: *(Calling down.)* Oi, Mark! There's 'orse up ere.

MARK: 'orse?

DWAYNE: Must be Bolt's. I'm gonna try it on for size. Ride into town like John Wayne. Only I'm John Dwayne! Geddit?

MARK: You are comin back, aren't ya?

DWAYNE: Mark. For fucksake. Chillax. It's me. It's Dwayne.

MARK: But Dwayne… Dwayne? Dwayne!

Rattlesnakes rattle from all around now. MARK stamps at them and drags his unconscious brother into the dimming light. He rescues his camcorder too, clutches on to it for dear life.

MARK: We just gotta sit ere and wait. Dwayne'll be back soon. Oh yeh. Yeh. Yeh, you can always rely on Dwayne…

(Dawning realisation.) We're fucked.

MARK films himself.

MARK: *(To camera.)* So. Welcome to Supersition Mountain... and the Lost Dutchman's Gold Mine... That's Slim. E's unconscious. Again. Dwayne's done a runner... Behind me is Elias Bolt, a treasure hunter… e's dead… there's the gold… and there – I dunno if you can see? – are some deadly poisonous rattlesnakes… say 'ello snakes…

Rattlesnakes rattle.

MARK: And I'm Mark Gunwallow… and I think… I am about… to die –

The camera bleeps.

MARK: Outta film. Better get a fuckin good mark for this.

He sits. Opens his clenched fist – in it is the Masonic Ring.

SLIM: *(Coming round.)* Huh…

MARK: O'right?

SLIM: Where's Dwayne?

MARK: E got out.

SLIM: Lucky escape. How?

MARK: Climbed up Elias Bolt.

SLIM: Oo?

MARK nods to the hanged man. SLIM gets to his feet and checks him out.

SLIM: Aw.

MARK: Reckon you could climb up Bolt now that yer conscious?

SLIM: I'd love to but I kent… me arm dun't feel so good…

MARK: Yours too. Broken?

SLIM: Bitten.

MARK: That ain't good…

The mine creaks.

MARK: Dwayne took some gold to prove we found it. E'll come back.

SLIM: It ain't gold. It's fake. It's worthless.

MARK: Oh?

SLIM: This ain't the Lost Dutchman's. This is the…

(Shows MARK the tourist leaflet.) Glory Nugget Mine. Local tourist attraction. Picked a good one, eh? Looks like the real thing.

MARK: You fooled me.

SLIM: I got summin to confess, Mark. The Peralta Stone is all bollocks.

MARK: Not Apache handiwork?

SLIM: St. Day Nursery School. Dun't you recognise it? You made it, ya spod. When you was four. Outta clay or some shit. Mother's Day present.

MARK: I dun't remember.

SLIM: And Daddy never told me on his deathbed that we ad to come ere… Daddy told me on his deathbed to tell you that e loved ya but that you weren't 'is son. E told me to give you this…

(Produces the letter.) E couldn't speak the words, so he left the job to me… and *I* couldn't speak the words… until ten minutes ago, when they accidentally popped out.

MARK: How long've you known?

SLIM: When I was 12 I got hit by a Datsun Cherry. Got sent 'ome. Caught mother and Seth together upstairs.

Nuthin sordid. Just… in each other's arms. You was just born. Guess mother told Daddy just before she… Abel Gunwallow was a strange bloke. Unhappy most days. There musta bin summin good she saw in 'im… but maybe that goodness just dried up? But e was o'right –

MARK: E was a twat.

SLIM: Yeh. E was. And now you find your real dad is an even bigger twat. And yer brother drags you 'alf way across the world and almost kills ya to tell you all this, and e's the biggest twat of em all.

MARK: You ain't a twat, Slim. You was the one looked after me. You brought me up. Ere. This dun't belong to me.

MARK offers up the Masonic Ring. SLIM takes it, then slings it into the darkness.

SLIM: Mark.

(Offers the letter.) Take this off me hands for fuck's sake.

MARK takes the letter. He strikes a match and burns it.

MARK: I dun't need to read it. You told me what I ad to know. There it is. End of story.

The rattlesnakes rattle.

MARK picks up the rolled newspaper and attempts to light it when something stops him. He opens the paper and stands beneath the fading light from the shaft.

MARK: *(Reads.)* Lost Gold Mine Fortune Found.

SLIM: What? Read it.

MARK: *(Reads.)* The legendary Lost Dutchman's Mine was yesterday thought to have been finally unearthed, along with its considerable catchment in gold ore. The State of Arizona Department of Mines and Mineral Resources estimate the astonishing haul at 4.9 million dollars.

SLIM: Aw shit.

MARK: *(Reads.)* The infamous history of the mine and its much sought after fortune was relegated to the annals of local myth. However, three days ago a resident of Apache Junction, 21 year old Bobby… Jo… Parker… contacted the department claimin to have fresh information as to the whereabouts of the mine…

SLIM: Fuck.

MARK: *(Reads.)* When asked how she'd happened upon the new information, Miss Parker simply stated that pages of a diary had fallen into her possession which contained first-hand knowledge.

SLIM: No no no no no –

MARK: *(Reads.)* The Lost Dutchman's Mine was found remarkably close to the now-abandoned Glory Nugget tourist attraction…

SLIM: Bobby Jo.

MARK: No wonder e 'ung imself, readin this.

SLIM: Dwayne musta told 'er everything. E ad the diary that night. Showed it to 'er. She musta pinched the last couple of pages…

MARK: Maybe they was in on it together?

SLIM: Where did e say e was goin?

MARK: To fetch 'elp. But that e'll be back soon.

SLIM: Yeh. Oh yeh, you can always count on Dwayne.

(Sings to himself.) 'No matter how I struggle and strive… I'll never get outta this world alive…'

Beat.

We're on our own now, brother. We're on our own…

The hanged man's boots revolve slowly above them. The rattlesnakes rattle. MARK produces his emergency supply of Hobnobs and offers one to SLIM.

MARK: Biscuit?

SLIM gives him a look.

THE END

GRAND GUIGNOL

Grand Guignol was first performed on 29 October 2009 at the Drum Theatre Plymouth.

CAST *(in alphabetical order)*

PROFESSOR TARR / ANDRÉ DE LORDE / DR GORLITZ / ONE-EYE	Jonathan Broadbent
HENRI / PAULAIS / DR MARBOIS / CHARRIER / GATEAUX / NIKOLAI / NORMANDY WITCH	Philip Brodie
DR ALFRED BINET	Keir Charles
MAX MAUREY / EDGAR POE / LEVEL / THE SISTER	Robert Demeger
JEAN / CHIEF GUARD / RATINEAU / DE MORA / PHILLIPE / JOSHUA / HUNCHBACK	Samuel James
NURSE FETHER / SECOND GUARD / MAXA / SONIA / VERONIQUE / CLAIRE / LOUISE	Emily Raymond

CREATIVE TEAM

Director	Simon Stokes
Sets & Costumes	Francis O'Connor
Lighting Designer	Bruno Poet
Sound Designer	Adrienne Quartly
Casting	Lucy Jenkins
Translation of original scripts	Anthony Wise

PRODUCTION

Set, Props and Costumes	TR2 Theatre Royal Plymouth Production Centre

Act One

The Grand Guignol Theatre, Paris. 1903.

The theatre was once a chapel. What remains are the vaulted ceilings, oak beams, pew seats, carved angels looking down from above, and the smell of incense that still pervades after all these years.

The stage itself is a proscenium arch. The curtain (red) is in.

Through the auditorium is an aisle, at the back of which is an entrance/exit to the Outside World.

The place is dimly lit. The atmosphere tense, smoky, mysterious. Suddenly, three loud knocks!

The curtain rises to reveal a small stage set for 'The System of Tarr & Fether' by André de Lorde.

The setting is an austere psychiatrist's study in a mental institution somewhere in the French countryside.

At the back, some French windows, beyond which is a balcony with a 'very high drop'. The study itself has a desk cluttered with the usual detritus (files, stationary, an ink blotter, etc). There is a chair. There are two doors – the main door leads to the rest of the building, the other to an adjacent room.

It is a hot, heavy afternoon. The main door slowly opens.

Enter HENRI (chiselled, dashing, heroic).

HENRI: There's no one here, Jean.

Enter JEAN (younger, wide-eyed, cautious).

JEAN: Doors unlocked? No guards on the front gates? What sort of madhouse is this?

HENRI: I'm sure when we locate this Professor Tarr all will become clear. And please refrain from calling his renowned psychiatric hospital a 'madhouse'.

The sound of distant wailing.

JEAN: What in God's name – ?

HENRI: It sounded like… people being tortured!

HENRI throws open the French windows. He steps out onto the balcony.

HENRI: It's coming from down there!

JEAN: Careful, Henri! A fall like that could easily kill a man.

HENRI: Whoever it was, they've calmed down again now.

A muffled thump from behind the other door.

JEAN: What was that?

HENRI: What was what?

JEAN: I heard something.

HENRI: You and your imagination.

A muffled thump.

JEAN: There!

HENRI: It came from behind that door…

They approach the other door cautiously.

HENRI: Somebody there?

JEAN: Perhaps it was the madhouse mouse.

Suddenly, enter PROFESSOR TARR (wild-eyed, an eccentric edge). He closes the door behind him and glares at the two startled men.

HENRI: Good afternoon.

TARR stares at them.

HENRI: We'd like to speak with Professor Tarr, director of this institution. My name is Henri Jeunet. This is my colleague, Jean D'estoc. We're journalists for *L'Information*.

JEAN: One of the most well-regarded periodicals in all of Paris.

PROFESSOR TARR: You're a long way from the city, gentlemen.

HENRI: Indeed. Professor Tarr invited us here to interview him on his revolutionary new methods for treating the insane…

PROFESSOR TARR: Did he now?

HENRI: Yes. I have here his letter of confirmation.

As HENRI produces a letter from his jacket pocket, TARR snatches it. Finding a letter opener on the desk, he slashes the envelope, reads the letter all too quickly, then crumples it into a ball.

HENRI: Excuse me, monsieur! That was personal correspondence from Professor Tarr!

PROFESSOR TARR: And who do you presume you are talking to?

JEAN: *You're* Tarr?

PROFESSOR TARR: I am he.

A distant rumble of thunder. The two journalists react, looking about them.

PROFESSOR TARR: For too long now the insane have been treated like animals, subjected to unspeakable methods… they should be pitied, not abused.

A muffled thud from behind the door.

PROFESSOR TARR: For the love of God, I told him to be quiet!

He disappears within.

HENRI: Curious fellow.

JEAN: He gives me the chills!

HENRI: Jean, as an apprentice journalist on your first assignment there's one thing you must learn: when fishing for a scandalous story, show no fear.

JEAN: Show no fear.

TARR re-emerges, smiling.

PROFESSOR TARR: My apologies, gentlemen. A special case. The poor lunatic is beyond even my help.

JEAN: A lunatic? In there?

HENRI: Professor, your hand!

TARR's left hand appears to be bleeding.

PROFESSOR TARR: Oh. Just a scratch.

He finds a roll of bandage from the desk drawer, dresses it. As he does this:

PROFESSOR TARR: Surprised me with a straight razor. Where he found that, I don't know! He's heavily sedated now.

Enter NURSE FETHER (glassy-eyed, slightly ethereal), from the main door.

Ah! Allow me to introduce my esteemed colleague, Nurse Fether.

(To NURSE FETHER.) These are two journalists from the city, come to question our methods and observe our patients.

NURSE FETHER: It isn't a pretty sight down there, Messieurs. Poor beasts, howling away…

HENRI: But surely things have improved since the implementation of your wonderful new system, Professor?

PROFESSOR TARR: My system, my system… Yes… Things have indeed improved, monsieur…

HENRI: I'm fascinated to know how it all works.

PROFESSOR TARR: The method I have conceived for curing the mad I call 'The System of Soothing'. By this I mean not only do we *indulge* their whims, we actually *encourage* them! Reductio ad absurdum!

JEAN: Forgive me, Professor, I am no psychiatrist –

NURSE FETHER: In layman's terms, picture a patient who actually believes they are a chicken. The System of

Soothing would recognise their mania as positive fact, and we would treat the patient as if they were one.

JEAN: As if they were a chicken?

NURSE FETHER: Believe me, monsieur, a handful of corn a day goes a lot easier on the institution's budget!

She and TARR laugh hysterically. More wailing from below.

NURSE FETHER: *(Opens the window, looks down.)* Oh, the lamentable wailing of the mad!

JEAN: *(Aside, to HENRI.)* I'm not sure who's worse. The staff up here or the patients down there!

HENRI: Something's not right, Jean.

JEAN: *(Tugging at his collar.)* And this heat's insufferable.

HENRI: The calm before the storm… Come on.

HENRI marches for the main door but TARR bars his way.

PROFESSOR TARR: Where are you going?

HENRI: I want to see your patients, Professor!

Outside, it's grown dark. A loud clap of thunder. A flash of lightning. TARR and FETHER shriek.

NURSE FETHER: What was that?

HENRI: Why, just the storm, woman!

PROFESSOR TARR: The storm?

NURSE FETHER: The storm! Lightning! Thunder! It has come for us!

PROFESSOR TARR: It is here! The thunder is here!

NURSE FETHER: Where?

PROFESSOR TARR: *(Pointing at JEAN.)* There! *He* is the thunder!

JEAN: Me? Thunder? Don't be ridiculous!

PROFESSOR TARR: We have him! We have the thunder!

TARR pushes JEAN back onto the desk. FETHER ceremoniously hands TARR the letter-opener.

HENRI: Unhand him, Tarr!

FETHER takes an ink-blotter from the desk and strikes HENRI with it. He collapses.

JEAN: Oh God! Henri! Help me!

Another thunderous boom!

NURSE FETHER: Silence the thunder!

PROFESSOR TARR: Yes! The thunder must be silenced!

TARR and FETHER hold JEAN down as TARR stabs out his tongue with the letter opener.

NURSE FETHER: Get it out! Get it out!

JEAN emits terrible blood-choked screams. TARR yanks the tongue out of his head, pinched between finger and thumb.

PROFESSOR TARR: The thunder is silenced!

HENRI: *(Coming round.)* What have you done…?

PROFESSOR TARR: *(To NURSE FETHER.)* Send the thunder back from whence he came!

NURSE FETHER hauls JEAN's spasming body out of the window. JEAN goes over. FETHER loses her balance. They scream as they fall.

HENRI: Jean!

(To TARR, hysterical.) It was his first assignment, you monster! His first assignment!

TARR clucks like a chicken, tries pecking the floor.

HENRI: You're insane. Insane, I tell you!

PROFESSOR TARR: Keenly observed, monsieur. Perhaps your article should state that the system still has one or two… *(he produces a straight razor)* glitches?

He comes for HENRI, wide-eyed and grinning.

HENRI: No! Help! Help!

PROFESSOR TARR: You can shout all you like. There's no one to help you here... in the *madhouse.*

HENRI: Help me!

Suddenly, in burst CHIEF GUARD and SECOND GUARD (played by the same actors as JEAN and NURSE FETHER), through the main door. They swiftly disarm TARR and throw a strait-jacket over him.

CHIEF GUARD: Fun's over, my friend.

PROFESSOR TARR: Don't touch me! Don't you know who I am? I'm Professor Tarr!

SECOND GUARD: Nice try, Hachette.

CHIEF GUARD: *(To other GUARDS, unseen.)* Take him back to the cells, and make sure he *stays* there this time! *(Comes back in.)* What happened here?

HENRI: *(Shaking.)* Tarr... Professor Tarr... he killed Jean...

CHIEF GUARD: That wasn't Tarr. Tarr is the director of this institution. His name is Hachette. Incurably insane. Ringleader of the inmates. Very dangerous. You're lucky to be alive. He escaped this morning. Bastard put a straight razor to my throat. Locked us up in his own cell. He and his accomplice. A woman. Have you seen her?

HENRI points to the window. The SECOND GUARD runs to it, winces when he sees the two bodies far below.

SECOND GUARD: *(Deep voice.)* Fallen to her death, chief.

HENRI: *(To himself.)* A fall like that could easily kill a man... Or woman.

CHIEF GUARD: Couldn't you hear us screaming down there? Clamouring to get out?

HENRI: That was *you*? But if he wasn't the professor, then... *(Something dawns.)* When we arrived, he said he was in there with a patient...

CHIEF GUARD: Patient? There isn't any –

HENRI: He said they attacked him with a straight razor!

SECOND GUARD: Look. Seeping under the door!

HENRI: Blood!

Indeed, a pool of dark red seeps from under the door.

CHIEF GUARD: Stand back!

CHIEF GUARD breaks the door down and runs in. SECOND GUARD follows. Pause. A horrified scream. The SECOND GUARD staggers out, hand clamped over mouth.

HENRI: What has he done? What have you seen?

CHIEF GUARD: It's Professor Tarr. The *real* Professor Tarr! Help me get him out!

They carry in the corpse of the real PROFESSOR TARR, his face horribly mutilated.

CHIEF GUARD: His face! Slashed to ribbons! We can only pray that death came swiftly.

The corpse shudders to life and wails in unimaginably agony.

HENRI: *(Clutching his head.)* He's alive! The poor animal! He's *still* alive!

Tableau of Horror!

A terrified gentleman, DR ALFRED BINET, fights his way through the audience.

BINET: Out! Out! I need to get out! Is there a doctor in… the… house…?

He suddenly faints, half-on, half-off the stage. The curtain drops over him, leaving his shoes protruding.

Enter MAX MAUREY, theatre manager. He stands before the curtain, centre stage.

MAUREY: A fainter! We have a fainter! Did you see that? He fainted through sheer terror, here, at this very theatre!

This is no cheap stunt! On my word, this is *real! (Looks at the fainter's feet)* Well I'll be damned…

(To audience.) Take care as you wind your way back through the dark, cobbled streets of Montmartre. For, as we know, *real* dangers lurk in those shadowy alcoves and alley ways. If you've 'enjoyed' this evening's entertainment come back soon, and bring your friends, because there's always more gore to be spilt, more chills to be felt and copious fresh horrors to be dealt out here at the *Theâtre du Grand Guignol!*

(Calling back.) A stiff brandy for our fright-rattled friend there!

BINET's feet disappear under the curtain.

MAUREY: Until next time, pleasant dreams!

He turns up-stage. The curtain flies out. Working lights come on.

MAUREY: Is he dead?

BINET is out cold in the armchair. Attending to him is MAXA, who played NURSE FETHER/SECOND GUARD. She fans him with two floppy severed arms. PAULAIS, who played HENRI, stands looking on from the other side, mopping his brow. RATINEAU, who played JEAN, wears a blood-splattered apron and busies around in his proper role of stage manager. He rolls up the puddle of blood and carries it off.

RATINEAU: Whatever he is, get him out. You know I can't abide punters on stage.

PAULAIS: Show some mercy, Ratineau. The poor lamb's out cold.

MAXA: I know how to rouse him.

MAXA leans close to BINET and emits a horrified scream! BINET sits bolt upright.

MAUREY: Welcome back to the land of the living, monsieur!

BINET: Oh God! I'm *in* the play!

PAULAIS: *(Handing him a hip flask.)* Drink this. It'll calm your nerves.

BINET: *(Taking it gingerly.)* Thank you. Is it blood?

MAXA: Don't be silly.

BINET drinks.

MAXA: It's poison.

BINET chokes.

PAULAIS: She's joking.

BINET drinks.

PAULAIS: It *is* blood.

He chokes again. BINET gathers his wits. He produces a notebook and pencil, and writes. The company look to each other.

RATINEAU: What's 'e taking notes for?

BINET: Oh. These are… initial thoughts and feelings. It's for my paper.

MAUREY: Paper?

(Mouths the word, to company.) 'Critic!'

The company are suddenly very interested and adjust themselves accordingly.

MAUREY: Now now, don't crowd the jittery gentleman. Give him air. Let him write.

(Leaning in close.) Honoured you could join us at our humble theatre of blood, monsieur.

PAULAIS: Honoured. Honoured. Honoured.

MAXA: Are you a virgin, monsieur?

BINET: I am a father of two, mademoiselle.

PAULAIS: She means – is this your first time at the Grand Guignol?

BINET: Oh. It is.

MAUREY: And having survived your first night would it be crude to enquire… what you thought?

BINET: It's what I *felt* that is significant. My heart is pounding, my hands are shaking, my nerves are shredded and, were it not for my pathetic constitution, my dignity would still be intact too!

MAXA: Your collapsing out of sheer fright paid us the highest of compliments!

BINET: If I may say, mademoiselle, you have an exceptional gift.

MAXA: Oh, say. Say away!

BINET: The intensity you conveyed… the torturous convulsions you displayed… the tragic emptiness you possessed when portraying madness… left me speechless!

MAXA: Oh. *Good.*

MAUREY: Behold, The Magnificent Paula Maxa. Mistress of the Macabre, Death's Divine Diva, and Montmartre's one and only Queen – *(she screams)* of Scream.

BINET: Incredible.

MAXA: You find Maxa blushing at your kind words, monsieur…

PAULAIS: And what of the other performances?

MAXA: Don't fish, you whore.

BINET: I have never seen such conviction, such emotion, such *truth*, on stage as I have tonight.

PAULAIS: If, perchance, I managed to make you believe that my own arms were chopped off and fed to me, then I can rest easy in the knowledge that I have, in some small way, succeeded in my task.

MAUREY: Georges Paulais. The Grand Guignol's leading man.

PAULAIS: I see myself as an archetype both heroic *and* intelligent.

RATINEAU: But don't believe everything you see in the theatre.

BINET: Oh, you were very good too!

RATINEAU: Shut up.

MAUREY: This young gore-hound is Ratineau, our stage manager, prop-maker, and secondary player.

MAXA: There's no horror he can't realise with his ghoulish materials, bubbling pots of fake blood and yards of rubber tubing!

RATINEAU: Don't give away the trade secrets!

BINET: You are a true craftsman, and a fine actor.

RATINEAU: Tell me. What was the moment that drove you to leave the theatre?

BINET: It wasn't so much a specific moment, more the intense cumulative effect of the entire evening. As the lights dimmed, I giggled like a school boy. But, thereupon, my nervous laughter swiftly gave way to fevered, icy sweats!

MAUREY: Suddenly you found yourself all awhirl in a cauldron of thrills!

BINET: And as each new play began, the noose closed a little tighter about my throat. Tighter… tighter… oooh!

MAUREY: *(To RATINEAU.)* I've never seen this level of reaction before. He was drawn in, gripped, chilled, thrilled and knocked out cold. He's positively *horrified.*

RATINEAU: That is the general idea, Max.

MAUREY: We've built good houses throughout this first season, but with a rave notice from our friend here we could see this place packed to the rafters. I could see myself a very rich man… Fetch de Lorde! He'll want to see the trembling effects of his writing in the flesh!

RATINEAU: *(Shouts to backstage.)* André! We have a fainter!

BINET: André? De Lorde?

MAXA: The premiere playwright of the Grand Guignol.

BINET: He's here? The Prince of Terror himself?

MAUREY: Our resident demented genius! Would you like to meet him?

BINET: I'm not entirely certain I would. I have heard such tales… Is it true he sleeps in a coffin? That he was raised in an asylum? That he writes his scripts in human blood?

PAULAIS: Yes but very rarely his own.

BINET: I ought to be going.

MAXA: Too late, I fear. Behold, he comes…

The theatre creaks. BINET looks about him, unnerved, as shadows lengthen and the company seem to warp grotesquely in their aspect. Somewhere, far off, a child weeps… A hand looms up from nowhere and touches BINET's shoulder.

BINET: *(With fright.)* Ahh!

Reality snaps back. Standing there is ANDRÉ DE LORDE – he is immaculately groomed, ruddy of cheek, and wearing a warm smile.

DE LORDE: Are you the fainter?

BINET: Monsieur de Lorde?

MAUREY: This is our Prince of Terror!

BINET: *(To DE LORDE.)* Yes, monsieur. My legs, indeed, betrayed me…

DE LORDE: So you were frightened?

BINET: Out of my wits.

DE LORDE: Oh, I'm so pleased.

BINET: I am still reeling from your collection of extraordinary plays.

DE LORDE: Scary stuff, eh?

BINET: Allow me to introduce myself. My name is Alfred Binet and –

DE LORDE: Binet? *Dr* Binet? From the Salpêtrière Asylum for the Incurably Insane?

BINET: I prefer Hospital for the Psychologically Unsound but… yes.

DE LORDE: I am a great admirer of your work!

BINET: You are?

DE LORDE: *(To the company.)* Dr Binet is one of Paris's leading lights in modern psychology. He's written many fascinating papers on the capabilities of the human mind!

COMPANY: Oh.

DE LORDE: The last I read, you were conducting a study on the creative mind.

BINET: An avenue I am still pursuing.

MAUREY: So you're not a critic?

BINET: Goodness, no. Merely a devotee of the theatrical arts.

MAUREY: But you said you were writing something for your 'paper'.

BINET: I am writing *a* paper to be published in *The Psychiatrist's Journal* next month.

PAULAIS: So he's not a critic?

MAXA: *(Drops the two prop arms immediately.)* Maxa has been tricked! All that effort…

MAXA and PAULAIS exit backstage.

RATINEAU: *(To DE LORDE, a whisper.)* Get him off the stage. I don't want him nosing around.

DE LORDE: *(A whisper.)* But it's Alfred Binet!

RATINEAU: *(A whisper.)* I want him gone by the time I get back.

RATINEAU exits to the Outside.

MAUREY: Right. Well. I'm going to count the takings. And then I'm going to get pissed.

MAUREY exits.

On stage, BINET and DE LORDE stand looking at each other. Awkward silence.

BINET: Monsieur de Lorde.

DE LORDE: Dr Binet!

BINET: I came here this evening for a reason. The new paper I'm writing is a study on creative behaviorism in children and chess players. After tonight's phantasmagoria, I want to add playwrights to that list! Would you consider discussing the topic further?

DE LORDE: What topic might that be?

BINET: I wish to interview you on your working practises.

DE LORDE: Oh?

BINET: I'm very curious to know why you would write such lurid entertainments. I would like to know where all this horror comes from!

DE LORDE: Where it all comes from?

BINET: What do you say?

DE LORDE: I would be honoured, doctor. But only on one condition. If I allow you to pick my brain, then you must allow me to pick yours. Reciprocal research.

BINET: Reciprocal research?

DE LORDE: I wish to know more about the field of psychiatry. For my plays. I'm a stickler for detail.

BINET: Of course. Anything to be of service.

DE LORDE: Excellent.

BINET: Excellent. Well, it's late. My wife will be wondering where I am! Tomorrow? Here? After the show?

DE LORDE: After the show. Thank you for fainting, doctor. It means a great deal to me. They sometimes shudder and they sometimes scream, but you were the first to respond in the truly correct manner!

BINET: The terror was all mine. Look at that. *(Presents his hand.)* Still shaking.

BINET exits to the Outside World.

DE LORDE: Dr Alfred Binet…

Enter RATINEAU from the Outside World. He has the late edition of 'L'Information'. It has a headline on it: LE MONSTRE DE MONTMARTRE!

RATINEAU: He's struck again! The Monster of Montmartre!

DE LORDE: That's the third murder to happen on our very door step. It chills the blood…

RATINEAU: Want the gory details?

DE LORDE: Certainly not!

RATINEAU: Come on. You love this stuff. It's inspiration!

DE LORDE: These are innocent women, Ratineau!

Beat.

How was the victim found?

RATINEAU: Same as the others.

DE LORDE: Dear God. He's honing his craft.

RATINEAU: But this is new… they say he's left a mark on 'em. A symbol cut into their flesh…

DE LORDE: What kind of symbol?

RATINEAU: Authorities say it can only best be described as… a five-pointed star.

DE LORDE: A pentangle. An icon of the dark arts. That suggests that these killings are ritualistic, quite possibly Satanic, in motive.

RATINEAU: Bloody hell…

DE LORDE: Madmen are at liberty, Ratineau, and monsters live within us all…

RATINEAU: Yup. It appears so.

MAXA and PAULAIS enter from backstage in coats and hats.

PAULAIS: *(Re: RATINEAU's paper.)* Look, it's splashed across the front page! I just think the presence of a gentleman might offer you some protection.

MAXA: So might this.

She produces a huge butcher's knife from her coat.

RATINEAU: Is that one of my props?

MAXA: I'll bring it back tomorrow.

PAULAIS: Maxa, really, I should accompany you home.

MAXA: Thank you darling, but a girl needs more than an actor on her arm what with that nasty bastard running about.

PAULAIS: He goes after woman on their own, so they say.

RATINEAU: Prostitutes.

PAULAIS: What's that?

RATINEAU: They've all been prostitutes. So far.

MAXA: I have nothing to fear. I am Maxa.

PAULAIS: Then… could you walk me home?

MAXA: Ha.

PAULAIS: Safety in numbers!

RATINEAU: I thought your mother was in tonight, Paulais? She'd scare off any knife-wielding maniac.

PAULAIS: She left after the third play. Once again, her hunger for drama was overcome by her thirst for gin.

MAXA: Oh, darling.

PAULAIS: I try to please her! Really, I try! Maman. My greatest critic…

Enter MAUREY, elated.

MAUREY: We're in profit! A small profit, but a profit nonetheless! Who wants a drink?

MAXA: Max?

PAULAIS: On the house? Really?

RATINEAU: Quick!

MAXA: To the Clare de Lune! At once!

They all exit in a hurry.

MAUREY: Not you, de Lorde. You need to write. Conjure more horrors for the next season. We had one fainter tonight! I want them *all* fainting!

DE LORDE: But that would require the plays to become more… extreme.

MAUREY: Good! Spill more blood! Show more flesh! That's what the people of Paris want to see! Nothing sells better than guts and tits!

DE LORDE: But –

MAUREY: I know you've got depraved stories of your own forming in that sick mind of yours. Unleash them, boy. Commit them to paper. Write that play!

MAUREY exits to the Outside.

DE LORDE: Easier said than done, Max.

DE LORDE removes his jacket, rolls up his sleeves, lights a candle, sits at the desk. DE LORDE knocks three times…

From the bowels of the theatre, a distant, eerie chanting… whispering… a child sobbing… The theatre's very bones creak.

VOICE: Time crawls close to midnight nearly,
He bends to write, all weak and weary
Over parchment, pen in hand
Not so unlike the play before –
Whilst I nodded, clearly napping
Suddenly there came a tapping
As of someone gently rapping,
Rapping on my chamber door!
'Tis some playwright!' I mutter –
'By the name of André de Lorde!'
A playwright this, and nothing more…

Enter EDGAR ALLAN POE, with satanic theatricality, a stuffed raven perched on his shoulder.

POE: You rang, de Lorde?

DE LORDE: Hello, Edgar.

POE: I take it the last play went well?

DE LORDE: It was a great success. All thanks to you.

POE: May you rot for stealing my work!

DE LORDE: I didn't steal, monsieur! I only adapted *Tarr & Fether* at your suggestion. I would never have dared to otherwise.

POE: But now you call upon me again…

DE LORDE: I have to write another one…

POE: And you called me. You called because you need me.

DE LORDE: I beg you, go easy this time?

POE: Writing isn't 'easy'. Writing is agony given shape on the page.

DE LORDE: And grows more agonising with every word…

POE: I presume you'll be wanting another of my stories for 'ease'?

DE LORDE: Actually, this time I thought I'd try one of my own?

POE: Did you now?

DE LORDE: Maurey desires the boundaries to be pushed.

POE: And you think you can better the horrors of Edgar Poe?

DE LORDE: Of course not, monsieur! What am I without you? I couldn't escape your influence if I tried!

POE: Exactly! Everything you create comes from me. Never forget that!

DE LORDE: Never!

POE: Does this new work have a title?

DE LORDE: I call it… 'Laboratory of Hallucinations'.

POE: Sounds like one of mine.

Beat.

Well? Pick up the pen, draw up the ink, and write.

DE LORDE's trembling hand picks up the pen. He stares at it.

POE: Afraid? It's only a play, de Lorde.

DE LORDE: It's only a play…

Beat, steels himself.

To set the scene… we find ourselves in a… country house which also doubles as a clinic for the brain surgeon, Dr Marbois.

POE: And what is his character?

DE LORDE: He is brilliant, but brutal.

POE: Of course he is. And so, what happens?

DE LORDE: *(Straining to create.)* He… has… a beautiful wife named… Sonia. But… she has fallen in love with another man –

POE: Who?

DE LORDE: A neighbour. Let's call him de Mora. They have a plan to elope, to be free of Marbois for good! Sonia and de Mora meet that very afternoon –

POE: Where?

DE LORDE: Some nearby ruins. It's all very innocent.

POE: But?

DE LORDE: But…

DE LORDE grabs a costume rail from the wings, grabs a white lab coat, adopts the frantic movements of a mad doctor.

DE LORDE: Whilst Marbois is conducting his experiments –

DE LORDE grabs a crate of props (rusty tools, a bunch of tatty flowers, a melon, etc) from the other side.

DE LORDE: De Mora is brought to the clinic.

POE: He is?

DE LORDE: On his way to meet Sonia, his car over-turned, and some villagers unwittingly brought him to the doctor for saving…

POE: Go on.

DE LORDE: De Mora's skull is –

POE: Horribly fractured! Only Marbois has the power to save him!

DE LORDE: Yes! But on preparing de Mora for emergency brain surgery, the doctor finds something on his person!

POE: What?

DE LORDE: A love letter!

POE: From Sonia!

DE LORDE: Insane with jealousy, hell-bent on revenge, Marbois cracks open de Mora's skull!

DE LORDE messily lops off the top of the melon and gouges out the flesh.

And begins to snip vital lobes in the helpless man's very brain!

POE offers a pair of scissors. DE LORDE takes them and snips at the melon –

POE: And then what happens?

DE LORDE: Enter Sonia! She is horrified to discover her lover's skull sawn open, his brain exposed, now near-demented, a love letter besplattered with blood, her wicked husband fully aware of their infidelity!

POE: And then?

DE LORDE: *(Crazed now.)* Marbois tells Sonia that with this final snip de Mora will be forever rendered a mindless, gibbering idiot!

POE: Yes!

DE LORDE: But de Mora, the rational side of his brain now cut adrift and lost forever, rises from the slab, overpowers Marbois and straps *him* to the table!

POE: Yes! Yes!

DE LORDE: And does to the demented doctor what was indeed intended for him!

DE LORDE holds the scissors against his own head. In his other hand, a lump hammer. He takes careful aim –

DE LORDE: Until there is nothing on stage… but *suffering*!

DE LORDE goes to hammer the scissors.

Tableau of Horror!

Darkness. The metal-clunk-and-skull-cracking sound of scissors being repeatedly hammered into DE LORDE's skull accompanied by agonising screams.

Beat. Then… fulsome applause. MAXA, PAULAIS, RATINEAU take their bows.

PAULAIS, as MARBOIS, has a pair of scissors sticking out of his head. MAXA has a bouquet of red roses in her hands. RATINEAU is splattered in blood, and has his brains exposed. All appear humbled by the response.

The company turn up-stage and exit. Curtain drops in. Before it, BINET and DE LORDE. BINET has a notebook and pencil. DE LORDE has a bandage about his head marked with a dot of dried blood.

BINET: What is this obsession you have with frightening people?

DE LORDE: I'm not sure it's an obsession…

BINET: What happened to your head?

DE LORDE: Oh, nothing. A little writing accident.

BINET: Dangerous business, eh?

DE LORDE: It can be.

BINET: Tell me about your childhood?

DE LORDE: Have we started the interview?

BINET: Yes, I suppose we have. Is that all right with you?

DE LORDE: Please. Proceed.

BINET: Your childhood –

DE LORDE: Yes.

BINET: Rumours abound that you were raised in an asylum!

DE LORDE: If only I were *that* interesting.

BINET: Playwrights, actors, lunatics – all are eminently fascinating to me!

Beat.

Tell me about your parents…

DE LORDE: My father was a physician. My mother, a pianist. They separated when I was nine.

BINET: A traumatic time for anyone, not least a child.

DE LORDE: They sat me down, explained the situation –

BINET: But there was violence.

DE LORDE: It was all very amicable.

BINET: *(Writes.)* No violence…

DE LORDE: Mother soon re-married –

BINET: And you felt that your father had been replaced by another man. You grew isolated, angry –

DE LORDE: Actually it was my dear stepfather who fostered my passion for the theatre. He was an actor. Introduced me to the masters – Sophocles, Euripides, Shakespeare –

BINET: But, in seeing your true father less and less, you found yourself prone to uncontrollable adolescent emotions which, over the years, you learnt to bury, and now express through the writing of horror theatre?

DE LORDE: I saw my father each weekend, doctor.

BINET: Are you still in contact with your parents?

DE LORDE: Both, sadly, are gone…

BINET: How did they die?

DE LORDE: Has anyone survived this gruelling analysis with their wits intact?

BINET: It's a harmless interview. If you want gruelling, you should try one of my intelligence tests. I drive my poor daughters to distraction.

DE LORDE: You experiment on your own daughters, doctor?

BINET: Nothing ghoulish about that! Merely gathering data!

DE LORDE: Croaked the insane psychiatrist as he drilled a hole into his loved one's pretty skull.

BINET: Good God, de Lorde!

DE LORDE: Now that's a play worth writing!

Suddenly, enter POE!

POE: De Lorde!

Horror cacophony! Smoke and light! He stares at DE LORDE, who is paralysed with fear.

DE LORDE: Ahhh!

BINET: *(Can't see POE at all.)* Is everything all right?

DE LORDE: Oh God! Not now!

BINET: I'm sorry?

DE LORDE: *(To POE, despairing.)* Why are you here?

BINET: We made an appointment.

DE LORDE: Leave me be!

BINET: Very well. Perhaps I should come back?

DE LORDE: Please! I beg you!

POE: You cannot write without me, de Lorde!

DE LORDE: Oh God!

BINET: André?

POE: Not without my help!

DE LORDE: Give me peace!

POE: You shall find none until you have squeezed your last drop of pain out onto the page.

DE LORDE: I beg you! For my sanity's sake –

POE: Too late for that!

POE approaches DE LORDE. BINET comes between them.

BINET: André?

DE LORDE: *(Wild-eyed.)* Help me! Please help me, Alfred!

BINET: Of course! Of course!

DE LORDE: Say you will! Say the words! Say it!

BINET: I will help you, André!

And like that, POE vanishes. DE LORDE looks to where POE once was. BINET observes, fascinated, unnerved.

DE LORDE: You did it. Thank you, doctor.

BINET: For what?

DE LORDE: Forgive me. I must look... mad to you.

BINET: André, what just happened?

DE LORDE: Think nothing of it.

BINET: I thought you wanted my help.

DE LORDE: Oh, I do Alfred. I do. A new play must be written! And you are the man to help me write it!

BINET: Me? I don't know the first thing about writing plays!

DE LORDE: Think of it merely as an experiment! Shall we collaborate?

BINET: I can't deny I'm wildly curious!

DE LORDE: Good! So. To set the scene... *(stops, listens to the theatre, looks about him for POE – but there's nothing)* A doctor – let's call him Charrier – has a laboratory – one of those fancy annexes built on the side of his isolated country house! The doctor has a daughter. Her name is...

BINET: Véronique? He loves her very much!

DE LORDE: Yes. But unnaturally so.

BINET: Oh.

DE LORDE: He displays this in Act One, caressing her hair and back in an overly tactile manner.

BINET: Inappropriate obsessions bordering on fetish – perhaps denoting his own abuse as a child?

DE LORDE: I like that. Now, conflict: she is engaged to a handsome young man –

BINET: Perhaps an apprentice to Charrier?

DE LORDE: Good! Of whom Charrier is very jealous. It's suggested that he's tried to put a spanner in the works of their wedding. They know. But he doesn't know they know!

BINET: That's drama!

DE LORDE: The doctor is obsessed with his work. He's close to a breakthrough. Something chillingly prescient…

BINET: I read something in *The Psychiatrist's Journal* the other day about resuscitation of the human brain via electro-stimulation.

DE LORDE: In the name of science, a noble and life-saving cause! But what if such a procedure were to be conducted long after death had taken place?

BINET puts a hand over his mouth.

DE LORDE: Is it working its horrors upon you?

BINET nods.

DE LORDE: 'I'm going to visit grandmother. I'm taking the car. I'll only be an hour. I know a shortcut!'

BINET: I'm sorry?

DE LORDE: That's what Véronique says, and she takes her fiancé with her…

They start to move closer.

DE LORDE: While they are gone, Dr Charrier has a visitor…

BINET: He does?

DE LORDE: The town executioner.

BINET: Oh my. What does he do?

DE LORDE: He brings news that a criminal is soon to be guillotined, and that the body will be available for experimentation.

BINET: Charrier doesn't… does *he*?

DE LORDE: He does! Before he leaves, the executioner tells the story of a decapitated corpse whose hands suddenly *clamped* so tightly around his arm that the priest had to cut through the dead man's fingers with a hack-saw! The executioner exits…

BINET: Something horrible is coming!

DE LORDE: Dr Charrier's lunatic desire has been carefully placed to suggest that he will stop at nothing to achieve his twisted goal! And then… and then…

BINET: The corpse of the criminal arrives?

DE LORDE: The corpse of the *daughter.*

BINET: Véronique's *dead?!*

DE LORDE: Véronique took her short cut, driving around those narrow country lanes. You see, a carefree young woman very much in love does not tend to regard the speed at which she is hurtling, does not possess the reflexes needed to slow down for the break-neck bend. The fiancé –

BINET: Philippe!

DE LORDE: Struggles free of the twisted wreck but Véronique, her golden hair soaked in blood, is dead. Her broken body –

CHARRIER: Still warm.

VÉRONIQUE (MAXA) is laid out on the table. CHARRIER (PAULAIS) and PHILIPPE (RATINEAU), injured, stand over her.

CHARRIER: I can save her!

DE LORDE: Philippe protests –

PHILIPPE: No, Charrier!

A wind howls, a shutter rattles.

DE LORDE: The doctor makes his preparations…

CHARRIER fixes a strange crown of copper wiring and contact points to VÉRONIQUE's bloody head. He tightens three conductive screws into her skull. The grinding of metal against bone is heard.

CHARRIER: We must make absolutely certain all six electro-conductors have pierced the skull and are embedded deeply within her brain!

PHILIPPE: This is an abomination!

CHARRIER: You must get the better of your nerves, Philippe! It's the only way to save your precious Véronique now!

CHARRIER rips open her bodice. Lightning crashes. BINET looks away. CHARRIER plunges a ghastly-looking needle into her chest.

CHARRIER: A secondary electrode into her heart, inserted just above the breast…

PHILIPPE: Charrier, I beg you…

CHARRIER: Throw the switch, Philippe! Full power! We must move quickly! Flesh decomposes!

(stroking her hair)

You shall live again, my beautiful! You shall live again!

DE LORDE: The wind howls! A shutter blows open!

The shutter blows open. Wind howls in.

BINET: Ahhh!

DE LORDE: It's alright, Alfred, it's only a play!

BINET: It's only a play, it's *only* a play!

CHARRIER: The switch, Philippe! *Now!*

PHILIPPE throws a switch on a machine. A shower of sparks. A strange blue light glows from dials, the ampoule flickers and an eerie electrical hum builds in intensity. Strange sounds start emanating from VÉRONIQUE's throat.

CHARRIER: It's working. Look, Philippe! She's twitching! Reaching up!

PHILIPPE: No! *NO!* It cannot be!

DE LORDE: As she rises, he kisses his daughter's hands – which suddenly spasm! Grip tight about his throat! Tight! Tighter! The dead girl's fingers squeeze the air from her father's windpipe! Her nails sinking deep into his soft flesh!

DE LORDE strangles BINET.

BINET: *Arrrrrrggggghhhhhhh!!!!!!*

DE LORDE: And behold, our play!

BINET: It's written?

DE LORDE: 'The Horrible Experiment' by André de Lorde and Alfred Binet.

BINET: Oh no, I hardly did anything!

DE LORDE: I insist!

BINET: I helped write a play! How thrilling!

DE LORDE: You helped more than you can ever know, doctor.

BINET: So what happens now?

DE LORDE: Now Alfred, we stage it!

They vanish, and let the play reach its climax with full-blown theatrics (ampoule and device glowing, sparking, the eerie electric whine at its height):

VÉRONIQUE's hands clasp around CHARRIER's throat. He gasps.

PHILIPPE: Véronique?

CHARRIER: My throat! Philippe!

PHILIPPE: The current! The current is doing this!

CHARRIER: The *switch*... the... *sssswii...*

VÉRONIQUE now stands, eyes wide, staring deep and dead. CHARRIER's on his knees.

CHARRIER: I'm choking...!

PHILIPPE goes to throw the switch to stop the current – another shower of sparks!

PHILIPPE: Oh God! It won't turn off! It won't turn off!

CHARRIER: Her fingers... Philippe... saw... through... her fingers...

PHILIPPE finds an array of surgical instruments nearby – he picks up a medical bone-saw. He starts to saw through VÉRONIQUE's knuckles. Blood.

CHARRIER: Quicker! *Quuuuickkk-errrrrrr...*

Lightning flashes! Thunder booms! The electric hum is unbearable now! VÉRONIQUE turns and stares into PHILIPPE's eyes... PHILIPPE stops sawing.

CHARRIER: Help... me...!

PHILIPPE: No, Charrier. I won't.

PHILIPPE drops the saw.

CHARRIER: Do as I say!!!

PHILIPPE: You had this coming! We knew you had plans to sabotage our wedding. She told me. And she told me all about you. The things you did to her as a child! This is her revenge! Congratulations, doctor. It seems your experiment... is a *success!*

PHILIPPE laughs dementedly. VÉRONIQUE continues to squeeze. Blood oozes through her fingers. CHARRIER chokes horrifically.

Tableau of Horror!

The curtain drops. Wild applause.

Enter MAUREY through the curtains, followed by DE LORDE and BINET.

MAUREY: Fainters! Pukers! Walk-outs! They're leaving in droves, then coming back for more! Congratulations, de Lorde, you sick animal! Whatever you're dreaming up with the weak-kneed doctor works a treat! This new repertoire is twice as twisted, which means the tickets can be twice the price!

DE LORDE: With Dr Binet, I have discovered a new approach to writing. We have a fine and fruitful collaboration!

BINET: I do nothing but stand around, I swear.

DE LORDE: But your influence in the work is palpable. Your expertise lends each play a legitimacy that I have long quested for and never found. Until now.

BINET: And I came to pick *your* brains!

MAUREY: I'm having to put medical staff on the front door. The damned audience has to sign a waiver before they enter absolving us of responsibility in case they die of fright, yet they're queued up round the block whilst a crazed killer stalks the streets! Does it deter them? Does it bollocks! The Grand Guignol is an unmitigated success, de Lorde!

DE LORDE: I couldn't be happier for you, Max.

Enter PAULAIS and MAXA from backstage in civilian attire.

PAULAIS: ... and there I am, playing the grandest theatre in all of Paris. It's a full house, all priests, and I'm completely naked. I can't remember any of my lines and my mother sits there in the front row, amongst a sea of horrified faces and cries, 'He's no good! He's just no bloody good!' and then this enormous snake comes slithering out of the darkness –

BINET: What play is this?

MAXA: This is no play, man. This is a terrible nightmare he used to have.

PAULAIS: How would you interpret that dream, doctor?

BINET: The crushing weight of a mother's expectations?

PAULAIS: Oh, he's good.

MAXA: But now the nightmares are gone!

PAULAIS: Just like that!

BINET: Interesting. It's as if performing André's horrors on stage alleviates your subconscious fears.

MAXA: Or perhaps it's the relief of being employed?

MAUREY: Nonsense! It is simply the confidence that comes with success!

PAULAIS: The strange thing is, I somewhat miss the dream. It was a horror to draw upon. I pray to the gods my brilliance does not fade in the same way my fears have!

Enter RATINEAU from the Outside.

RATINEAU: There's a Police Inspector outside wants a word with you, Paulais.

PAULAIS: The authorities? What is it regarding?

RATINEAU: Best talk to the Inspector yourself, eh?

Exit PAULAIS to the Outside.

DE LORDE: Is everything all right?

RATINEAU: It's his mother. She's been found dead.

MAXA: What?

MAUREY: Oh!

BINET: God!

DE LORDE: Dead?

RATINEAU: They found a body behind the chemist on the Rue Agile.

MAXA: How did she die?

RATINEAU: They're saying it's murder.

The company gasp.

RATINEAU: Evidence suggests… The Monster of Montmartre.

BINET bites his fist.

DE LORDE: Evidence, Ratineau?

RATINEAU: Had his signature all over it. Tongue hacked out. Eyes scooped from her skull. Belly sliced open. Guts removed. Meat hook through the ankles and left hanging from a lamp post, bleeding her last from the gash in her throat.

MAXA: Ghastly, ghastly business.

RATINEAU: It gets worse. Madame Paulais was, as we know, a woman of considerable size. The fixing on the lamp must've broke… she fell into the alley, where the rats were waiting. Said it took two days to identify the body. The only discernible distinguishing marks? A bunch o' five pointed stars carved with a surgeon's precision into her flesh.

BINET does all he can to stop himself being sick.

RATINEAU: Oh, the Inspector wondered if there was any tickets left for Friday night?

MAUREY: Tell him we'll give him a couple of house seats.

RATINEAU: Keep 'em sweet, eh?

RATINEAU exits.

BINET: This could herald severe trauma for Paulais. How close was he to his mother?

DE LORDE: He was terrified of her. Hence his nightmares.

MAXA: If you ask me, she got what she deserved.

Exit MAXA.

MAUREY: I do hope this doesn't affect sales…

The curtain drops. BINET, before the curtain, is alone with his notebook.

BINET: Each play always climaxes with an act of extreme violence, the spilling of blood and a typically agonising death. I am convinced that the themes of these plays are in cycle in de Lorde's consciousness. But why? Could his prolific creative output be itself some form of catharsis? Is it strange that such intense and brutal horrors emanate from such a seemingly sweet, good-natured man?

(To himself.) His childhood… His childhood…

Enter DE LORDE from backstage.

DE LORDE: That's the first sign of madness, talking to yourself.

BINET: I'm pulling together your psychological profile.

DE LORDE: And what have you deduced?

BINET: That you have a generous spirit and the heart of a ten year old boy!

DE LORDE: Yes, and I keep it in a pickling jar on my bedside table.

BINET: Ha.

DE LORDE: Maurey is demanding another play.

BINET: I thought we might attempt to dig a little deeper into your psyche first?

DE LORDE: Digging, digging, always digging.

BINET: Now tell me, your mother –

DE LORDE: Alfred, I've told you all about my childhood. I'm not going to suddenly remember some long-lost trauma which shaped my consciousness and made me a writer of horror theatre! You're a bag of nerves but I'm convinced there's no *one* incident from your past which made you a doctor of psychiatry.

BINET: Actually… there is.

DE LORDE: Is there?

BINET: When I was five, my parents sent me away to school in Nice. A ghastly place. Vast, cold, echoing dormitories. The older boys would goose me, lock me in cupboards, flick matches through the gaps, piss in my milk. And they all bowed to the ringleader – Gregor Gateaux.

DE LORDE: I bet there was nothing sweet about him.

BINET: Gregor existed solely to make my life a living hell. And he was inventive too… Did you know if someone dips your index finger in a cup of water whilst you are asleep, you involuntarily wet yourself?

DE LORDE: I didn't know that.

BINET: Gregor Gateaux did, and utilised the phenomenon to full effect!

(Distant.) But for all the elaborate japery he conjured up, it was the simplest trick that pushed me over the edge… When the steward called lights-out, all hell would break loose. I would wait, nobly biding my time, until each and every one of those monsters had fallen asleep. Then I would creep as silently as I could down the corridor to do my ablutions. But someone was watching… in the dark… and that someone had laid a trap…

DE LORDE: Gregor Gateaux.

BINET: Relieved, fresh of breath and longing for sleep, I threw back the sheets –

DE LORDE: *(Seeing it.)* Yes?

BINET: That devil! So terrifying, even now –

DE LORDE: *Yes?!*

BINET: I threw back the sheets, and there… before me… grinning, skinless in the moonlight! He had placed –

DE LORDE: What, man? What?

BINET: A fabric skeleton!

DE LORDE: Oh. Oh, that's a good one.

BINET: Admittedly it doesn't sound much now but as a child it was very frightening.

DE LORDE: No, no! Fabric skeletons? Terrifying when you aren't expecting them!

BINET: I screamed all through the night until my parents came to collect me. Oh, how the boys pointed and laughed, pointed and laughed… All except Gregor. He just sat in bed with this little smirk on his face. Why did he do those things to me? What had I ever done to him? Why was this boy so predisposed to torture? What makes a person who they are? If I wanted to get to the bottom of these questions, if I myself was to find some understanding in Gregor's maliciousness, I realised that I would have to learn the mysterious byways of the human mind. So I did.

DE LORDE: Do you know what became of him?

BINET: The last I heard, Gregor Gateaux had suffered the self- imposed fate of most school bullies.

DE LORDE: Killed himself?

BINET: Joined the police force. I often think about what would happen if I ran into him on the street…

DE LORDE: What would you do?

BINET: I would sit him down, discuss his problems in depth… then skewer his beady eyes out!

DE LORDE: This place is having an effect on you, doctor.

BINET: I blame you entirely!

Beat, with hatred.

Gregor Gateaux.

DE LORDE: Do you know, your story's helped me dredge up something from my past.

BINET: Oh?

DE LORDE: My father used to lock me up in rooms with dead people.

BINET: He what?

DE LORDE: Yes. He used to take me along with him when he visited patients. Some had minor ailments but some were dying. Or dead. His job would be to sign their certificates. I would wait outside the door while he saw to them and imagine such horrors. One time, I whipped myself into a frenzy. Seeing that I was terrified, father dragged me into the tiny room and locked me up with the corpse so that I would learn how not to be afraid of death.

BINET: Did it work, in your opinion?

DE LORDE: Yes. I am unafraid of death.

BINET: You are also utterly obsessed with it.

DE LORDE: Papa did what he thought was best for a lily-livered nine year old boy.

BINET: Why didn't you tell me about this earlier?

DE LORDE: I've only just remembered it. Haven't thought about it in years.

BINET: André, the man locked you up with a dead person! Only *now* do you remember it?

DE LORDE: People. Dead *people.*

BINET: He did it repeatedly?

DE LORDE: Oh, yes! He even shut me up with my mother.

BINET: Your *mother*? God! Oh, God!

DE LORDE: Alfred, it was fine. I didn't look at her once, though Lord knows father did his damnedest. 'Look at her! Look at her!' She was so terribly damaged from the accident, you see? And he was there, wailing like a lunatic. Which, it transpired, he was. They dragged him screaming to the Salpêtrière Asylum.

BINET: Wait. Your mother died in an accident?

DE LORDE: She had been playing for the sisters at the local convent. A slaughterhouse wagon was passing. The horse bolted. Ploughed into the chapel. Nuns and blood everywhere. Mother didn't die immediately…

BINET: And your father was deemed insane?

DE LORDE: She was broken… so horribly horribly broken…

BINET: That is an extremely traumatic experience for anyone, not least a nine-year-old boy!

DE LORDE: Trauma? Nonsense! It's all part of growing up. Death is a lesson of life, man.

BINET: No psyche experiences such scarring and gets away with it! This new information changes everything! I want to help you, André.

DE LORDE: But you *are* helping me Alfred. Writing was agony before. Now it's a joy! I can't tell you why. Call it the mystery of creation. My torment is banished now that I no longer have to collaborate with Poe.

BINET: Poe?

DE LORDE: Edgar Poe. The famous American short story writer.

BINET: I know Poe. Poe's dead. What do you mean you 'collaborate' with him?

DE LORDE: It's complicated.

BINET folds his arms and waits.

DE LORDE: Edgar Poe was a great influence on me in more ways than one. He would come whenever I had to write.

BINET: The episode you suffered from recently…?

DE LORDE: Was the last time I saw him.

BINET: But now you no longer have these… visitations?

DE LORDE: I have no use for him now that you're here. Thanks to you his shadow has no hold over me whatsoever!

(To the theatre.) Do you hear that, Edgar? You have no power over me, you malicious bastard! I beat you! I beat you back into the darkness!

The curtain goes out to reveal the stage stripped back.

RATINEAU sets two chairs and a costume rail with dresses, upstage.

RATINEAU: I hate to interrupt your insane rant André but can I ask you to vacate the stage?

BINET: We're in the middle of something, Ratineau.

RATINEAU: Tell that to Maxa. She'll be here in minute. For a rendezvous.

BINET: It's late. My wife will be wondering where I am.

DE LORDE: Don't go. We should write. While the muse is with us.

BINET: It's with you, André. Not me. Another time perhaps.

RATINEAU: *(To DE LORDE.)* Could you pop down to the workshop? I'd like to try and gouge your eyes out.

DE LORDE: We'll be right there.

RATINEAU: Alone?

Exit DE LORDE and RATINEAU backstage. BINET frantically scrawls notes.

BINET: At last! Subject revealed defining traumatic incident in childhood. Several, in fact! Dead mother. Father incarcerated. Also revealed delusional proclivities. Edgar Allan Poe…

Beat.

My God. He's insane.

Enter MAXA.

MAXA: I've been watching you, doctor. I've been observing you 'observe'. Noting down our strange little rituals and practises.

BINET: A privileged insight into the artistic world.

MAXA: Horseshit. What are you trying to do with André?

BINET: I'm not sure I quite understand…

MAXA: You wouldn't be trying to cure him of his precious malady, would you? He's an artist. His emotions are heightened, pulling like the tide one way and then the other. I don't expect you to understand, but it's true. I ask you kindly: leave him the way he is. Assist him by all means, but don't apply any of your newfangled psycho-analytic gibberish on him.

BINET: What are you trying to say, Maxa?

MAXA: We need him tortured. We need him tormented. We need his plays.

BINET: I appreciate your dedication to the genre but… surely there are other theatres? Other roles?

MAXA: *(Darkens.)* Dr Binet, I am the most assassinated actress in the world.

Throughout the following, she slips out of her clothes (hanging up the butcher's knife she carries about with her nearby) and into a stunning white dress.

MAXA: In the brief time we have been producing André's work, I have been shot by firing squad, hung, drawn, quartered, burned alive, crucified, devoured by a mountain puma, kissed by a leper and stabbed through the heart. I have been crushed flat by a steamroller, disembowelled by slaughter-men who then stole my intestines. Sliced into ninety-three pieces by an invisible Spanish dagger, and stitched back together again by a Samaritan. I have screamed 'Murder!' more times than you've have hot dinners! I am, as was said in *L'Information*, 'The Sarah Bernhardt of the Rue Chaptal'. My six minute on-stage decomposition without the use of make-up is now legendary. All in Paris know the name of Maxa, and when they hear it, shiver. So if it appears as if I am slightly protective of my reputation, it's because I have earned it. I'll be damned if some curious academic is going to get in my way by killing the golden goose! Do me up.

She turns her exposed back to BINET. He obediently does up the final button on the dress.

MAXA: Now if you'll excuse me, I'm meeting a devotee of mine. Someone who wishes to bow before the altar of Maxa. Go find André and help him write another play, there's a good boy.

Flustered, BINET exits backstage.

MAXA: *Other* theatres? *Other* roles?

Enter a man with a bouquet of red roses. He sees MAXA elegantly poised on stage, ready for him.

MAXA: Don't be afraid. I'm not going to eat you. I… am Maxa.

MAN: Yes. You are.

MAXA: We finally meet in the flesh, monsieur Gateaux.

GATEAUX: Please mademoiselle, call me Gregor.

MAXA beckons him closer.

GATEAUX: I didn't dare hope you'd actually see me.

MAXA: The least I could do for such a committed aficionado.

GATEAUX: *(He hands her the roses.)* These are for you…

MAXA: More roses? How sweet. Please.

She pats the empty chair. He sits.

GATEAUX: You look to die for. Would you die for me? I mean, would you do one of your deaths, right here, for me?

MAXA: Do you have a favorite?

GATEAUX: I loved the bullet you took in 'The Ultimate Torture', the way your body just… *fell.*

She gets shot and falls.

GATEAUX: And then there's the dance you performed when doused in gasoline and set alight…

She is set alight.

GATEAUX: The scalpel-slashed throat, that gurgling sound you made…

She clutches her throat, gurgles.

GATEAUX: The premature burial, crushed and broken under all that dirt… the sudden whip-crack hanging… the madwoman, all drenched in blood… all drenched in blood…

MAXA hypnotically performs a series of gruesome deaths. GATEAUX is spellbound.

Enter MAUREY from wings followed by DE LORDE and RATINEAU. They head down stage. RATINEAU carries a fake severed arm. He tinkers with its gory mechanism. They don't notice MAXA's display.

MAUREY: And how goes the collaboration with Binet?

DE LORDE: I fear for the poor doctor. He told me the curious story of how he was tormented as a child. There is a terror in his soul, one deep and immovable. Perhaps that is why he is drawn to the Grand Guignol? Those that fear life by day may be granted release here by night! Catharsis.

MAUREY: I meant, where's the new bloody play?

DE LORDE: It's coming. I have a title. 'Lesson At The Salpêtrière'!

Behind, GATEAUX stands before MAXA as she performs. Seized with passion, he grabs her throat and begins to strangle her. She grabs her butcher's knife and tries to stab him. He catches her wrist. They struggle.

MAUREY: I don't give a fig what it's called. Just make sure it's more horrible than 'The Horrible Experiment'!

DE LORDE: Oh, it will be! It promises to be our most terrifying play yet. Ratineau, how would one go about showing the effects of an acid-scarred face?

RATINEAU: Well, the top layer of skin would smoulder, crack, then liquify. The eyelids would be the first to go. Hair. Then the flesh itself would dissolve and peel from the bone, drippin' like hot wax – yeah. Should be easy.

MAXA: Help!

They turn.

RATINEAU: *Bloody hell!*

RATINEAU leaps into action and renders GATEAUX unconscious with the severed arm. He dumps GATEAUX in the chair. MAXA collapses. DE LORDE runs to her side.

DE LORDE: Maxa, are you alright?

MAXA: Sick… perverted… bastard!

She staggers to her feet.

RATINEAU: I knew I shouldn't have let some punter onto my stage! I knew it!

MAXA: He attacked me!

RATINEAU: He's the Monster!

MAUREY: He can't be!

DE LORDE: Who is he?

MAXA: His name is Gateaux. Inspector Gregor Gateaux.

RATINEAU: Nothing sweet about him.

MAXA: He adored me!

DE LORDE: Wait...

MAXA: Then he betrayed me!

DE LORDE: Gregor Gateaux?

MAXA: He applauded me!

RATINEAU: What is it André?

DE LORDE: How extraordinary...

MAXA: And then he killed me!

MAUREY: Out with it, man!

DE LORDE: Could it be that Maxa's deranged fanatic is also, in fact, the childhood torturer of Dr Alfred Binet? Inspector Gateaux. It *has* to be the very same...

RATINEAU: So what are we going to do with him? We can't hand him over to the authorities if he *is* the authorities.

DE LORDE: I have an idea. To set the scene... Maxa, one of Paris's leading actresses craves hot-blooded revenge upon the man who attacked her. The man, Gregor Gateaux, sits unconscious... tied to a chair by Ratineau the stage-manager...

DE LORDE hands RATINEAU a coil of rope. RATINEAU works fast.

MAUREY: De Lorde, what are you doing?

DE LORDE: Asks Max Maurey the theatre manager. Apprehensively. Ratineau frantically picks up his pace, quickly realising what fiendish plot de Lorde is constructing! Ratineau fetches The Rejuvenation Machine!

Exit a frantic RATINEAU to wings. GATEAUX stirs.

DE LORDE: Gateaux stirs! Time is short. Maxa slips out of her immaculate dress –

MAXA takes off her dress.

DE LORDE: Theatre manager Max Maurey looks on. Apprehensively.

MAUREY, apprehensive.

Enter RATINEAU with a strange cuboid machine (dials, wires, head clamp, etc) on wheels.

RATINEAU: The Rejuvenation Machine! One of my finest makes.

DE LORDE: … proclaims Ratineau and dives off to the opposite wing to find the headless corpse from 'Chop! Chop!' – not forgetting to take Maxa's white dress with him!

Exit RATINEAU with dress. GATEAUX groans.

DE LORDE: Gateaux groans, consciousness almost fully regained!

MAXA: Are we going to kill him? I wish to kill him, like he killed me! When can I kill him, André?

DE LORDE: Cries the vengeful-hearted Maxa as she climbs into the Rejuvenation Machine!

MAXA does as she's told.

DE LORDE: Theatre manager Max Maurey looks on. Apprehensively.

MAUREY: What's going to happen?

DE LORDE: Ah ha! Hooked, aren't you?

Enter RATINEAU with a headless female body in MAXA's white dress under one arm, a severed head under the other, and a pot of blood in his hand. RATINEAU lays the body on the floor before the unconscious GATEAUX and carefully sets the head at the neck of the dummy...

RATINEAU: I have developed nine types of blood for the productions here at the Grand Guignol. Blood that trickles, blood that gloops, blood that performs the arterial spray. Fresh blood, dark blood, blood that scabs.

He splatters blood artistically around the corpse, and on the head's wound.

RATINEAU: Facial gore, coagulate gore – and this one... for special occasions. I don't mean to blow my own trumpet but I am bloody good.

He puts the knife in GATEAUX's hand, paints it red, and artfully splatters him.

DE LORDE: And with everything set, the show begins!

The lights snap to the requisite atmosphere.

GATEAUX: Where am I?

The company play horrified.

DE LORDE: Gregor Gateaux?

GATEAUX: *(Straining at his bonds.)* What is this?

DE LORDE: What have you done?

GATEAUX: Eh?

DE LORDE: You killed our leading lady. Chopped her head off with a butcher's knife!

DE LORDE grabs MAXA's 'head' from the floor and thrusts it into GATEAUX's face. He shrieks.

GATEAUX: Oh good Christ! That wasn't me!

Throws knife down in horror.

I didn't touch her, I swear!

DE LORDE: Let's ask Maxa herself, shall we?

DE LORDE takes the head, his back to us, and wires it up to the machine with RATINEAU's help.

GATEAUX: I don't know how it happened! It was an accident! I didn't mean to! She attacked *me* with that knife! God forgive me! I grew weak in her presence! She has *powers*! So intoxicating! I lost control! I'm only a man, for Christ's sakes! Flesh and blood!

DE LORDE: Ratineau, activate the Rejuvenation Machine!

RATINEAU throws a switch. The machine fires up, hums, glows. MAXA's decapitated head bursts into life with a scream.

MAXA: Revenge! I want revenge on the man who cut off my head!

GATEAUX: *(Horrified.)* How are you doing that?

DE LORDE: Is this the man who killed you, Maxa?

MAXA: Him! Him! Yes! *Hiiiiiiiiiiiim!*

GATEAUX: No! We were just having fun! Playing games! I swear!

MAXA: *Heeeee kiiillllllled meeeeeeee!!!*

DE LORDE: And that's what you like to do, isn't it monsieur? Play games? You've played games as far back as when you were a little boy. At school! In Nice!

Enter BINET from wings.

BINET: What's everybody doing?

DE LORDE: Right on cue!

BINET looks at the horrors before him.

DE LORDE: Do you recognise him, Gregor? Dr Alfred Binet?

GATEAUX: Who?

BINET sees GATEAUX and shrieks.

BINET: *(Shaking with fear.)* Gregor Gateaux!

GATEAUX: I don't know him. I've never seen him before in my life!

BINET: You terrorized me with a fabric skeleton!

GATEAUX: *(A faint memory.)* Oh..

DE LORDE: *(Offering knife.)* Avenge yourself, doctor.

BINET: What? No! I need to be… rational. I need to understand his behaviour. After all, he was only a child… we were all… just… children…

MAXA: If you won't do it –

MAXA bursts out of the machine, stalks over to DE LORDE and takes the knife.

MAXA: Then I fucking will!

GATEAUX: Please don't kill me – !

MAXA plunges the knife into GATEAUX's stomach. GATEAUX shrieks. MAXA sinks her hands into GATEAUX's gut and hauls out COILS OF INNARDS. GATEAUX, screaming, can't believe his eyes.

MAXA: Maxa… is… avenged…

(Offering knife.) Binet?

GATEAUX: *(Realising he's not dead.)* This place is a madhouse!

BINET: *(Darkening.)* Gregor Gateaux… you don't have any idea the suffering you've caused me.

BINET can't control it any longer. He runs at GATEAUX. He gathers up the rubber intestine, wraps it round GATEAUX's neck and throttles him.

DE LORDE: Alfred!

MAXA, MAUREY and RATINEAU try and drag him off.

MAUREY: Alfred, your killing him!

BINET: I know!

RATINEAU: You *do* know this is all fake, don't you?

BINET: Yes! No! I don't know! I just know I hate him! I hate you, Gregor Gateaux! And I want… you –

He yanks the intestine tight. GATEAUX goes puce. His eyes bulge.

BINET: *Dead!*

GATEAUX goes limp. The company recoil.

Tableau of Horror!

Act Two

Tableau of Horror!

BINET screams, his head in his hands – the picture of crumbling sanity. As quickly as it appears, the image is gone.

The curtain flies out to reveal the company assembled.

RATINEAU: But the question remains: who is the Monster of Montmartre? Gregor Gateaux?

MAXA: If it is him, the murders should stop now that the pervert's been carted off to the asylum!

PAULAIS: He won't stay in there long. The police look after their own.

MAXA: If he *was* the Monster it would have been *my* blood on this stage, not Ratineau's homemade stuff!

PAULAIS: If only I'd been here and not at chapel burying my poor mother's remains…

RATINEAU: It has to be Gateaux. He's prime material. I think we caught the Monster, and gave him a dose of his own medicine!

Enter MAUREY from the Outside.

MAUREY: How's morale amongst the troops? Are we all surviving?

MAXA: Times have been trying, to say the least.

MAUREY: Dearest Maxa. Paris's precious paragon of peril, have you recovered from your terrifying ordeal?

MAXA: Bruises fade, Max. It's the psychological damage that runs deep…

MAUREY: The Great Paulais! Losing a mother is a tragedy I've yet to contend with given Old Maman Maurey's apparently indestructible nature. I cannot imagine what you've been through.

PAULAIS: Getting there slowly, Max.

MAUREY: And Ratineau? You've coped with such challenges admirably, and even under such pressures, your craft has never wavered.

RATINEAU: Thank you, monsieur.

MAUREY: I want my company to be happy. I want them eager to perform. So look after yourselves. It's a nasty world out there. Did you hear? The Monster of Montmartre has killed again.

COMPANY: What?!

MAUREY: Old Gougon the fruit seller. Strung up by his ankles not one hundred yards from this very theatre. Three five-pointed stars etched into his ancient flesh.

RATINEAU: Three?

MAUREY: I thought you might have heard. Poor Gougon.

Exit MAUREY.

RATINEAU: Well it ain't Gregor Gateaux.

PAULAIS: Oh God, *why?!* Why all this murder? All this senseless, senseless murder!

MAXA: Old Gougon the fruit seller…

PAULAIS: But wait. This doesn't make sense. Old Gougon wasn't a prostitute!

Beat.

Was he?

RATINEAU: And The Monster's never killed a man before. And the three symbols? Old Gougon… what did 'e ever do to anyone?

MAXA: I didn't like his rattling cough. Spluttering tuberculosis all over the plums.

RATINEAU: Who is this Monster?

PAULAIS: It's terrifying. Could be anyone. Could be Max Maurey for all we know! Ha!

RATINEAU: For all we know, The Monster could be standing on this very stage.

MAXA: But that would make one of you two… *him.*

PAULAIS: Me? Kill my own mother?

RATINEAU: *(To MAXA.)* What makes you so sure it's a 'him'? André's plays have taught me a lot about character – don't think just because you're the only female in this crowd you're exempt from suspicion.

MAXA: You accuse *me* of being The Monster?

RATINEAU: You take a butcher's knife with you every time you walk home.

MAXA: For protection! In case 'he' strikes!

RATINEAU: A well-constructed alibi.

MAXA: Well, what about you and your perverse love of severed limbs and spurting blood?

RATINEAU: I'm too obvious.

MAXA: Oh, are you?

RATINEAU: Yes! And besides, it's me job.

PAULAIS: I am an actor. A man of many faces, many guises. But the face you see before you now is no mask, I assure you. It is flesh forged with intention. Know this! I will not rest until I have The Monster on his knees, begging. He may look upon this face, and into these eyes, but he will find no mercy. Only the desire for justice. And on my mother's grave, I shall administer it!

RATINEAU: But we still don't know who he is.

PAULAIS: No.

The curtain comes in, masking the company.

Enter DE LORDE, in front of the curtain, leafing through a script. BINET, somewhat frayed now, follows in behind. They stand before the curtain as the others whisper – seen, perhaps, backlit, in silhouette.

RATINEAU: Binet could be The Monster. 'E's prime material.

MAXA: Yes! Bumbling. Bookish. Family Man. A clever cover for a killer!

DE LORDE: *(Re: script.)* This is a good one, Alfred. 'Lesson At The Salpêtrière'. It has tension and terror in just the right measure!

RATINEAU: Wait. I've cracked it. It's de Lorde! 'E's prime material. Murdering to inspire his own plays whilst adopting a facade of sweet nature, the perfect front to hide a crazed –

DE LORDE: I can hear you. I'm not The Monster.

PAULAIS: Just eliminating suspects, André.

DE LORDE: Eliminate them elsewhere, could you? Dr Binet and I have work to do.

The COMPANY wander off, backstage.

BINET: Gregor Gateaux was right. This place is a madhouse.

DE LORDE: Oh, Alfred. It was fun and games.

BINET: He is now an inmate of the Salpêtrière Asylum!

DE LORDE: How ironic. Your place of work, and the setting for our latest play. Is that life imitating art or –

BINET: This isn't funny, André. We drove him insane!

DE LORDE: Serves him right, the bully.

BINET: I could've killed him with that rubber intestine!

DE LORDE: But you didn't.

BINET: I was in a frenzy! You tricked me! You and your company!

DE LORDE: Forgive me. I was only trying to help.

BINET: I'm the psychiatrist! I'm supposed to help you! And I don't mean with the writing!

DE LORDE: I told you. I'm fine.

BINET: Ha! You need help, André. More than you know.

DE LORDE: Is that so?

BINET: You are addicted to the creative act.

DE LORDE: You make it sound like a bad thing.

BINET: You are compelled to write because you have a mystery burning within you that will not be extinguished. The writing of each play is an exploration of that mystery!

DE LORDE: Go on.

BINET: Theme. Character. Setting. You tell the same story over and over again.

DE LORDE: Do you accuse me of repeating myself, monsieur?

BINET: I'm not talking plot, I'm talking about story – *your* story. The subconscious framework inherent in all of your writing.

DE LORDE: Yes, of course. My 'traumatic childhood'.

BINET: Precisely! The story of your father, his madness and your mother's tragic death – this all remains unresolved within you.

Beat.

But if you chose to face it, I could cure you!

DE LORDE: Face what?

BINET: Every time you create, you put yourself in a particular state of mind. You open a door. A door in your mind. A door through which your subconscious is permitted to rise up and run rampant!

DE LORDE: A door? Do I?

BINET: If we could somehow keep the door open and find that specific moment when you were with your dying mother –

DE LORDE: I never looked upon her, doctor. How can I confront a memory I don't even have?

BINET: I have pioneered an experimental psychiatric technique that involves dramatic re-creation of repressed events.

DE LORDE: You'd set the scene?

BINET: It is my hope that it could lead to a single curative result.

DE LORDE: Catharsis?

BINET: It is called re-enactment therapy.

DE LORDE: You wish to re-create my mother's death?

BINET: If you'd permit me.

DE LORDE: And if this procedure was successful?

BINET: Your trauma would be laid to rest.

DE LORDE: And I would be liberated of all the horrors inside my head?

BINET: You would.

DE LORDE: But what of my writing?

BINET: It is possible that by removing this core trauma you would lose your compulsion to write.

DE LORDE: And then where would I be?

BINET: It can only ever be your choice.

DE LORDE: My choice is to keep writing plays with you, Alfred.

BINET: No.

DE LORDE: No?

BINET: We have to stop.

DE LORDE: Stop what?

BINET: This collaboration of ours.

DE LORDE: Why?

BINET: Things are getting out of hand.

DE LORDE: But we've so much more to write!

BINET: I want to help you. And I believe I can. But I will not write with you any more. It's too dangerous. I can't do it. I'm sorry, André.

BINET exits to the Outside.

DE LORDE: Alfred? Alfred!

The theatre creaks ominously. Somewhere in the dark, a child sobs…

DE LORDE, script in hand, exits through the curtain.

The curtain flies out revealing a stage loosely set for a rehearsal of 'Lesson At The Salpêtrière'.

RATINEAU hurriedly positions a trolly that rattles with bottles of acid. PAULAIS and MAXA leaf through their scripts and get into rudimentary costume and wigs.

DE LORDE enters in a white lab coat.

DE LORDE: Is everyone ready?

PAULAIS: I was born ready, André.

DE LORDE: To set the scene… we find ourselves in the clinical laboratory of the Salpêtrière. A hospital for the insane, but also, as it is in reality, a place of psychiatric study. We are in a large bright room. There is a workbench.

Microscopes. Anatomical pieces pickled in formaldehyde. Scientific apparatus. Chemical phials. Flasks of acid… I shall portray Dr Gorlitz, head lecturer. Making his welcome return to this stage after a brief period of bereavement, Georges Paulais as my prized intern, Nikolai –

PAULAIS: Hungry for it, André. Hungry.

DE LORDE: And mademoiselle Maxa, just recently recovered from a vicious attack by a psychopath obsessed with death, shall portray Claire.

MAXA: A young patient.

DE LORDE: Indeed. Places everyone.

The lights dim as the scene is set.

DE LORDE: *(As GORLITZ.)* Nikolai, hypnotise the patient.

(As DE LORDE, reading from script.) The patient flails violently as an assistant tries to restrain her.

RATINEAU, as JOSHUA, in white coat, runs to MAXA, as CLAIRE, and wrestles her as if she's wild. PAULAIS / NIKOLAI grapples her from behind.

MAXA: *(Reading, flailing.)* You can't do this to me! The insane are not to be treated like animals!

PAULAIS: Steady on, darling. It's only a read-through.

MAXA: The author asked me to flail.

DE LORDE: *(As GORLITZ.)* An intriguing case, gentlemen. The patient's name is Claire. Six months ago she claimed to have been paralysed and raped by an intern student, her virginity taken against her will. Accusations were dismissed when said patient could not recall the face of her assailant. To complicate matters further it was discovered that this 'virgin' had two children already.

(As DE LORDE.) The interns laugh.

PAULAIS and RATINEAU laugh.

MAXA: *(Quiet, building in intensity.)* I was not lying. I told you, I was paralysed. He paralysed me!

DE LORDE: She flails again!

(As GORLITZ.) Enough of this nonsense! Nikolai, put the woman under!

MAXA struggles against RATINEAU's hold as NIKOLAI slowly approaches.

MAXA: I will *not* be one of your scientific studies!

She sees his face and freezes with horror.

CLAIRE: *You.*

NIKOLAI: What's the matter with her?

CLAIRE: You were the one who paralysed me!

NIKOLAI: You're right, Dr Gorlitz. She *is* delusional. Lock her away immediately!

CLAIRE: Yes! Lock me away! Stop me from talking! Whilst you continue to conduct your vile experiments! Whilst you abuse helpless patients! Sick! Perverted! Despicable! Well, I won't let it happen again! Not to me! Nor to anyone! For what you did, I shall be revenged!

She flings a flask marked SULPHURIC ACID in his face. He screams in agony.

NIKOLAI: *Arrgghhhh!!!* It burns! Oh God, it burns!

(Breaking character, as PAULAIS.) Sorry, can we stop there? That water went *right* in my eye.

DE LORDE: No! Keep going! The acid is eating its way into your flesh!

PAULAIS: *(As NIKOLAI, staggering back over the workbench.)* *Aaaaarrrrrrrgggggghhhh!!!!!*

MAXA: I hope it's *agony*, you animal! You sick, sick animal!

DE LORDE: Claire is dragged out.

(to RATINEAU)

Drag her out!

RATINEAU: *(Manhandling a wild MAXA off.)* I'm tryin'!

DE LORDE: *(As GORLITZ.)* What in God's name did she throw at him?

RATINEAU: *(Returning as ASSISTANT.)* An entire flask of sulphuric acid, doctor!

PAULAIS/NIKOLAI: *(From behind them.) AHHHHHHHHHH!!!*

DE LORDE: *(As GORLITZ.)* Ammonium compresses, Joshua! And quickly!

PAULAIS: Oh! The agony! I'm suffering! Please! Kill me –

Helping him up onto the bench, they reveal his hideous, acid-scarred face – the smouldering flesh melts away like wax from his bones.

RATINEAU: *(As JOSHUA.)* It's too late for that, doctor.

DE LORDE: *(As GORLITZ, looking at PAULAIS / NIKOLAI.)* You're right. The acid has already penetrated the bone structure. Dear God! There is nothing we can do… but wait for the poor man… to die!

PAULAIS / NIKOLAI howls in convulsions of pain.

VOICE: *(From auditorium.)* Stop! Stop! For the love of God, stop! I have seen enough!

The company peer into the darkness. Standing there is CLAUDE LEVEL, theatre critic.

DE LORDE: *(To company, whispers.)* Did anyone know Claude Level was in?

RATINEAU: Who?

COMPANY: Critic.

MAXA: Perhaps the most influential in all of Paris.

RATINEAU: Oh.

LEVEL: What kind of diseased mind do you possess, de Lorde? Vengeful half-naked young mad women raped by interns? Phials of acid thrown in to people's faces? All in the name of 'entertainment'? With such 'staged' violence publicly available, is there any wonder why a crazed killer stalks our streets, shedding blood that is oh so very real? To those of us who wish to live in a safe, clean and guarded society, I shall urge the public to boycott this seeping wound of a playhouse. This reprehensible and morally irresponsible back alley side-show is the sickening proof of precisely what happens when the lunatics take over the asylum!

PAULAIS: So… he didn't like it?

DE LORDE: Monsieur Level, are you suggesting I'm inspiring The Monster of Montmartre to kill, kill and kill again?

LEVEL: I'm saying that any drunken slob could stumble in off the street, watch one of these sordid little skits and mimic the horrors he has seen!

DE LORDE: I fear The Monster would murder whether he had seen my plays or not.

LEVEL: Your 'plays' are infecting society, de Lorde.

DE LORDE: No, monsieur. They merely reflect it.

PAULAIS: *(Stepping forward.)* If I may, André? Monsieur Level, after having watched a production of 'Hamlet' have you ever felt the desire to stab someone behind an arras?

LEVEL: No.

PAULAIS: Make someone go so mad they drown themselves?

LEVEL: No.

PAULAIS: Poison your mother?

LEVEL: No.

PAULAIS: I rest my case.

LEVEL: I wasn't aware you were making one.

PAULAIS: My beloved mother was the fourth victim of the Monster, Level. She was taken from the street having left the Grand Guignol early. Had she not been watching through a gin-soaked haze, perhaps she might have lasted the evening. Perhaps I could have escorted her home. And perhaps she would still be alive to this day… So it serves the booze-bloated old bitch right!

DE LORDE: Paulais –

PAULAIS: Ha, I say! Ha! I'm glad the Monster filleted the gassy old trout!

LEVEL: One of the more convincing performances I've seen from you, Paulais.

PAULAIS: Ah. Really?

MAXA: That was an insult, darling.

PAULAIS: Ah. Really?

LEVEL: I shall submit my critique tomorrow. The sooner this cesspit is shut down, the better.

MAXA: What did he say?

RATINEAU: Shut down?

PAULAIS: No!

DE LORDE: Wait, monsieur. Let's not be too hasty. I can make the necessary cuts. I can pull this play from the repertoire –

LEVEL: What good would that do? Your plays are all the same, de Lorde. Full of blood and madness, and I don't approve. Your influence must be severed so that innocent lives might be saved. Kiss your theatre good bye. The Grand Guignol… is dead!

Exit LEVEL to the Outside World.

PAULAIS: Dead?

MAXA: Dead. If the Grand Guignol is dead, then… what of Maxa?

RATINEAU: Who reads the reviews anyway? Sod him.

DE LORDE: If it was any other critic, Ratineau, I'd be inclined to agree. But this is Claude Level of *L'Information*. The moral compass of this city. What he says goes.

PAULAIS: What are we going to do, André?

DE LORDE: He's on a crusade to close us down. There'll be no stopping him.

MAXA: Perhaps it's not a bad thing.

PAULAIS: Maxa?

MAXA: We can still do the plays, can't we André? Just… no audience…

PAULAIS: What are you saying? The Grand Guignol is nothing without a crowd.

MAXA: You weren't attacked by him! You haven't felt the fanatical grip of a regular about your throat!

PAULAIS: *(Aghast.)* She fears her beloved audience…

MAXA: We don't know who they are, where they're from, or why they've come.

PAULAIS: Maxa darling, they've come for *me*. And you.

MAXA: Who are they really? Out there. Watching us night after night. I say we close the theatre to the public, but continue to perform!

DE LORDE: But Maxa, what of the applause at the end? Isn't that what it's all about?

MAXA: We can *pretend* to hear it!

She takes a curtain call to deathly silence. The company view MAXA with deep concern.

Enter MAUREY from the Outside.

MAUREY: I just saw that puritanical arsehole Claude Level make his exit. Did he like it?

COMPANY: No.

MAUREY: Shit.

MAXA: Where were you, Max? We needed you here!

MAUREY: I was at the Hotel Chevalier raising capital for the next season. Christ, I can't be everywhere at once!

RATINEAU: He's gonna close us down.

MAUREY: On what grounds?

PAULAIS: He thinks the Grand Guignol is inspiring The Monster of Montmartre to kill.

MAUREY: Not a bad idea for a play that, de Lorde.

DE LORDE: Max! This is serious!

MAUREY: It's only one man's opinion. It'll take more than a slating in *L'Information* to deter the people of Paris from coming!

DE LORDE: He knows how much society needs a scapegoat for these murders. If you ask me, we're done for.

PAULAIS: He can't shut us down! He just can't! I have re-emerged transformed from a tempest of grief! The only glimmer of light was that I might play this stage again!

MAXA: It is not for the first time in Maxa's life that she realises no matter what she does, she cannot win. There is nothing to be done but wander the darkened streets of Montmartre in the hope that The Monster finds and eviscerates this now useless body…

MAUREY: Fucking actors. Can we stop the notice from going to press? Can Claude Level be bribed?

PAULAIS: No. I knew him once. We started off together as apprentice clerks in the prefecture. A lifetime ago now. It was before I had The Calling. No, Claude Level cannot be bought. Even as a lowly clerk he was top of his league. His staunch, crystal-cut moral standards set him head and shoulders above the rest of us. He's a good man. Clean living. God-fearing. Hard worker. No wife. No children. He lives alone. No dependants… He wouldn't be missed…

The company listen more closely to PAULAIS, slightly unnerved with what he is getting at.

PAULAIS: A theatre critic's racket is a cut-throat one. There are any number of young pretenders desperate to take his place…

MAXA: Paulais?

PAULAIS: Just say… *just say…* we invited Claude Level here tonight under the pretence that we wanted to implement his criticisms to better our performance, it is wholly possible he might not survive the journey back through Montmartre…

DE LORDE: What are you saying?

PAULAIS: I'm saying, he could quite easily fall victim to the Monster's attack.

MAUREY: Are you suggesting we employ The Monster to lurk outside the theatre and pounce him?

PAULAIS: I'm suggesting it would *appear* that the Monster got him. We've all read the papers. We know how this beast kills. Indeed, I've seen his vicious handiwork in gruesome detail. It can be replicated – with a sharp blade and a steady hand.

DE LORDE: Paulais –

MAXA: The Monster *does* kill men now…

DE LORDE: I can't believe what I'm hearing!

PAULAIS: I cannot have the nightmares return! I will fight to the death to keep this place alive, no matter the cost. What say you, company? Shall we dispatch of this individual before he dispatches us?

MAUREY: Think we could get away with it?

DE LORDE: Max!

MAUREY: I'm with Paulais. I've invested too much in this old place to see it close down just as it's getting going!

PAULAIS: Maxa?

MAXA: Nothing is more precious to me than my craft, my reputation, my costumes… my lovely, lovely costumes…

Beat, dark.

Kill him.

Exit MAXA, backstage.

PAULAIS: I will bring him back here, then?

DE LORDE: Paulais, this is insane!

PAULAIS: It must be done.

PAULAIS pulls his collars up and exits Outside.

MAUREY: There. Problem solved.

RATINEAU: When we say we're going to kill Claude Level, do we mean 'fake' kill him or *actually* kill him?

MAUREY: Ratineau, would you be a dear and prepare the writing desk?

RATINEAU exits backstage.

DE LORDE: We're going to kill a man, just like that?

MAUREY: He's not a man, de Lorde. He's a theatre critic.

DE LORDE: I wish for the Grand Guignol to stay open as much as anyone but… to take a life for it?

MAUREY: Oh, come on. You're the master of murderous motives. Surely you've one reason to bump Level off?

DE LORDE: He *did* dismiss my work out of hand.

MAUREY: Well there we are, see? He deserves to die.

DE LORDE: We cannot kill Claude Level and that's final!

RATINEAU brings the desk in.

MAUREY: But we need another play, de Lorde.

DE LORDE: Dear God…

MAUREY: Princess Wilhemina of The Netherlands has been touring Europe, spending her dead husband's fortune like it's going out of fashion. Since she's been in Paris, she has attended this theatre every night. She adores the Grand Guignol. It appeals to her base nature. She wants to invest, de Lorde. She wants to send us around the world! But… there's a catch.

DE LORDE: Here we go.

MAUREY: She desires to see a play that contains death by knitting.

DE LORDE: Knitting?

MAUREY: The Dutch, eh?

DE LORDE: She can't just request a death! This is my work! It comes from within!

MAUREY: I've already told her you've written it.

DE LORDE: You've already told her?

MAUREY: She was so very excited. Her purse twitched and gaped.

DE LORDE: Perhaps she'd like some clog dancing in there as well?

MAUREY: She's asked me to marry her, André.

DE LORDE: I see.

MAUREY: She's royalty. I could hardly say no. She's wilful. Strong. Damned strong as it happens.

Beat.

So. Do you think you could write it? This could be the play that makes all of our fortunes.

DE LORDE: Yes, until the next one…

MAUREY: It's love, André. Love.

DE LORDE: If it'll make you happy… why not?

MAUREY: Where's the harm, eh? Find the good doctor and get writing.

DE LORDE: Binet is gone, Max.

MAUREY: Well, you didn't need him anyway. You are the twisted genius, de Lorde. You are our Prince of Terror. Alone, your vision will be pure and unencumbered! Maestro, your desk awaits…

The desk, chair and writing equipment sit in an ominous light. Exit RATINEAU and MAUREY.

DE LORDE circles the desk, sits.

DE LORDE: And so, to set the scene… To set the scene… To set… the scene… We find ourselves in a… in a… a…

But nothing comes.

Damn you, Alfred. Damn you, Max. Damn you all…

DE LORDE knocks on the table three times. Smoke and light! A ghostly choir! Enter POE.

POE: Deadlines tear his soul so deeply,
He hopes and prays ideas come cheaply
But alas! He returns, cap in hand,
Not so unlike the play before –
He tries to write, his thoughts now seeping
So, suddenly comes the beggar creeping,
And Edgar Poe is laughing, weeping!

Weeping for the poor de Lorde!
'Tis that playwright!' I splutter
'Who said of me he did deplore!
But what is this? He's back for more!'

POE grabs DE LORDE.

DE LORDE: Oh God! No! Please!

POE goes to skewer DE LORDE's eye out with the ink pen, when –

Enter BINET from the Outside.

BINET: André!

POE vanishes like a vampire at dawn. DE LORDE collapses.

BINET: I knew it. I should never have left.

DE LORDE: I need your help, Alfred.

BINET: Of course. We must begin the re-enactment therapy at once.

DE LORDE: No. I need your help to write one last play.

BINET: Very well. One last play. Besides, the therapy will work more successfully with you in a heightened state.

DE LORDE: We shall conduct the therapy as we write?

BINET: Or would that be madness?

DE LORDE: What's the worst that could happen?

BINET: That I mishandle the procedure and leave you in a state of permanent psychosis.

DE LORDE: It's a risk worth taking.

BINET: To set the scene?

DE LORDE: To set the scene!

The curtain comes in.

Enter MAUREY, through curtain.

MAUREY: Do forgive my intrusion at this critical point of the evening. You are about to watch the last play. There are doctors on standby in the foyer, for there will be scenes of madness, and murder, and the shedding of copious blood! Oh God, so much blood! Author de Lorde has made good on his promise and forged a twisted masterpiece. This is the horror show to end all horror shows! No refunds, not tonight – no matter what happens! May God have mercy on us all. *Mesdames et messieurs*, I give you the final play of the evening… 'Crime In The Madhouse'!

Exit MAUREY through curtain.

Three loud, sudden knocks. House lights die. The curtain rises with a bloodcurdling scream.

The stage is set for a production of 'Crime In The Madhouse'.

A room in the Saint-Léger, an archaic mental institution: white-tiled walls, a door on each side (one to the corridor, the other to an adjoining room), a window at the back, through which greenish moonlight pours. A crucifix hangs on the wall above a shelf. A sturdy armchair in the corner. Two small beds. Between them, sat against the wall, a cast-iron stove.

LOUISE (MAXA), a young mad girl in a blonde wig, sits up in bed, and screams again.

LOUISE: Sister?

Enter THE SISTER (MAUREY), a sour-faced nun with a night-lamp, which casts an eerie orange glow.

THE SISTER: What? What's the matter, child? What's all this shrieking?

LOUISE: They're doing it again!

THE SISTER inspects the two sleepers in the other bed as DE LORDE and BINET speak from the sides of the stage.

DE LORDE: And so it begins…

BINET: Are you in this one, André?

DE LORDE: Of course, Alfred. We're all in it. All of us.

THE SISTER: *(To LOUISE.)* They merely mutter prayers in their sleep, which is more than can be said for you, my little heathen!

LOUISE: Sister, they torment me!

BINET: Let us piece together the motifs so redolent in your work, André.

DE LORDE: Tell me, doctor.

BINET: As always, there is torment. Both psychological and, ultimately, physical. This, I believe, is a representation of the torment you suffered as a child.

THE SISTER: Old and mad they may be, but the Hunchback and the Normandy Witch are quite, quite harmless.

LOUISE: You don't believe me…

(In despair.) I hate it here at the Saint-Léger Hospital for the Incurably Insane!

BINET: The setting? As it often is, a madhouse. The terrible place your father was taken.

LOUISE: *(With dread.)* The worse thing is when *she* creeps in from the other room… the hag with one eye!

THE SISTER: Ah yes. 'One-Eye'.

BINET: And your obsession with eyes, tongues, brains –

LOUISE: I tell you, they're plotting something horrible against me!

THE SISTER: Louise! Firstly, that adjoining door is locked and only I have the key. Secondly, One-Eye is paralysed from the waist down and hasn't risen from her bed in precisely six years… six years since she went insane… six years since she murdered her own child… Now I suggest you stop these silly hallucinations – or you will never, ever leave this asylum, do you understand?

(Kindly.) Sleep now, child. Here. Take my knitting wool, and these needles…

She produces a ball of wool and needles from nowhere.

THE SISTER: Tonight, knit. For it will calm your mind.

BINET: The seeding of seemingly innocent domestic implements as potential tools for violence…

LOUISE stares ahead, frightened.

THE SISTER: I'll leave them here, on the shelf beneath the statue of Christ Our Saviour.

A mournful bell rings out.

THE SISTER: The mournful bell rings out! It calls me to my duties in the chapel of rest…

She leaves the lamp on the shelf too, then exits. The bell stops. LOUISE watches the two beds, looks to the adjoining door. Distant organ music eerily drifts in from the chapel, along with the nuns singing hymns.

LOUISE: The comforting echo of nuns at prayer…

She sinks down to sleep. Suddenly, HUNCHBACK (RATINEAU) and NORMANDY WITCH (PAULAIS) sit up with a grunt. They are wild-haired, deep-voiced grotesques.

NORMANDY WITCH: Have y'got the rope?

HUNCHBACK: No rope, no!

NORMANDY WITCH: She told us to get rope! Tear your bed sheets up! Use your teeth to rip'm!

The sound of effort and the tearing cloth.

LOUISE: *(Bolt upright.)* What's going on there?

The crones freeze and feign snoring.

LOUISE: I know you're not asleep! Oh, I can't stand this torture! Trapped, alone –

HUNCHBACK: You're not alone, my dear.

NORMANDY WITCH: You're with us.

They climb out of bed and lurch towards her, cackling.

NORMANDY WITCH: Was it the cry of the cuckoo that woke you?

LOUISE: Sister!

HUNCHBACK: She won't hear. She's in chapel.

LOUISE: Keep away, I tell you! Keep away!

Suddenly, a strange gurgling howl from the adjoining room, and the sound of a key in the lock.

HUNCHBACK: It's her!

LOUISE: No!

NORMANDY WITCH: She's coming!

HUNCHBACK: Pray!

NORMANDY WITCH: Pray!

They speak in tongues, cross themselves frantically.

LOUISE: The door… The door!

BINET: And often, there is a door, behind which lies a mystery, some unseen horror, an answer, a truth!

LOUISE: Help me somebody!

Suddenly, enter POE from behind it.

POE: De Lorde!

DE LORDE: No!

BINET: What is it? What do you see?

POE: You are in your mother's room…

DE LORDE: I am… I am in…

DE LORDE, seeing MAXA in bed, turns away in horror.

DE LORDE: She's there! Broken! Dying!

BINET: Who?

DE LORDE: My mother!

MAXA / LOUISE sits in bed, staring.

BINET: The re-enactment therapy has begun. Can you see her, André?

DE LORDE: No. I will not look.

POE: Look at her, boy.

DE LORDE: No, father.

POE: Look at her.

DE LORDE: I will not look at her!

BINET: Of course! Poe is a psychological manifestation of your father! They're one in the same!

POE: Look at her, André.

DE LORDE: I'm too afraid!

BINET: This is it! *This* is the event that changed your life! This one scene altered everything inside you! What you saw, what you *didn't* see – shaped your very consciousness!

POE: Look upon your mother before she dies.

DE LORDE: She's not going to die!

POE: Life leaks from every wound!

BINET: You must look, André.

DE LORDE: *I WILL NOT!*

DE LORDE lunges at POE. He grabs him by the throat and strangles him viciously.

POE: *(Gasps.)* André…!

BINET: André!

DE LORDE: Leave… me… alone!

POE dies.

Tableau of Horror!

MAXA: André, what have you done?

DE LORDE: I did it, Alfred! I confronted him! And I won!

PAULAIS: He's dead.

RATINEAU: You strangled him with your bare hands!

DE LORDE: Poe is vanquished! I am free!

MAXA: André, you killed...

MAUREY slips lifelessly from DE LORDE's grip.

DE LORDE: *(Confused.)* Max? I killed... Max? I don't understand...

BINET: Oh God!

RATINEAU: We should hide the body.

MAXA: *(Re: the audience)* It's a bit late for that!

PAULAIS: Drag Maurey off!

DE LORDE and RATINEAU haul the body off stage.

BINET: Is he dead?

PAULAIS: *(To audience.)* Dead? He is dead! In our *play*, he is dead! He is, of course, not *actually* dead! For this is merely theatre, and not real in any way!

MAXA: Now what should we do?

PAULAIS: We should... We should...

Enter DE LORDE.

DE LORDE: Continue! We should continue!

BINET: André! Wait!

DE LORDE disappears backstage. BINET follows. We return with a crash to 'Crime In The Madhouse'.

LOUISE: I know you're not asleep! Oh, I can't stand this torture! Trapped, alone –

HUNCHBACK: You're not alone, my dear.

NORMANDY WITCH: You're with us.

They climb out of bed and lurch towards her, cackling.

NORMANDY WITCH: Was it the cry of the cuckoo that woke you?

LOUISE: Sister!

HUNCHBACK: She won't hear. She's in chapel.

LOUISE: Keep away, I tell you! Keep away!

A strange, gurgling howl comes from the adjoining room. Then, the sound of a key in the lock.

HUNCHBACK: It's her!

LOUISE: No!

NORMANDY WITCH: She's coming!

HUNCHBACK: Pray!

NORMANDY WITCH: Pray!

They speak in tongues, cross themselves frantically.

LOUISE: The door… The door! Help me somebody!

She makes a dash for the main door when –

LEVEL: *(Standing in auditorium.)* Cease this depravity at once!

Enter DE LORDE in eyepatch and wig.

DE LORDE: Claude Level!

MAXA: He came.

PAULAIS: Oh yes.

RATINEAU: I'd forgotten about him.

LEVEL: You wanted to see me, de Lorde?

DE LORDE: I did? I… did. Monsieur, you are here for good reason. Look what horrors I have brought upon the world! I am sick, Level. I seek your… moral guidance…

LEVEL: Guidance? Rather you seek to bribe me into not publishing… this!

He produces his critique. The company freeze.

LEVEL: *(Joining them on stage.)* Yes. My damning critique, committed to paper, yet to be submitted. I'm on my way to the editor's office right now. Strange to think that this delicate document is all that stands in the way of society's downfall… or, indeed, its salvation.

PAULAIS: *(Draws a knife.)* You aren't printing that notice, Level! I have killed before and I will kill again! That's right! *I* am The Monster of Montmartre! I slaughtered my own mother in cold blood, so disembowelling you will be easy.

MAXA: Level!

(Draws a knife.) I am The Monster of Montmartre! I murdered to study the way the body writhes in the throes of death. And if you post that notice I shall gut you from gullet to groin!

DE LORDE pulls a knife.

DE LORDE: Level!

LEVEL: Oh for heaven's sake…

RATINEAU: Well, if everyone else is… *(Draws a knife.)*

BINET enters from backstage to find LEVEL surrounded with glinting knives.

LEVEL: If everyone's quite finished…?

(Drawing a huge butcher's knife from his coat.) I… AM THE MONSTER OF MONTMARTRE.

The company's knives droop.

PAULAIS: You cannot be…

LEVEL: Montmartre is a sewer over-flowing with filth. Prostitutes, drunks and vagabonds swarm the backstreets and boulevards. I have watched them, playing their parts, pretending to live, when all they do is infect our world with their sickness! They had to be judged. So I critiqued them. Savagely.

RATINEAU: Claude Level. I bloody knew it!

DE LORDE: Of course it's Level. The mask of piety and righteousness is evil's most familiar face.

LEVEL: You would know, de Lorde.

RATINEAU: Wait. Before all the screamin' and the bleedin' starts, I got a question. The symbols. The Satanic pentangles you cut into their flesh… what was that all about?

LEVEL: Nothing sinister. Simply an iconographic review of their deaths based on a star system of one to five. Some of them were very truthful in their dying. Far more truthful than they ever were in life. Your inebriated mother, Paulais, I awarded a four. She was so truthful. So truthful it *hurt.*

PAULAIS: Maman!

MAXA: How can you live with yourself?

LEVEL: How can you? I see the effects of your diabolical works! Disgusting! Sordid! Filth-making! But I shall restore order to this world. This building used to be a church, you know… and so it shall be again!

LEVEL raises his blade high – but before he can get a swing in, the company seize the chance, and stab him violently to death.

Tableau of Horror!

BINET: Is he…?

PAULAIS: *(To audience.)* Dead! He is dead! In our play he is… dead. He is… of course… not *actually* dead. For this is merely theatre… and not real… in any way.

LEVEL is dragged off stage.

We crash back to 'Crime In The Madhouse'. Strange gurgling howl… sound of key in lock…

HUNCHBACK: It's her!

LOUISE: No!

NORMANDY WITCH: Pray!

HUNCHBACK: Pray!

Speak in tongues, cross themselves… door creaks open…

LOUISE: The door… The door! Help me somebody!

Enter ONE-EYE (DE LORDE) – a brutish, terrifying madwoman, a patch over, well, one eye. She throws LOUISE back on the bed.

ONE-EYE: Light!

HUNCHBACK hurries over with the lamp. The crones leer and drool. LOUISE goes to scream but ONE-EYE clamps a hand over her mouth.

ONE-EYE: Normandy Witch? Bind her wrists. Hunchback?

HUNCHBACK: Ugh?

ONE-EYE: Fetch me the knitting needles The Sister was kind enough to leave behind on the shelf beneath the statue of Christ Our Saviour.

ONE-EYE snatches the needles from HUNCHBACK.

ONE-EYE: *(To NORMANDY WITCH.)* What's taking so long?

NORMANDY WITCH: The cloth is stiff, One-Eye!

ONE-EYE: Cloth? Stiff? Stiff with starch! I asked for *rope* not bed sheets! Soak it. Soak it, you idiots, and dry it on that damned iron-plate stove there!

NORMANDY WITCH finds a brimming bedpan and moistens the cloth.

LOUISE: What do you want from me?

ONE-EYE: Nothing, my little bird, but your pretty eyes.

LOUISE: My eyes…?

ONE-EYE: They are not yours!

HUNCHBACK: Ha ha!

NORMANDY WITCH: Ha ha!

LOUISE: No!

HUNCHBACK takes the wet cloth and throws it on the stove – it hisses and steams.

ONE-EYE: A cuckoo bird has flown inside your head. It nests there still! Now I shall do you a favour, and set that wretched bird free!

LOUISE: Please God!

ONE-EYE: A cuckoo flew into my head once, dear, but I got it out! See?

ONE-EYE lifts her eyepatch for LOUISE. She chokes with horror.

ONE-EYE: Now, my child, let One-Eye cure you…

(brandishes the knitting needle)

With this!

LOUISE: I don't want to die!

ONE-EYE: You won't die, dear. You just won't have any eyes!

LOUISE struggles.

ONE-EYE: Gag her!

HUNCHBACK ties the steaming cloth across LOUISE's mouth. She screams. They tie her hands to the bed with the other strips.

ONE-EYE: Starched cloth! Stupid hags!

ONE-EYE feels LOUISE's face. In her other hand is the knitting needle… She brings the needle down HARD into LOUISE's eye socket! LOUISE spasms and screams.

ONE-EYE: There's a good girl.

LOUISE: Oh God! *My eye!!!*

ONE-EYE: And now for the other one!

She skewers the other eye. Blood squirts. LOUISE screams again.

LOUISE: *ANNNNNDDREEEEEEEEE!!!*

BINET: *(From the auditorium.)* André? André, you're actually hurting her!

ONE-EYE: See the blood flow… like the blood of my children…

ONE-EYE laughs hysterically, flaps her arms like a bird, and dances around LOUISE's writhing body. BINET steps onto the stage, and goes to LOUISE / MAXA. He wrenches the needle from her head, an eyeball skewered on the tip –

Blood and vitreous fluid pours from her gory eye-holes. MAXA shudders with agony.

BINET: Maxa!

NORMANDY WITCH: But… where is the bird?

HUNCHBACK: Yes. Where is the cuckoo?

LOUISE gives one last agonising scream. Blood everywhere.

ONE-EYE: The bird has flown! Cuckoo! Cuckoo!

HUNCHBACK: We've been tricked…

NORMANDY WITCH: She tricked us!

ONE-EYE drags HUNCHBACK to the stove. She forces HUNCHBACK's face toward the hot-plate.

ONE-EYE: Starched sheets! I'll teach you!

HUNCHBACK: What? Wait, One-Eye! Please, I –

Steam rises. Flesh sizzles. HUNCHBACK howls.

HUNCHBACK: *Arrrggghh!* Oh God, wait, André! It really burns!!! *Stop!*

ONE-EYE lifts HUNCHBACK's melting head up by the hair, then smashes it down HARD on the edge of the iron stove. HUNCHBACK is finally dead. NORMANDY WITCH looks terrified.

NORMANDY WITCH: There never was a cuckoo…

ONE-EYE darts behind NORMANDY WITCH and slits her throat with a knife.

PAULAIS: *Dead! I am… actually… dead – !*

PAULAIS, blood spurting through his fingers and all over the back wall, drops dead. Blood and bodies everywhere. But this time, no Tableau of Horror…

BINET: You killed them. You killed them all.

DE LORDE: I did it for you, Alfred.

BINET: For me?

DE LORDE: They didn't want me cured. So I got rid of them. Now nothing stands in the way of my treatment. Isn't this what you wanted?

BINET: I don't understand…

DE LORDE: The re-enactment therapy! It has shed light on a darkened scene long-forgotten.

(He listens.) There is… a hammering –

Three loud knocks reverberate through the theatre.

DE LORDE: And the door gives way with a crash as two asylum wardens burst in! They find me there with my parents. My mother, dead. My father, insane. They transport him to the laboratories of the Salpêtrière! They strap the poor man to the chair, inject him with chemicals, and they *drill*. They drill a hole into his skull and bore deep into his very brain…

The theatre starts to BLEED.

BINET: André, the re-enactment therapy has failed. You are in a fugue state, a psychotic flux. We must leave here at once!

A strange, hypnotic whispering comes from all around, stopping him dead.

COMPANY: Come, doctor… join us, Alfred… don't be afraid…

Slowly, MAXA, eyeless, rises from the bed. Then PAULAIS stands, his throat still leaking, followed by RATINEAU, his face horribly burnt. BINET can't believe what he's seeing.

COMPANY: Sit… sit down… sit down here, doctor… sit down…

An ominous-looking high-backed chair on wheels is brought forth by EDGAR POE. Attached to the chair's back, a sinister-looking drill device. They sit BINET down. His wrists and ankles are then strapped. The drill hangs above his head.

DE LORDE: The pounding heart. The shredded nerves. The reeling senses. You understood the effect this theatre had more than anyone, Alfred. You. The Fainter!

The drill begins to whir.

BINET: Oh God, no!

DE LORDE: So I know how much you'll appreciate this.

BINET is gagged, his head clamped into position with a strap. The drill begins to descend… BINET struggles to no avail. The COMPANY stand by, watching.

DE LORDE: And to answer your question, Alfred: Why do I write such horrors?

The drill descends…

DE LORDE: I write purely to please. To delight. To thrill.

The drill reaches the top of BINET's head. There is pure terror in his eyes.

And it is my hope that somewhere in the darkness, my father is smiling…

BINET: *(Struggles with all his might.)* André! Please! I beg of you!

DE LORDE: Don't worry, doctor. It's only a play…

BINET: It's only a play it's only a play it's only a play it's only a play it's only a *plaaayyyyyy* –

The drill starts to grind into BINET's skull. BINET's eyes bulge, blood trickles. The COMPANY bend in to watch. DE LORDE smiles as BINET screams in unimaginable agony.

The curtain crashes down on this ***Tableau of Horror****.*

Darkness.

THE END

HORSE PISS FOR BLOOD

Horse Piss For Blood was first performed on 24th February 2012 at the Drum Theatre Plymouth

CAST (in alphabetical order)

DUSTY	Philip Brodie
LEVINE	Gregory Gudgeon
IRIS	Amy McAllister
GERTRUDE	Veronica Roberts
VIRGIL	Alex Robertson

CREATIVE TEAM

Director	Simon Stokes
Set & Costume Designer	Francis O'Connor
Lighting Designer	Colin Grenfell
Sound Designer	Adrienne Quartly
Casting	Lucy Jenkins CDG & Sooki McShane CDG
Accent Coach	Mary Howland
Fight Director	Kev McCurdy

PRODUCTION

Set, Props and Costumes	TR2, Theatre Royal Production and Education Centre
Production Manager	Nick Soper
Stage Manager	Sarah Alford-Smith
Deputy Stage Manager	Caroline Meer
Assistant Stage Manager	Dan Shearing
Drum Theatre Technician	Matt Hoyle
Wardrobe Mistress	Cheryl Hill

CHARACTERS IN THE PRESENT

VIRGIL PLOY (late 20s)

GERTRUDE PLOY, his mother (50s)

DUSTY ST. DAY, her husband (late 20s)

IRIS ROSCROW, a Nancekuke woman (late 20s)

DR EVERETT LEVINE, a psychiatrist (as he comes)

CHARACTERS IN 1976

ARTHUR PLOY, Virgil's father (30)

YOUNG GERTRUDE, (late 20s)

JERRY ZUNDER, an American scientist

WING COMMANDER LIONEL GOUT

THE OWLMAN, a cryptid phenomenon

NOTE

The action takes place in Cornwall, in 1976 and the present.

Nancekuke is a village on the North Cornish coast (rocky, wind-swept, sheer). Mawnan Woods is on the South (wooded, eerie, estuarine). In the play, it appears as if they are in close proximity to each other. In reality, however, they aren't.

Apart from this one glaring fabrication, everything else is real.

Darkness.

GERTRUDE: *(A voice.)* 'Twas said it began as a bedtime story, to keep the children of the village sweet. 'You best be good as gold now, girl, or The Owlman of Mawnan will come for ya.'

1976. Mawnan Woods. Night.

YOUNG GERTRUDE appears from nowhere. She is breathless, terrified and heavily pregnant. She shines her torch at anything that moves.

GERTRUDE: *(A voice.)* 'Twas said that the mere sight of the fiend was a sign that terrible things were to befall the world. 'Twas said that when the Owlman came and cast 'is shadow over the land, you knew the end was near…

Something is in the darkness with her. It moves through the trees. She stops breathing.

GERTRUDE: *(A voice.)* But 'twas worse still if the monster looked you square in the eye. For Death would come to ya, swift and sure…

YOUNG GERTRUDE: *(Whispers to herself.)*

Shut yer eyes, shut yer eyes
Keep 'em closed against the night
If the Owlman sees ya
Then yer sure to die of fright –

Silence. She opens her eyes. She looks behind her. Nothing. She looks around her. Nothing. She makes to go forward. Suddenly, the creature is before her. THE OWLMAN. It emits a horrific shriek. YOUNG GERTRUDE screams. Darkness.

GERTRUDE: *(A voice.)* Thass what I believed anyway.

The Present. Nancekuke. The Ploy Home.

The Ploy home is a dilapidated cliff-top house. At the back, there's a door to the outside world and a large window, double glazed, with cliffs beyond. There is a tatty armchair, and a small kitchen table and chair to the side. Elsewhere, a large grotty fridge, a cassette tape deck, a picture of Bob Marley on the wall, and some stairs leading to the upper part of the house.

GERTRUDE PLOY, a monster of a woman, slowly descends the stairs. She has dreadlocks, wears tatty Rasta-themed lounging clothes, bumbag (where she keeps her papers and drugs and mobile phone) and a dressing gown. We may or may not notice that, beneath the gown, on her left-hand side, a strange lump protrudes.

DR EVERETT LEVINE stands at the front door (open). Wind whistles outside. He wears an overcoat and carries a briefcase.

DR LEVINE: Mrs Ploy?

GERTRUDE: Come in and close the door, ya prat.

He closes the door. The wind cuts dead.

DR LEVINE: Wow. Wild out there.

GERTRUDE: We're on a cliff.

DR LEVINE: Yes, I suppose you are. Dr Everett Levine.

GERTRUDE: Geezer from Bodmin nuthouse.

DR LEVINE: St. Lawrence's mental hospital, yes.

GERTRUDE: I can smell the madness on ya.

DR LEVINE: I had a pasty in the car. Mrs Ploy, I came here to talk about your son.

GERTRUDE: Izze dead?

DR LEVINE: No! God, no. Your son is very much alive.

GERTRUDE: Siddown.

He sits.

DR LEVINE: I… appreciate you agreeing to see me. I think it's important we discuss this matter face to face.

GERTRUDE: Mind if I smoke?

DR LEVINE: Not at all.

GERTRUDE: Spliff.

DR LEVINE: Oh.

GERTRUDE: Or do you frown upon this sorta thing?

DR LEVINE: Is it for medicinal purposes?

GERTRUDE: Religious ones.

She throws a look to Bob Marley on the wall.

DR LEVINE: Ah. Sir Bob. *Aii-ree.* I shall turn a blind eye…

He tries to ignore her as she unzips her bumbag and starts skinning up. She eyes him suspiciously.

DR LEVINE: So. About Virgil.

GERTRUDE: Whass e done, then? Murdered again?

DR LEVINE: Nothing of the sort. After ten years in our care, I can safely say he is completely rehabilitated.

GERTRUDE: Shit.

DR LEVINE: I thought you'd be happy.

GERTRUDE: 'appy? 'appy? 'ardly!

DR LEVINE: Your son is no longer sick, Mrs Ploy. He's much better now.

GERTRUDE: E'll never be better. Tis in 'is blood to be nuthin but pure evil!

DR LEVINE: Virgil isn't evil, Mrs Ploy. I came here to tell you he can come home.

GERTRUDE: No way! No fuckin way, man! E ain't comin back ere!

DR LEVINE: Mrs Ploy –

GERTRUDE: Thought e was incarcerated up Bodmin for good! Thass what you people told me!

DR LEVINE: I didn't, I'm sure.

GERTRUDE: Well, some fucker like you! Dr Hairy-hoof or –

DR LEVINE: Heirrennhoffer. He passed away some years ago. His patients were put into my care. Treatments have improved radically since then.

GERTRUDE: Answer's no.

(To herself.)

Hopin e was dead…

As GERTRUDE starts to smoke her considerable joint, DR LEVINE takes VIRGIL's inches-thick profile from his briefcase and flashes through the pages.

DR LEVINE: Virgil has shown remarkable consistency over these past few years. You would've known all this if you'd responded to my letters.

GERTRUDE: Any letters I got from Bodmin I burnt.

DR LEVINE: And you changed your number without informing us. You were difficult to track down.

GERTRUDE: I was hopin for 'impossible'.

DR LEVINE: Why don't you want him back?

GERTRUDE: The boy is deranged, doctor. Sick in the head! After what e did…

DR LEVINE: Virgil is fully aware of what he has done, Mrs Ploy. He wants to make amends.

GERTRUDE: Huh!

DR LEVINE: He's looking forward to seeing his mother.

GERTRUDE: Dun't pull that sentimental heartstring shit wimme.

DR LEVINE: I wasn't. I was just saying –

GERTRUDE: I've moved on. Things 'ave changed. I'm a Rastafarian now.

DR LEVINE: So I see but –

GERTRUDE: I got Bob now.

DR LEVINE: Just try to think of this as a fresh start.

GERTRUDE: Fresh start? Wi' that psycho?

DR LEVINE: He hasn't suffered a violent episode since he came to us.

GERTRUDE: Once a killer always a killer.

DR LEVINE: Virgil hasn't killed anybody, Mrs Ploy.

GERTRUDE: E tried to kill me! 'ave ya got that in yer flashy folder, Mr Bodmin?

DR LEVINE: Came at you with a kitchen knife, I know.

GERTRUDE: I shoulda smothered 'im at birth.

DR LEVINE: Oh, Mrs Ploy –

GERTRUDE stands before DR LEVINE, undoes her robe.

DR LEVINE: Mrs Ploy?

She displays her midriff. We may or may not see a disturbing brown tumour – a grapefruit-sized protrusion of flesh and hair and teeth bulging from her stomach. DR LEVINE violently recoils.

DR LEVINE: Wuh! Jesus! Sorry. *Shit!* What is *that*? A tumour?

GERTRUDE: Thass Nancy.

DR LEVINE: Nancy?

GERTRUDE: Me daughter.

DR LEVINE: Daughter?

GERTRUDE: Virgil's twin. Only she never made it out like that rancid bastard did.

DR LEVINE: Fetal reabsorption. I've read about the phenomena but I've never seen it with my own eyes.

GERTRUDE: What e think, doc?

DR LEVINE: You should get it removed.

GERTRUDE: Removed? Nancy? She's me pride and joy!

DR LEVINE: She might be malignant, Mrs Ploy.

GERTRUDE: *E* was malignant! After what e did to the poor dear. In utero. Nancy was always me fav'rite. Virgil was so jealous of Nancy. Thass why e tried to cut 'er from me with a kitchen knife. Scoop 'er out like she's ice cream. But she's mine, ya know? She's my little girl.

DR LEVINE: I have to open a window.

GERTRUDE: Don't let the 'eat out.

DR LEVINE: I need to breathe!

GERTRUDE: Siddown!

He sees something through the glass. Looks away. Looks again.

DR LEVINE: The strangest thing. There's a sheep outside… and from here it looks like it's got two heads.

GERTRUDE: Thass Jeffry.

DR LEVINE: I'm sorry?

GERTRUDE: Dun't be. You'll find e's quite content.

DR LEVINE: What? Who is?

GERTRUDE: Jeffry, ya tit.

DR LEVINE: *(Paranoid.)* What do you mean Jeffry? Who is Jeffry?

GERTRUDE: You just said *I thought I saw a sheep with two heads* and I replied *Thass Jeffry.*

DR LEVINE: Jeffry?

GERTRUDE: Jeffry.

DR LEVINE: Jeffry the two-headed sheep?

GERTRUDE: Jeffry the Sheep wi' Two 'eads.

DR LEVINE: Is this village renowned for its deformed livestock? What is this place? Where the hell am I?

GERTRUDE: D'ya not knaw of Nancekuke, doctor? Of its pale, poisoned skies and its toxic-black heart? How the accursed earth belches death into the world and 'ow all livin things, from the fish in the sea to the birds in the air, enter this vile realm 'alf made, mutated, or jus' plain dead? 'specially when The Owlman of Mawnan flies... I'da thought Virgil would've spilt 'is guts 'bout this place. Cus e's King Freak of it all. Lord Aberration 'isself.

DR LEVINE: Why are you telling me all this?

GERTRUDE: *(Intense pause, then...)* Stoned.

He watches GERTRUDE open the fridge (mouldy remains of things inside), break off a chunk of cheese and nibble it. She ponders, deep in thought.

DR LEVINE: You know, Mrs Ploy? I think you're right. Perhaps this isn't the best environment for your son to come back to.

GERTRUDE: Bring 'im 'ere.

DR LEVINE: What?

GERTRUDE: You heard me. Bring the bugger back.

DR LEVINE: You said you didn't want him.

GERTRUDE: I've changed me mind ab'm I, Mr Bodmin?

DR LEVINE: Yes, but... I'm not so sure now.

GERTRUDE: You offered. I'm acceptin.

DR LEVINE: I know but... it's not very healthy here.

GERTRUDE: E's cured inne?

DR LEVINE: He is, yes –

GERTRUDE: Then I agree to take 'im.

DR LEVINE: I don't understand this sudden turnaround.

GERTRUDE: Gib'm to me Levine or I'll toss ya like a bullock.

DR LEVINE: You'll what?

GERTRUDE: I've ad a ponder, and I knaw just what to do with that nasty no-good nutcase of a Nancy-killin 'orse-piss-for-blood-spillin spawn-o'-the-devil evil li'l fucker that e is!

1976. A chemical weapon testing station below Nancekuke.

'Sinister Purpose' by Creedence Clearwater Revival comes out of tinny speakers.

JERRY ZUNDER, an American military scientist, nods to the beat. He is dressed in gasmask and bio-suit. A green light is on above the door. It changes to red. Through the viewing hatch we see something furry in a cage. Green smoke rises up and surrounds the cage. The cage violently bucks and jumps. When the smoke clears, the creature, a rabbit, is dead. Light changes to green again. JERRY fetches the rabbit from the chamber. He flops it on the table, removes his bio-gear, picks up the phone.

JERRY: Yeh, hi. Clean-up in Station 4, please. 'kay. Thanks.

He goes to a fridge, opens it. It's chock-full of grim looking chemical containers of various qualities – and his packed lunch. He eats a sandwich and studies the dead rabbit.

JERRY: Say, what's up Bugs? You'll be pleased to know that your death was not in vain, soldier. You've confirmed for the Ministry of Defense that o-ethyl S-2 diisopropylaminomethyl methylphophonothiolate still works adequately.

He takes a bite of sandwich.

JERRY: And if the gas don't kill ya the name sure will!

Beat.

(Whispered.) Sorry, Bunny. They made me do it. And now I gotta dissect ya.

(Puppets the rabbit.) Aw, Jerry. D'ya have to?

(His voice.) Yes, I do. I have to cut out your brain and lungs and examine them for tissue damage. It's the way we do things down here.

(As rabbit.) Can't we just listen to Creedence and chill?

(His voice.) That would be nice, wouldn't it?

(Rabbit.) Yeh.

(His voice.) Sure, we can listen to Creedence.

(Rabbit.) Is this *Cosmo's Factory* that's playing?

(His voice.) No. This is *Green River.*

(Rabbit.) I like *Mardi Gras.* That's a great record.

(His voice.) Mardi Gras? What the hell are you talking about? *Mardi Gras* is, like, their worst album.

(Rabbit.) It is?

(His voice.) Yeh. Tensions in the band meant that Tom Fogerty split leaving John, Doug Clifford and Stu Cook to forge on regardless. The result was mediocre at best. And because it wasn't the full line-up, you can't even really call *Mardi Gras* a Creedence record.

(Rabbit.) You don't get out much do you, Jerry?

Enter RAF WING COMMANDER LIONEL GOUT, unbeknownst to JERRY. He switches the music off, making JERRY jump.

GOUT: Hello Jerry.

JERRY: Wing Commander Gout. I didn't hear you come in.

GOUT: Please, Jerry. Call me Lionel.

JERRY: Really?

GOUT: We're all good friends down here.

(Seeing rabbit.) What's this the result of?

JERRY: Well, Lionel, that's one drop of 0-ethyl S-2 diisopropylaminomethyl methylphophonothiolate.

GOUT: VX.

JERRY: What's VX?

GOUT: It's the shorter name for 0-ethyl S-2 diisopropylaminomethyl methylphophonothiolate.

JERRY: Wait a second. Are you telling me 0-ethyl S-2 diisopropylaminomethyl methylphophonothiolate has a shorter name?

GOUT: Yes, Jerry. VX.

JERRY: Dang. Wish I'd known that sooner. I woulda saved a heck of a lotta time talking to rabbits.

GOUT: Hah.

JERRY: You'll be pleased to know this delightful Cold War vintage still kills things horribly.

GOUT: Violently attacks the central nervous system, doesn't it?

JERRY: Impairs the vision. Liquifies the lungs. Results in agonising death. Pretty pokey stuff.

GOUT: That's the boys at ICI for you.

JERRY: Ten times more toxic than most G-agents.

GOUT: Seem to remember it was first developed as a pesticide.

JERRY: *(Peeling a banana.)* That's what it is. Compound organophosphate. If funding dries up you could sell it to the local farmers round here for crop spray.

GOUT: We tried that already.

JERRY: I was joking.

GOUT: We sold it to South East Asia to kill creepy crawlies on banana trees. They then shipped the bananas back to us. Before we discovered it was best used as a chemical weapon.

JERRY stops chewing.

GOUT: That was a long time ago now. We've covered our tracks and all the poorly people have gone away.

JERRY: Sheesh.

GOUT: And what else are they making you test?

GOUT opens the fridge and gazes into it.

JERRY: Porton Down want results on everything we have stockpiled here.

GOUT: That's a frightfully long list, Jerry.

JERRY: Oh. You know me. I live to give.

GOUT takes one canister out of the fridge – it has a yellow and black skull and crossbones on it.

GOUT: Tri-oxine 432.

JERRY: *(Tenses.)* Be careful with that canister, Lionel. The housing's a little loose.

GOUT: And what does this one do?

JERRY: On inhalation it drives you insane. Completely and utterly insane.

GOUT: Insanity Gas? Exciting!

JERRY: It's a prototype. It's never been used in the field. Vietnam was the closest it came but…

GOUT: Ah. An American recipe? Like Momma's good old home-made apple pie.

Pause.

JERRY: To what do I owe the pleasure of your company, Lionel?

GOUT: Jerry, I have some rather distressing news. We've hit a snag. Environment are coming down on us hard. They're –

Enter ALFRED PLOY, early 30s, in work overcoat. He wheels in an MOD bucket and mop.

ALFRED: Clean-up?

JERRY: Hey Alfred. In the test chamber.

ALFRED: I'll fix they flanges, too.

JERRY: Thanks.

ALFRED goes to the testing chamber. He cleans.

JERRY: You were saying?

GOUT: We're being shut down, Jerry.

JERRY: What?

GOUT: 'The harbouring, testing and continued manufacture of chemical and biological weapons is seen as illegal in the eyes of international law'. We have to vacate the premises immediately. Now, here's where it gets tricky, Jerry. We were supposed to stop manufacturing nerve gas in '58.

JERRY: But we haven't.

GOUT: No, Jerry. We haven't. And with this place to close we must hide the evidence of production otherwise we're all for the chop.

JERRY: Hide the evidence?

GOUT: Get rid of everything. Immediately.

JERRY: Everything?

GOUT: Everything.

JERRY: But the dumps are at capacity. We can't bury any more on-site.

GOUT: Then you'll have to think of some other alternative.

JERRY: Me?

GOUT: I know you're not happy here, Jerry.

JERRY: Oh, I wouldn't say that. I have plenty of dead rabbits for friends and… *(He wells up.)* You MOD SOBs said I could surf here. That's why I came to this shithole. I was promised. Great surf!

GOUT: Surfing, Jerry, is not the prime concern here. The prime concern is the chemical capability this country can boast in the event of another war.

JERRY: I know I know I know, but I haven't been allowed out since I got here. I ain't seen the goddamn sun let alone Hang Ten on my longboard!

GOUT: Do me this one favour and I'll release you.

JERRY: You'll let me go surfing?

GOUT: You'll be back to sunny California with considerable pension and benefits before you can say… what do surfers say, Jerry?

JERRY: Cowabunga?

GOUT: 'Cowabunga'. But we have to work quickly, Jerry. The quicker the better.

JERRY: Transport it by road?

GOUT: Far too risky.

JERRY: Seal it in here?

GOUT: Environment wants the place left empty.

JERRY: Shit. Think, think, think.

GOUT clocks ALFRED wiping the window.

GOUT: Can he hear us in there?

JERRY: Alfred, can you hear us in there?

ALFRED shakes his head, blows his cover. GOUT beckons him to come out.

GOUT: You shouldn't have heard that conversation, lad.

ALFRED: What conversation, sir?

GOUT: Don't play dumb with me…

(Reads name tag.) Ploy.

ALFRED: Yes, sir. Sorry, sir.

JERRY: Don't go too hard on him, Lionel. Alfred here does a fine job. Don't ya?

ALFRED: I do me best, sir.

GOUT: He also possesses a keen talent for eavesdropping in confidential matters of defence.

JERRY: C'mon, Lionel. Give the guy a break. This is a secret chemical weapons plant. Things get said all the time, right?

ALFRED: *(To GOUT.)* It's o'right, sir. I treat my work with the utmost discretion.

GOUT: Do you now?

ALFRED: I've signed the Official Secrets Act, ya knaw?

GOUT: I know.

JERRY: He knows.

ALFRED: I didn't mean to listen in. It's just… I caught wind me job might be on the line. And I need me job, sir. I really do.

JERRY: 'course ya do, Alfred. Man's gotta have a job.

ALFRED: I recently wed, see? I got responsibilities.

JERRY: You got a family on the way?

ALFRED: We 'ave.

JERRY: That's nice. Ain't that nice, Lionel?

GOUT gives JERRY a look.

GOUT: So you like working here, Ploy?

ALFRED: I like havin a job. Me father was a farmer but I never took to silage. And if you dun't take to silage round ere there ain't much else to choose from.

GOUT: Local chap are you, Ploy?

ALFRED: You couldn't get more so.

GOUT gives JERRY another look.

ALFRED: You seen that house on the cliff stands alone to the west of ere?

JERRY: No. But I can picture it in my mind's eye.

ALFRED: Thass bin a Ploy 'ouse for six generations. I was born there. Right on the kitchen floor.

GOUT: I know the property. It's on our land.

ALFRED: Ah. Well. See, this land was owned by the farmers. My father bein one ob'm. When you fellas moved in –

GOUT: We requisitioned it. And we allowed you to keep your home, didn't we Ploy?

ALFRED: You did.

GOUT: And we could just as easily take it away.

ALFRED: You wouldn't do that, would ya? My father said a deal was struck. They shook on it.

GOUT: Oh, well, if they *shook* on it…

GOUT gives JERRY another more pointed look.

JERRY: Lionel. You're freakin' me out, man.

GOUT: I'm presenting you with a possible solution to your problem, Jerry.

JERRY: What problem?

GOUT: Didn't you want to go surfing?

JERRY: Yeh.

(Twigs.) Oh. Yeah!

Beat.

(Bad acting.) Say, Lionel, I know this facility has met its untimely end as a nerve gas factory, but this will remain MOD property, right?

GOUT: From now until the end of all creation.

JERRY: Ain't you gonna need a skeleton staff to keep things ticking over?

GOUT: You mean someone who can keep a close eye on things after we're packed up and gone?

JERRY: Precisely.

GOUT: Who do you suggest?

JERRY: Why, Alfred here would be great! What about Alfred?

GOUT: Alfred?

ALFRED: Aww, that sounds –

JERRY: Great. Lionel here will see that it is done.

ALFRED: Just like that?

JERRY: Just like that.

ALFRED: Thank you, Jerry. Thank you, sir. I'd be glad to stay on. Keep an eye on the place. You can trust in me.

JERRY: Oh. But before we extend your contract, might you know of anywhere in the local area where we might be able to dump some unwanted equipment?

ALFRED: Stick it in me garridge if you like?

GOUT: This stuff is sensitive, Ploy. And there's a lot of it.

ALFRED: Oh. You mean –

JERRY: Materials, machinery, containers, that sorta thing. It needs to be buried deep. *Real* deep.

ALFRED: You wanna dump all they chemicals somewhere round ere?

JERRY: Forget it. Just a thought. I'm sure you'll have no problem finding work elsewhere, even if it means going back to the farm –

GOUT: Which we will have to requisition unless –

ALFRED: Sally's Bottom. Sally's Bottom. You could take it there.

GOUT: Tell us about Sally's Bottom, lad.

ALFRED: Well. Tis old copper workins. A mine shaft. Right near ere.

GOUT: Is it deep?

ALFRED: Ellish deep. Ole Sal runs right out under the sea.

GOUT: Sounds ideal.

ALFRED: But we dun't wanna poison the soil. That wouldn' be funny.

JERRY: Mine spoil's riddled with arsenic anyways. What's a drop of VX thrown into the mix?

GOUT: Dump the stuff tonight under cover of darkness. I cannot impress upon you the delicacy with which you must undertake this mission, Ploy.

ALFRED nods, wracked with the ramifications.

GOUT: *(To JERRY.)* Surf's up, dude.

JERRY: Gee thanks, Lionel.

GOUT: That's Wing Commander Gout to you, Jerry.

Exit GOUT.

Present. House.

There is a plastic banner up which reads WELCOME HOME! Neon-orange orange squash and cheesy Wotsits in a bowl on the table. GERTRUDE is on her mobile.

GERTRUDE: Barb? Tis Gertrude Ploy. You hear whass gone on? E's bin seen again, Barb. The Owlman of Mawnan. Hear what happened to Grace Pucky? I knaw. Shame. Tis why I wanted to talk to you Barb, and talk to you specifically. Dark days are upon us once again. What can we do, Barb? What can anyone do? Well… I might 'ave a solution for ya. One I'd be willin to share. With you, Barb. But only with you…

Outside the window, DR LEVINE appears with VIRGIL PLOY. DR LEVINE opens the door.

DR LEVINE: Mrs Ploy?

GERTRUDE: Barb, I gotta go. I'll call ya back dreckly.

She hangs up. LEVINE has a present (flat, rectangular) under his arm. VIRGIL has a bunch of withered flowers in one hand, and an old Puma sports bag stuffed with clothes in another.

DR LEVINE: He's here.

GERTRUDE: Aw.

GERTRUDE goes to the fridge for cheese.

DR LEVINE: Virgil, would you mind waiting outside for a moment?

DR LEVINE enters. Closes the door. VIRGIL remains outside. He stands awkwardly at the window, watching his mother.

DR LEVINE: *(Opening briefcase.)* If I can just get your signature on these release forms?

(With pen and papers.) Sign here, please?

She signs.

DR LEVINE: I also wanted a quick word with regards to Virgil's re-housing program.

GERTRUDE: Oh yeh?

DR LEVINE: Try to refrain from exposing Virgil to situations of high stress, if you can. And here, please?

She signs.

DR LEVINE: The therapies I've practiced on him are based on Eastern meditative techniques –

GERTRUDE: 'ippy shit.

DR LEVINE: And it's crucial he enters a stable environment at this early stage. He shouldn't ingest any artificial colours, preservatives, additives or high-sugar foods. Plenty of fresh fruit and vegetables. Brown rice. Pulses. Lentils. That sort of thing. Organic diet, if you can. Healthy body, healthy mind. That's our philosophy at Bodmin. And here, please?

She signs.

DR LEVINE: I'd also request that you go easy on the drug abuse in his presence.

DR LEVINE hands her copies of the release forms.

GERTRUDE: Will that be all, doctor?

DR LEVINE: No, there is one more thing. I am incredibly proud of the work I have achieved with Virgil. I've spent a lot of time untangling a myriad of densely constructed fantasies from inside his head, and I now believe he is as good as he's ever been. I would hate to see all my hard work go to waste. And so I ask you, Mrs Ploy, to treat him gently during these first few days of reintegration.

GERTRUDE: Fantasies? What fantasies?

DR LEVINE: When he first came to us he believed in many strange things.

GERTRUDE: Like what?

DR LEVINE: Like a terrible winged creature that would haunt these parts. Clearly, this 'monster' personified his endangered sense of security. The malignant force that took his father away. He feared that if he saw this beast, it meant –

GERTRUDE: The end was a-comin.

DR LEVINE: And if it looked him in the eye –

GERTRUDE: E'd die. Thass The Owlman of Mawnan. E's real.

DR LEVINE: Mrs Ploy, The Owlman was a figment of his imagination. Please don't start telling him it's real.

GERTRUDE: Oh, but I tell no fibs, doctor. The creature's bin sighted again of late. Sylvia Crabbe up Tregasko saw it cavortin in 'er back garden! Dick Cutter ad it fly out in front of 'is van up 'igh lanes. They lived to tell the tale. Grace Pucky wadn't so lucky.

DR LEVINE: She died?

GERTRUDE: 'Shut yer eyes, shut yer eyes
Keep 'em closed against the night
If the Owlman sees ya
Then yer sure to die of fright!'

DR LEVINE: Mrs Ploy –

GERTRUDE: And lo, The Owlman cometh! 'arbinger o' doom! Angel o' Death! Upon 'is flight, the land will choke and suffer once more! Dark times are upon us! Dark times indeed!

DR LEVINE: Good grief.

GERTRUDE: Let 'im in.

DR LEVINE: Yes…

DR LEVINE opens the door. Enter VIRGIL.

GERTRUDE: Virgil?

VIRGIL: Mother.

GERTRUDE: Welcome 'ome, boy.

VIRGIL: *(Re: flowers.)* Got ya these. They was fresh when I bought 'em.

GERTRUDE: I'll put 'em in the bin.

DR LEVINE: How does it feel to be back?

VIRGIL: Strange.

DR LEVINE: Has it changed much?

VIRGIL: A little. I see you've ad double glazin put in.

GERTRUDE: Keeps the place airtight.

VIRGIL: Oh, I can feel the diff'rence.

GERTRUDE: Tis no longer the drafty ole shack it once was, doctor.

DR LEVINE: No.

VIRGIL: And I see you've ad yer 'air done.

GERTRUDE: I'm a Rastafarian now.

VIRGIL: Great.

Pause.

DR LEVINE: Oh look, Virgil. Your mother's laid on quite a spread for your return.

GERTRUDE: Wotsits'n squash.

DR LEVINE: Oh, and I almost forgot –

He hands VIRGIL a flat, rectangular package.

VIRGIL: I did not expect this.

VIRGIL unwraps it.

VIRGIL: My certificate of sanity.

DR LEVINE: We put it in a frame for you.

VIRGIL: Looka that mother. Proof! Proof that I'm cured and A-1 up ere!

Pause.

GERTRUDE: You should prolly be gettin back to Bodmin, right doc?

DR LEVINE: I suppose I'd better had.

GERTRUDE: Me and the boy got a lotta catchin up to do.

DR LEVINE: Of course.

VIRGIL: Dr Levine… I dunno how to ever thank you.

DR LEVINE: There's no need.

GERTRUDE: All part o' the service, right doc?

DR LEVINE: If you need me, you know where I am.

VIRGIL goes to embrace DR LEVINE who stops him with a hand on the shoulder. He gives him a pat.

DR LEVINE: Good luck, Virgil.

DR LEVINE gives GERTRUDE a look, then exits. VIRGIL, at the window, watches him go. GERTRUDE pulls the banner down, scrunches it up, takes the bowl of Wotsits and sits. The house falls silent.

VIRGIL: S'good to see you, mother.

GERTRUDE: I wish I could say the same.

VIRGIL's smile fades.

GERTRUDE: Last time I saw you, you was chasin me round the table with a kitchen knife.

VIRGIL: I was unwell.

GERTRUDE: Unwell? You was nuts.

VIRGIL: Dr Levine is one o' the top psychiatrists in the county. E sorted me right out.

GERTRUDE: Did e suck the poison out yer soul while e was at it?

VIRGIL: Ain't no poison in me soul, mother. There ain't no poison nowhere.

GERTRUDE: Zat what Dr Levine told ya?

VIRGIL: It's what I knaw of myself.

GERTRUDE: Like you d'knaw whass fuckin what.

VIRGIL: I knaw I believed some pretty strange things back then. But thass the old me. I'm the new me now. Tis my 'ope that you take comfort in that fact and let me be the best son I can to you. It may take some time but… I'm confident we can get to be like a proper mother'n son some day.

GERTRUDE: Mmmmmmmmm.

She devours a Wotsit.

Virgil, there's summin you should know… While you was in the loony bin gettin fixed I took another 'usband.

VIRGIL: Oh. Really?

GERTRUDE: Yes.

VIRGIL: You… married… again?

GERTRUDE: Is that so 'ard to believe?

VIRGIL: No.

Beat as he assimilates this.

Thass wonderful news, mother. You deserve a good man. What wi' father bein gone for so long. Congratulations. I'm over the moon for ya. Oo is the lucky fella?

GERTRUDE: Well, see now, ere's the thing… You know 'im of old.

VIRGIL: Do I?

GERTRUDE: Can you guess oo e might be?

VIRGIL: Not a clue.

GERTRUDE: Old school pal of yours.

VIRGIL: E's my age?

GERTRUDE: I shall bring 'im down?

VIRGIL: Is e ere?

GERTRUDE: E's me 'usband. Where else would e be? *(Calling up the stairs.)* Dusty? Dusty darlin, Virgil's ere.

VIRGIL pales.

VIRGIL: Dusty… ?

GERTRUDE: You remember Dusty St. Day, dun't ya?

Enter DUSTY ST. DAY from upstairs. DUSTY is VIRGIL's age but sleazy and ridiculous.

DUSTY: O'right, Virgil. Long time no see, mate.

VIRGIL: Dusty.

GERTRUDE: 'member 'im?

VIRGIL: Yeh. I remember Dusty.

DUSTY: 'spect I was the last bugger you was expectin to see livin ere in yer 'ouse married to yer muvver, eh Virge?

VIRGIL: You married *Dusty*?

DUSTY: She said yes, Virge. She said yes.

VIRGIL: 'ow did this happen?

GERTRUDE: Dun't ask me.

DUSTY: I's installin yer windas, wan' I, sweetpea?

GERTRUDE: Windas. You was.

DUSTY: *(Winks.)* You needed a refit.

GERTRUDE: This is all Dusty's work.

DUSTY: 'ottest August bank holiday weekend on record it was.

GERTRUDE: Dusty's a dab-'and wi' the double glazin.

DUSTY: There's an art to it Virge, and let no prick-ass from Chacewater tell you otherwise.

GERTRUDE: Sledge 'ammered the whole damn wall down e did.

DUSTY: Word of advice, Virge: never use linseed oil putty. Eats the rubber seals. Causes premature mistin. Then yer fucked.

DUSTY takes VIRGIL's certificate of sanity and proceeds to cut lines of cocaine on it.

GERTRUDE: I wanted insulatin, in readiness for the winter.

DUSTY: I ad a summer deal on. Install now. Get it 'alf price.

GERTRUDE: So I called'n up. Got'n in.

DUSTY: I thought I'd run into you Virge, but 'course you was up Bodmin Loony Bin.

GERTRUDE: And as I sat ere watchin 'is little ass skip about –

DUSTY: Like I said. 'Twas 'ot as 'ell.

GERTRUDE: 'is bronzed shoulders slick wi' sweat –

DUSTY: 'Twas in no way intended as a come-on.

GERTRUDE: I was struck be a beautiful idea.

DUSTY: Tis the way I work in 'eat.

GERTRUDE: I thought: Dusty's double glazin should be in every 'ome in Nancekuke. Nancekuke and beyond!

DUSTY: But I never got time to chase people up.

GERTRUDE: So I thought: 'ow 'bout Dusty does the double-glazin and I come onboard as an administrative crutch?

DUSTY: All the while I'm rimmin the frames and I'm thinkin: I dun't remember Mrs Ploy lookin *that* good.

GERTRUDE: So I got up and shimmied over and looked 'im in the eye –

DUSTY: And me, I go all weak in the knee –

GERTRUDE: I make a business proposition.

DUSTY: And I propose marriage.

GERTRUDE: And ere we are. In business.

DUSTY: In love.

GERTRUDE: Partners in crime.

DUSTY: Heh.

GERTRUDE: Heh heh.

DUSTY: 'Twas some 'ot that August bank holiday, Virge.

GERTRUDE: But thass how it 'appened.

DUSTY: Match made in Heaven.

He snorts a line.

DUSTY: We're like two panes of glass, trappin tight the air between us and heatin it right up. Oh, we gotta lotta trapped air between us. She's perfect for me, Virge, I gotta tell ya. Digs all the things I dig, like smokin' spliffs and Bob Marley and gettin jiggy and eatin cheese and smokin spliffs –

GERTRUDE: And e can dance, too, this one!

She turns the tape player on. Bob Marley's 'Three Little Birds' plays. DUSTY dances erotically around GERTRUDE.

GERTRUDE: Looka that! Like liquid inne? Dusty darlin? You get me 'otter than a church hall urn!

She turns it off.

GERTRUDE: So, thass the big news. You got a new father.

VIRGIL: Eh?

DUSTY snorts another line.

DUSTY: Yessir! Dusty's daddy now, Virgil. Whadda ya make o' that? Sure, we went to school together but in the eyes of the law I am now your stepdad. Ain't that insane?

VIRGIL: Insane.

GERTRUDE: Now, on to the finer details regardin this set-up. Though me and Dusty are joyfully wed, we sadly kent 'ave kids.

DUSTY: Though Christ knaws we tried.

GERTRUDE: Tis Dusty's dream to 'ave a child to call 'is own.

DUSTY: Such a dream. Such a dream.

GERTRUDE: But 'twas shat upon wun't it, dear?

DUSTY: That was a dark day, babe. Wankin into a plastic cup in Trura –

GERTRUDE: In hospital.

DUSTY: And 'avin some asshole nurse tellin me there was summin up wimme semen. They said my seed was lazy, Virge. Lazy?

He lashes out at an invisible nurse. VIRGIL jumps.

GERTRUDE: The fact that we could not conceive was causin –

DUSTY: Heavy strains on the relationship.

GERTRUDE: And the business.

DUSTY: I was in a funk.

GERTRUDE: Lost all 'is mirth.

DUSTY: Got sloppy wi' the installations.

GERTRUDE: Started losin custom.

DUSTY: I felt like I'd ad me balls chopped off or summin.

GERTRUDE: I put a lotta effort into this scheme so I'd be damned if I was gonna let it slip through me fingers.

DUSTY: She saved me. Saved me.

GERTRUDE: So when Dr fuckin Levine shows up with news that you was sane enuff to come 'ome –

DUSTY: This is brilliant.

GERTRUDE: I got to thinkin Dusty's dysfunctional cus e kent fulfill 'is dreams of havin a child and the business is about to go tits-up. And ere's this Dr Levine sayin I gotta son I near 'nuff completely forgot about!

DUSTY: Could they both some 'ow… ?

GERTRUDE: *(To VIRGIL.)* Now I never wanted ya back. In any way. But I was prepared to make the sacrifice.

DUSTY: Your muvver is a fuckin saint.

GERTRUDE: So I thought. Virgil. E'll do.

DUSTY: Dusty gotta baby!

GERTRUDE: And ere you are!

DUSTY: I wanna teach the boy 'ow to kick a ball around. Like a good dad. Show 'im 'ow to take care of 'imself in the school yard. Cus, as I seem to remember, e wun't much fuckin cop at that at all! You wanna line, Virge?

VIRGIL: Best not.

DUSTY: And I wanna teach you my trade, Virgil. Pass on me skills. So you can carry on the glazin business when I'm (god forbid) dead and buried. I am so 'appy. Are you 'appy, cupcake?

GERTRUDE: Ooooh, I'm 'appy if you're 'appy, sweetheart!

DUSTY rubs the remnants on his gums and puts the certificate back on the wall.

DUSTY: I never thought I could be so bastard 'appy. I got me boy. My joy. My new tin toy. A dream come true. Never thought it'd happen. So if I'm 'appy and you're 'appy that just leaves Virgil. You 'appy Virgil?

Nightmare flashback –

DUSTY: O'right, Virgil you VIRGIN?

Flashback ends.

DUSTY: Virgil?

GERTRUDE: Oi! Cloth ears! You 'appy or no?

Beat. VIRGIL suddenly bolts for the front door.

VIRGIL: Dr Levine!

DUSTY grabs VIRGIL.

DUSTY: Where ya goin?

VIRGIL: I wanna go back to Bodmin!

DUSTY: You ain't goin anywhere, son. And you best do what yer daddy tells ya, or there'll be trouble!

Present. Cliff. Day.

Sound of sea, distant. Enter IRIS ROSCROW with great urgency. She has a backpack loaded with strange home-made equipment; equipment intended to send signals into deep space. She aims a small transmitter dish to the heavens and speaks into a C.B. radio handset.

IRIS: This is Iris Roscrow from the village o' Nancekuke. Sendin out a message out to any extra terrestrial or inter-dimensional beins that might just happen to be in the vicinity. Do you 'ear me, over?

Static.

IRIS: Is anyone there, over?

Static.

IRIS: If you can hear me, come and get me. I am in grave danger. Repeat: grave danger. Over!

Static.

IRIS: C'mon ya buggers, I've waited long enuff! I'm gonna close me eyes and count back from ten.

Beat.

10… 9… 8… 7… 6…

Enter DR LEVINE, along the cliff path. He is looking for something. He stops when he sees her.

IRIS: 5… 4… 3… 2 –

DR LEVINE: Excuse me.

IRIS: Shit-the-bed!

DR LEVINE: Sorry!

IRIS: Wow!

DR LEVINE: I didn't mean to –

IRIS: You came.

DR LEVINE: I did?

IRIS: I kent believe it. Wow!

DR LEVINE: Are you local?

IRIS: I am of this world, yes.

DR LEVINE: But you're from Nancekuke?

IRIS: You got my transmission?

DR LEVINE: What transmission?

IRIS: I sent it only moments ago but, heck, whass a voyage 'cross the cosmos to someone like you, eh? Tis a nano blip. A blink and a woosh and 'ere you shaggin are! You came in human form, I see.

DR LEVINE: Yes…

IRIS: I 'ppreciate that. My insignificant intellect would no doubt pop like a bug under a brick if you appeared to me as yer true self, am I right?

Beat.

Welcome.

DR LEVINE: Thank you.

Pause.

IRIS: Welp. I'm ready when you are.

DR LEVINE: For what?

IRIS: To be taken away.

DR LEVINE: Taken where?

IRIS: Back to where you came from.

DR LEVINE: I see.

IRIS: And the sooner the better if you ask me.

DR LEVINE: I'm afraid we're rather full up there.

IRIS: *(Looking up.)* Full? Up there?

DR LEVINE: Yes. Well. Bodmin.

IRIS: Bodmin?

DR LEVINE: Bodmin's a town.

IRIS: I dun't need you to tell me that, space man!

DR LEVINE: I'm not from outer space.

IRIS: What?

DR LEVINE: I'm a psychiatrist.

IRIS: You ain't alien?

DR LEVINE: I'm afraid not.

IRIS: Human?

DR LEVINE: My name is Dr Levine.

IRIS: Shaggin 'ell! I thought I was off!

DR LEVINE: You know, perhaps we could squeeze you in.

IRIS: Up Bodmin? No way. You lot are weird up there.

DR LEVINE: Hm.

IRIS: I'm in grave danger, ya knaw!

She picks up her C.B. handset, aims the transmitter and starts again.

IRIS: This is Iris Roscrow callin any alien life forms or inter-dimensional beins, over?

DR LEVINE: *(To himself.)* Must be something in the water…

IRIS: Ere. 'old this.

She gives him the transmitter.

IRIS: 'igh as you can, man.

DR LEVINE gingerly holds it aloft.

IRIS: Show some sense of urgency! I gotta get off this rock quick-sharp!

(Into C.B.) 'ello? Can you hear me?

(To DR LEVINE.) Up! Up!

DR LEVINE: What's the hurry?

IRIS: The Owlman of Mawnan flies again!

DR LEVINE: I see.

IRIS: Are you au fait with this phenomenon, doctor?

DR LEVINE: A little.

IRIS: Then you'll knaw if the creature is seen tis a sign of impendin apocalypse! And if the shagger looks you in the eye, yer dead as a door knob. It's taken poor ole Grace Pucky already!

DR LEVINE: So I heard.

IRIS: Number o' folk in the village seen 'im. I dun't wanna be next! Thass why I'm makin fast wimme getaway.

DR LEVINE: To another planet?

IRIS: I've bin in close contact with several alien civilisations for a while now. They owe me a favour or two. 'sides, there's nuthin for me ere. And I dun't wanna die. Higher! Tippy-toes!

He stands on tiptoe.

IRIS: Climb that fence there!

DR LEVINE: Look, I only came up here to –

IRIS: Hyup! Hyup! Hyup!

He tentatively climbs up on an old fence barrier, and attempts to balance. He holds the transmitter high.

DR LEVINE: And what sort of doom might The Owlman bring upon Nancekuke?

IRIS: Dun't tell me you ab'm noticed it.

DR LEVINE: ?

IRIS: That mean square-mile of sinister perimeter fence what protects a barren yet decidedly eerie couple of acres o' cordoned-off clifftop land to your left?

Wobbling, DR LEVINE turns.

DR LEVINE: I did wonder.

IRIS: The Keep Out signs. The security gates, razor-wired, alarmed and electrified. The ominous concrete structures that serve no purpose at all – or do they?

DR LEVINE: What is it?

IRIS: Chemical Defence Establishment Nancekuke. Secret Ministry Of Defence nerve gas factory.

DR LEVINE: Nerve gas?

IRIS: Oh, I got my theories 'bout that place…

DR LEVINE: Like what?

IRIS: They told us 'twas shut down in '76. But if 'tis empty, why keep the place sealed up like Area 51?

DR LEVINE: *(Remembering.)* Chemicals… Poison…

IRIS: They made Agent Orange on this pretty little cliff. Sarin. VX. Tri-Oxine 432. Experimental warfare gasses. Can you believe that? One drop of VX can kill a man, ya knaw.

DR LEVINE: And you think it's still down there?

IRIS: I think they're tryin to kill us off with a slow leak of deadly chemicals.

DR LEVINE: Why would they want to kill you off, Iris?

IRIS: Cus I knaw too much, doctor. I've dug too deep. And the bastards damn well know it.

DR LEVINE: And The Owlman is a warning that –

IRIS: They're wipin Nancekuke out!

DR LEVINE: That's a little far-fetched, don't you think?

IRIS: Birds are dyin. Fallin from the sky. For no apparent reason.

She picks up a rotted dead gull by the wing-tip and throws it off the cliff.

IRIS: Same as they did back in '76.

DR LEVINE: Why did the birds die in '76?

IRIS: Cus The Owlman was sighted. The land was blighted. Come on, doc. Keep up.

DR LEVINE: The factory shut down.

IRIS: Thass it.

DR LEVINE: And Virgil Ploy was born.

IRIS: *(Stops.)* Virgil Ploy? How'd you knaw Virgil Ploy?

DR LEVINE: He was my patient in Bodmin. I've just brought him home.

IRIS: E's ere?! Shit! That explains *everythin*!

DR LEVINE: It does?

IRIS: The 'igh levels of weirdness I can detect in the atmosphere! Virgil shaggin Ploy. Back in Nancekuke. With 'is mother!

Beat.

We gotta save 'im.

DR LEVINE: Why do you say that?

IRIS: E and 'is mother dun't mix.

DR LEVINE: It's all right. He's cured now.

IRIS: Yeh but she ain't! We gotta break 'im free, Doc! 'fore it's too late.

DR LEVINE: The last thing Virgil needs is excitement right now.

IRIS: You dun't understand. She's married again.

DR LEVINE: Mrs Ploy?

IRIS: And she's got dreadlocks now. Whass that all about?

DR LEVINE: Iris, this may sound strange but… Is there a mine shaft around here?

IRIS: There's many. This whole area is riddled like Swiss Cheese.

DR LEVINE: But is there one shaft in particular by the name of Sally's Bottom?

IRIS: There is.

DR LEVINE: Where?

IRIS: You are balanced precariously on its edge.

DR LEVINE realises that the fence he's been standing on is a makeshift barrier between the shaft and the cliff path. He almost loses his balance. He climbs down and peers into the shaft.

DR LEVINE: My god. It does exist. Is it deep?

IRIS: Ellish deep. Tunnels. Adits. Chambers. Shafts.

DR LEVINE: Have you ever been down there?

IRIS: Me and Virge almost did. Once. Years back now.
We was investigatin what happened to Virgil's father.

DR LEVINE: What stopped you?

IRIS: There's an old local sayin: 'You can g'down Sally's Bottom but you kent go up it.'

DR LEVINE: Iris, I think you're right. I think we have to get Virgil.

IRIS: I'll put alien contact on hold. You gotta look of deep consternation about you, Dr Levine.

DR LEVINE: I think I've made a terrible mistake.

Darkness.

GERTRUDE: *(Voice.)* The summer of '76 was knawn as the Summer of Weirdness. There was strange shit kickin off all over the place. All manner o' folk, even the straightminded among us, started to see things. Flying saucers over Portreath. Sea creatures in Falmouth Bay. And Owlmen in Mawnan Woods… The local press ad a field day when two sisters down on holiday wi' their family saw the monster in a tree by Mawnan church yard. The papers printed the drawings they'd made. Drawings of what they thought they'd seen. Blood-red eyes. Black claws. Wings spread wide. Soon, folks was seein 'im all over. The 'arbinger o' doom. A terrible portent of dark days to come…

1976. Cliff / mine shaft. Dead of night.

JERRY stands at the shaft mouth and loads chemical containers into a sling connected to a pulley. The sling is lowered down the shaft to the first-level workings where it is unloaded and stacked by ALFRED. JERRY wears full protective gear. ALFRED doesn't (just his overcoat). The work takes as long as it takes. Eventually, JERRY removes his mask and hollers down the shaft.

JERRY: That's the last of it, Alfred! Are you cool to handle it from here?

ALFRED removes his mask and shouts up.

ALFRED: Where ya goin?

JERRY: I gotta 747 and some Californian waves to catch.

JERRY steps out of his suit.

ALFRED: When do they come and cap it?

JERRY: Huh?

ALFRED: When do they come to cap the shaft?

JERRY: They're not!

ALFRED: What?

JERRY: They're not going to cap the shaft!

ALFRED: They kent just leave it open!

JERRY: Hey! It was your bright idea buddy!

ALFRED: But what if the containers are exposed!

JERRY: *(Laughing.)* Alfred? The containers aren't gonna *explode*!

ALFRED: No! Exposed! *Exposed*!

JERRY: Chill out, dude.

ALFRED: Jerry, I'm comin up!

ALFRED starts to climb up.

JERRY: *(To himself, spotting something.)* What the…

JERRY finds a cluster of forgotten canisters.

JERRY: Ahh, shit!

(Calling down.) Alfred, I forgot the Tri-Oxine!

The Tri-Oxine is dumped into the sling and starts its descent as ALFRED is halfway up.

JERRY: Careful with this, Alfred! It's nasty stuff!

ALFRED: *(Sees it coming.)* Jerry! Wait! I'm comin up!

JERRY sings Creedance to himself as he lowers the load. ALFRED sees it coming and rapidly descends and fumbles for his gas mask. At grass, JERRY feels the line go slack.

JERRY: Good work, Alfred! Nice knowing ya! Regards to the missis! Oh! And uhh… hide the evidence for me will ya?

He throws his suit and mask down the shaft. It lands in a heap.

ALFRED: *(Inaudible with gas mask.)* Jerry! Wait!

JERRY: Later, dude!

JERRY exits into the darkness, singing. ALFRED has a canister of Tri-Oxine in his hand. He removes his mask.

ALFRED: Jerry? Jerry! *JERRY?!*

In his hands, the Tri-Oxine canister suddenly springs a leak. Green mist spills from it. ALFRED chokes as he is enveloped.

The Present. House.

The certificate of sanity hangs somewhere visible. GERTRUDE is in her chair, on the phone.

GERTRUDE: Phylis. Tis Gertrude Ploy. You ad a think about my offer? There's 'alf price on the installation this week. And Dusty says e'll throw in a free squeegee.

Beat.

Dun't need double glazin? 'course ya need double glazin! Everybody need double glazin! Whassa matter with ya? Phylis, 'ave you taken a look round yer neighbourhood recently? If you dared to lift the lids on those saggy old eyes o' yours you would see that sinister forces are afut! There's summin in the air, Phyl. I can smell it. A poison. And folk round the village are droppin like flies… Claptrap is it? Well, I 'ope yer right Phylis. For your sake, I really do.

She hangs up.

GERTRUDE: *(Calls out.)* Dusty?

DUSTY and VIRGIL appear at the top of the stairs. VIRGIL has a large double glazed frame in his hands.

DUSTY: Just showin Virgil the ropes, sweetpea.

They descend.

DUSTY: OK. Let's go through it again. Varieties of window?

VIRGIL: There's single 'ang. Double 'ang. Sliders. Bay. Bow. Uhh… Casement?

DUSTY: Good.

VIRGIL: Hopper windas. Picture windas. Casement –

DUSTY: Said Casement.

VIRGIL: Shit. And…

DUSTY: Come on, Virgil. We bin through this!

VIRGIL: I kent remember.

DUSTY: Special shapes! Special shapes!

VIRGIL: Special shaped windas. Sorry.

DUSTY: Right. Models of door –

GERTRUDE: Dusty, I 'ate to interrupt this scintillatin' conversation but we 'ave a somewhat recalcitrant client in the form of Phylis Perranzabuloe.

DUSTY: Oh?

GERTRUDE: She ain't aware of the severity of these terrible times we'm livin in. She needs a little persuasion before she'll buy.

DUSTY: Not now.

GERTRUDE: Yes, now.

DUSTY: I'm passin on me skills.

GERTRUDE: Go see 'er, Dusty.

DUSTY: I bin workin all day, darlin!

GERTRUDE: So 'ave I.

DUSTY: Do I hafta go tonight?

GERTRUDE: Dun't make me discuss this ere!

Pause.

DUSTY: Virgil, take that and the other single-hangs out to me van, would ya?

VIRGIL tries the door.

VIRGIL: Locked.

DUSTY holds his hand out to GERTRUDE.

GERTRUDE: What makes you think e ain't gonna escape soon as that door's unlocked?

DUSTY: E wun't. Will ya, Virge?

VIRGIL: No.

DUSTY: And why wun't e run off? Cus e's eager to learn a trade off 'is old man. Aren't ya, Virge?

VIRGIL nods in agreement. GERTRUDE hands DUSTY the front door key (on a 'One Love' key ring). DUSTY unlocks –

DUSTY: *(To VIRGIL.)* Five lever lock. You lift it up once, twice, to lock it, yeh?

He opens the door. VIRGIL exits outside with window. They wait for him to disappear.

GERTRUDE: Are you completely stoopid?

DUSTY: What?

GERTRUDE: Dun't discuss this shit in front of Virgil. You'll blow everythin!

DUSTY: You started it.

GERTRUDE: I was bein discreet. Hence the use of the word 'recalcitrant'.

DUSTY: And you made a mockery o' my trade.

GERTRUDE: How?

DUSTY: By suggestin it was somewhat… dull.

GERTRUDE: Double glazin is dull, Dusty! There's no bones about it.

DUSTY: Tis a science!

GERTRUDE: Aw christ.

DUSTY: You undermined my authority then.

GERTRUDE: What authority?

DUSTY: My authority over Virgil.

GERTRUDE: Oh, did I?

DUSTY: I'm tryin to get the boy to respect me!

GERTRUDE: Then kick the shit out ob'm like you used to do!

DUSTY: I kent beat up my own son.

GERTRUDE: Stepson.

DUSTY: As much as I'd love to go back to the good ole days, it wouldn't be right. Just dun't make me look stupid again.

GERTRUDE: You dun't need me to do that, dear.

Enter VIRGIL. They fall silent. He goes upstairs and gets the next window. Once he's gone –

DUSTY: What the 'ell's that spus to mean?

GERTRUDE: I ain't got time for this. I gotta dozen other calls to make before tea. Just go and sort out Phylis Perranzabuloe.

DUSTY: I'd rather get stoned and chillax.

GERTRUDE: Do it, Dusty.

DUSTY: Tis my bastard business. I can do what I like.

GERTRUDE: Your –

VIRGIL comes down the stairs with a window. They fall silent. VIRGIL stops.

DUSTY: Nuthin to worry yerself about Virge. Me and yer mother just havin a loud chat is all. Grown-up stuff. Make sure they're ratcheted nice and tight, yeh? Goo' boy.

He exits outside.

GERTRUDE: Your business? Your fuckin business is it?

DUSTY: Oo's name is on the side o' that Citroën? Dusty St. Day's. Thass oo's.

GERTRUDE: You're just a front.

DUSTY: Oh am I?

GERTRUDE: You never made a penny til I come on board.

DUSTY: True.

GERTRUDE: I straightened you out. Gave you a purpose.

DUSTY: Ha!

GERTRUDE: I'm the brains o' this operation and dun't you forget it.

Enter VIRGIL. They fall silent. VIRGIL looks at them again.

DUSTY: *(To VIRGIL.)* What you gawpin at? Get that fuckin van loaded or I'll smash yer fuckin teef out!

Beat.

I didn't mean to shout. Sorry Virge. I'm under a lotta stress at the moment.

DUSTY hugs him.

DUSTY: You o'right? Goo' boy. Go on.

VIRGIL goes upstairs.

DUSTY: Look what you done! You've upset the child now!

GERTRUDE: Oh, shut up and get on with it.

DUSTY: Get on wi' what?

GERTRUDE: Wi' payin a visit to Phylis Perranzabuloe. Christ, tis like gettin shit offa blanket.

VIRGIL comes down stairs with a window. They fall silent. He exits.

DUSTY: O'right, I'll go.

GERTRUDE: Halle-fuckin-lujah.

DUSTY: But only if we kiss and make-up.

GERTRUDE: Make-up?

DUSTY: That was our first fight right there. I feel shaky. I need to feel desired before I can face the world again. Whadda ya say, honey-bunch?

He turns Bob on. Starts to dance before her. She looks on sternly.

DUSTY: You kent keep yer eyes off it, can ya?

GERTRUDE: 'course I can.

DUSTY: You kent resist it.

GERTRUDE: I dun't need it.

DUSTY: You do. You love it. Dun't ya?

(Wiggles closer.) Dun't ya? *(And closer.)* Dun't ya?

GERTRUDE grabs DUSTY in a firm grip. VIRGIL enters. He doesn't know where to look.

DUSTY: All done?

DUSTY locks the door, has the key in his hands.

DUSTY: Tomorra you can come watch me install 'em around the village. 'ow's that sound?

VIRGIL nods.

DUSTY: Any questions?

VIRGIL: Yeh. One.

(To GERTRUDE.) What happened to father?

DUSTY: What?

VIRGIL: I'm talkin to me mother. Mother? What happened to father?

DUSTY: I'm yer father, ya plank.

VIRGIL: Not you, Dusty. The other one. Me real one. Alfred Ploy.

GERTRUDE: We do not speak that name in this house!

VIRGIL: Alfred Ploy?

GERTRUDE: Ahh!

DUSTY: Whass goin on?

VIRGIL: Whass wrong with sayin 'is name?

GERTRUDE: You fuckin –

VIRGIL: Why kent I say Alfred Ploy?

GERTRUDE: Dusty, do summin for fuck's sake!

DUSTY: Like what?

GERTRUDE: 'it 'im! 'it 'im 'ard!

Whipped-up, DUSTY punches VIRGIL down behind the armchair and kicks him repeatedly. GERTRUDE comes round the chair to look at VIRGIL.

DUSTY: Virgil?

GERTRUDE: Dun't touch 'im.

DUSTY: E's out cold.

GERTRUDE: Thank god you was ere!

DUSTY: What was e sayin?

GERTRUDE: E started to go all funny in the head again. Just like e did ten year ago. 'hank you Dusty.

GERTRUDE cuddles his arm girlishly.

DUSTY: Pleasure, treasure.

GERTRUDE: 'hank you for protectin me.

DUSTY: Dusty's always ere.

GERTRUDE: Dun't I knaw it.

DUSTY: Forgot 'ow much I usta enjoy kickin 'im in.

GERTRUDE: I bet.

DUSTY: So?

GERTRUDE: Get that peach-of-an-ass up them stairs. And bring Bob, too.

DUSTY: I'll bring Bob if you'll bring Nancy.

GERTRUDE: Where I go, she goes.

They giggle. DUSTY turns Bob on, carries him with him as he dances up the stairs for GERTRUDE's pleasure. They exit. VIRGIL, battered and bloodied, crawls out from behind the armchair. He gets himself to his feet. He sees GERTRUDE's mobile. He tentatively keys in a number.

VIRGIL: *(Hushed.)* 'lo doctor… S'Virgil ere… If y'git this message, could ya come get me please? Things ain't workin out too well at 'ome and I would *reeeeally* love to come back to Bodmin. 'hanks.

'Stir It Up' drifts from upstairs. Bed springs squeak. VIRGIL stares at the ceiling with absolute horror. He hears DUSTY howl with pleasure as he gets spanked. VIRGIL covers his ears as it intensifies. The certificate of sanity falls from the wall and shatters. VIRGIL picks it up, its frame broken now. He drops it in the bin. Suddenly, DR LEVINE is at the window.

VIRGIL: Wow, that was fast.

IRIS appears beside him. They gesture to be let in. The door is locked. But the key has been left on the table by DUSTY. Quietly, VIRGIL unlocks it. Enter DR LEVINE and IRIS.

DR LEVINE: My god, Virgil –

VIRGIL: Shh! I'm fine.

DR LEVINE: Where's your mother?

VIRGIL: Upstairs wi' Dusty.

DR LEVINE: Who's Dusty?

VIRGIL: 'er new 'usband.

DR LEVINE: Ah.

VIRGIL: Thass them now.

They listen.

DR LEVINE: I see…

IRIS: Virgil.

VIRGIL: Iris.

IRIS: 'ow ya bin?

VIRGIL: Mad. You?

IRIS: Oh, you knaw…

VIRGIL: Yeh. I do. Why you ere?

IRIS: We came for you, Virgil.

DR LEVINE: We need you to come with us.

IRIS: Will you come with us, Virgil?

DR LEVINE: Say you'll come with us?

VIRGIL: Yeh. Sure. I'll come.

Beat.

Why? Where we goin?

Darkness.

GERTRUDE: *(Voice.)* When me and Alfred was courtin, we would take 'is father's old sail-boat up the Helford. The last time we ever went, I was fat with child. We took the boat round to Prisk Cove that day. 'Twas often a toss-up 'tween Prisk and Durgan. But Prisk was prettiest by far, I told Alfred, and that was that.

Present. Home.

GERTRUDE sits in darkness and smokes.

GERTRUDE: *(Voice.)* We pitched our leaky ole tent at the top o' the beach where the woods began. Prisk was all pebbles, see? No purchase for pegs. We spent the day walkin the length of the beach. 'Twas all stillness and strandlines, and the summer sun was scorchin. Come the afternoon, we wordlessly wandered through the woods, past the church, up the lane, on to the pub. There, we et, idly conversed with friendly faces and sank a drink or two. By the time the band started up round nine-ish, I'd ad enough of the place. I told Alfred I was goin back to the tent. 'Twas still light, even at that time. But fadin so fast you could almost feel the world turn right under yer feet. As I walked down them lanes, through the August dusk, I remember bein in love with the fact that there was just me. And me alone. Just me, the last light o' the sun, and the first few stars o' night. But as I rounded the bend, and sank into the long shadows o' the church and the woods up ahead, things began to change…

GERTRUDE: *(Listens.)* Virgil?!

Nothing. She stands.

Virgil?!

The Present. Clifftop. Night.

VIRGIL, IRIS and DR LEVINE stand around the shaft mouth. One by one, they descend the shaft on old iron rungs.

GERTRUDE: *(Voice.)* A breeze in the branches… only there was no breeze. *Strange.* Then, every livin thing in the church yard held its breath. Me included. The woods watched me. 'Twas then that me blood ran cold as ice. For I was wrong, ya see? I was not alone…

In a repeat of the Prologue, we hear the sound of running through thick forest. Panicked breathing. And terror.

Underground. First level workings. Torchlight.

VIRGIL: So what is it we're lookin for?

DR LEVINE: When we arrived in Nancekuke and I saw that you weren't exaggerating about the place, I started to fear the worst. I thought: What if Virgil had been right all along? You did, after all, have a mother just like you had described. There was a chemical weapons factory right where you said it would be. There is a disused mine shaft called Sally's Bottom. I started to think I'd made a terrible mistake. But then I thought: pull yourself together, Everett. There has to be a simple explanation to all of this. And that's what we're looking for.

VIRGIL: A simple explanation?

DR LEVINE: Yes. I believe the obsession you had with Sally's Bottom in Bodmin can be dispelled very easily. Let's put our minds to rest and see for ourselves that there's nothing strange or untoward going on down here. Then we'll achieve some closure!

IRIS: Was you obsessed with Sally's Bottom in Bodmin, Virge?

VIRGIL: I ad dreams.

IRIS: *I* ad dreams, too! They spoke to me in an alien tongue that I could strangely understand. They told me Sally's Bottom was one o' twelve landin sights back in '76 –

DR LEVINE: Iris, I'm trying to prove to Virgil that this mine shaft has no significance whatsoever.

IRIS: Prove to 'im or prove to yourself?

DR LEVINE: What are you implying?

IRIS: Nuthin.

DR LEVINE: You were implying something that's for sure.

IRIS: Dun't get paranoid, doc.

DR LEVINE: I'm not getting paranoid.

IRIS: E bin workin in the asylum too long, adn't e Virge?

VIRGIL's torchlight has found something covered by old, rotted tarpaulins…

IRIS: All I was sayin was you was freakin' out up on that cliff earlier. With the 'significance' of it all.

DR LEVINE: I wasn't freaking out. It was coincidence. I didn't realise Sally's Bottom existed. I thought it was part of Virgil's self-created personal mythology.

VIRGIL looks beneath…

IRIS: Oh, she real o'right. And she gotta long and sordid history. Not least by the fact that this may have bin the place where Virgil's father went missin.

DR LEVINE: All right. That's enough.

IRIS: We was close to figurin it out ten years ago, wadn't we Virge?

DR LEVINE: Virgil. I'm sorry. This was not a good idea. At all. Let's go back up.

VIRGIL throws it back to reveal ancient canisters of VX.

VIRGIL: Wait!

DR LEVINE: Virgil? What's this?

(Tries to read.) 0-ethyl S-2 di…

VIRGIL: Isopropylaminomethyl methylphophonothiolate. Or VX for short.

IRIS: Shit-house.

DR LEVINE: Shit-house? Why shit-house? What's 0-ethyl S-2 –

VIRGIL: Chemical weapons, doctor.

IRIS: And they bin ere a very long time.

DR LEVINE: My God.

VIRGIL: And there's more.

He throws back another tarp.

IRIS: And ere!

Another tarp.

DR LEVINE: And here.

DR LEVINE picks up a canister. IRIS snatches it and reads its markings in the torchlight.

IRIS: Tri-Oxine 432…

DR LEVINE: Virgil? I fear I may have misled you. This wasn't a madness you were suffering from. This was real. It's true! It's all bloody true!

VIRGIL: It's o'right, Dr Levine.

DR LEVINE: It's not all right! A secret horde of deadly chemical weapons has been dumped down a Cornish mine shaft! This is a conspiracy is what this is!

IRIS: Now yer talkin sense, doc.

VIRGIL: Iris.

IRIS: *(Innocently.)* What?

DR LEVINE: You said yourself back in Bodmin you believed Sally's Bottom had something to do with your father's disappearance.

VIRGIL: Yeh but I aren't positive. I dunno what all this… *(shines a light on the chemicals.)* means!

DR LEVINE: Your father worked at the factory. You know that. When they got word they were to close, he was no doubt press-ganged into assisting them with a complete evacuation. Probably against his will.

IRIS: Then what happened?

DR LEVINE: When the job was done, they would've covered their tracks in the best way they'd know how.

IRIS: They killed him?

DR LEVINE: They would've had to! If anyone spoke out about this –

VIRGIL: Doctor –

DR LEVINE: Disposed of the bodies down here.

IRIS: E's right, Virge. Tis the ideal place to dump chemicals and corpses.

DR LEVINE: They incinerated the files, and now they're trying to slowly poison the village of Nancekuke.

IRIS: Didn't I say that, doc?

DR LEVINE: You did. She did!

VIRGIL: Why would they try and wipe Nancekuke out?

DR LEVINE: Because… oh God, Virgil. To silence you.

VIRGIL: Me?

IRIS: And me, probably. I knaw some shit.

DR LEVINE: You were close to discovering all of this, Virgil.

IRIS: We both were.

DR LEVINE: You were about to expose them. What better way to keep you quiet than to incarcerate you for ten years in an asylum and have one of the best psychiatrists in the county convince you that all of this… is in your head?

VIRGIL: Dr Levine, this is all in yer head.

DR LEVINE: It's not! It's real!

VIRGIL: You've fabricated an elaborate belief system to enable your paranoid mind to cope with – *(Stops himself.)* Christ, you told me all this!

DR LEVINE: But it's right here, Virgil! It's plain to see!

IRIS: Wait. E's right. It *is* plain to see. This is all too obvious. They *wanted* us to find these canisters. This is a smokescreen to 'ide the truth. The real truth. The true truth. Virgil. Yer father was abducted by aliens.

VIRGIL: Oh, Iris.

IRIS: I'm just puttin it out there.

VIRGIL: What would aliens want wi' my dad?

IRIS: Same reason they want any one of us! To probe, to study, and to feed on our alpha waves!

DR LEVINE: They feed on our alpha waves? My God!

VIRGIL: Listen to yourselves! I'm spus'd to be the mad one!

DR LEVINE: But you're not mad, Virgil! You're completely sane!

VIRGIL: I knaw! Cus you just spent ten years unpickin all this stuff! Now yer tellin me I was right all along?

DR LEVINE: Yes!

VIRGIL: This dun't 'elp wi' my fragile mental state, doctor! Next you'll be tellin me the bleddy Owlman's real!

Enter THE OWLMAN from the shadows. They turn their torches off and hide in the darkness, terrified. From wherever he comes from, he should only be seen in silhouette. He hisses and whizzes.

IRIS: Oh my God…

DR LEVINE: What is it?

IRIS: Shut yer eyes, shut yer eyes
Keep 'em closed against the night
If the Owlman sees ya
Then yer sure to die of fright –

DR LEVINE: It's not… is it… ? It can't be…

VIRGIL: Yes, doctor. Tis the Owlman of Mawnan Woods.

IRIS: Dun't let the shagger look e in the eye, boys...

The creature removes something from its back – a drum of liquid, with hose and sprayer. He stretches, rubs his aching spine. Then removes gloves. THE OWLMAN starts to sing Bob Marley's 'Three Little Birds' to himself. He cracks open a Red Stripe and drinks. VIRGIL steps forward, trying to see what's going on. Suddenly –

IRIS: Club the fucker!

IRIS launches forward and smacks THE OWLMAN on the head with her torch.

THE OWLMAN: Ow!

VIRGIL: Iris, wait!

IRIS: Dun't look at 'im Virge!

THE OWLMAN: 'fuck's goin on?

IRIS: I got 'is head! I got 'is head!

THE OWLMAN switches a light on (garage work lights on cables). IRIS staggers away from him, an old gas mask has come away in her hands. THE OWLMAN is unmasked.

VIRGIL: Dusty?

THE OWLMAN: Shitshitshit.

DUSTY is dressed in a home-made costume (wings, claws, etc). In the dark it looked authentic. In the light, it's comical.

IRIS: Dusty?

DUSTY: What you doin ere?

IRIS: You're The Owlman of Mawnan?

DUSTY: Shit. This is bad. This is... *(He stumbles, dizzy.)* You whacked me some 'ard, Roscrow!

IRIS: I'd've dun't it harder if I'd knawn oo 'twas!

VIRGIL: I didn't knaw you two knew each other...

IRIS: We dun't.

DUSTY: We do. We ad a ding-dong. Did we not?

IRIS: Briefly. *(To VIRGIL.)* You was up Bodmin. I was des'prate.

DUSTY: Wadn't nuthin serious, Virge. Didn't last.

VIRGIL: How come?

DUSTY: She was weird. Way too weird.

IRIS: And Dusty met someone else. Didn't you, Dusty?

VIRGIL: Does yer wife know you come down Sally's Bottom and dress up as The Owlman, Dust?

DUSTY: Say you didn't see me, Virge.

VIRGIL: Does she, Dusty?

DUSTY: She'll kill me if she finds out. I was spus to go spook Phylis Perranzabuloe and –

(He stops himself.)

I've said too much.

IRIS: So you're the one oo's bin terrorizin Nancekuke.

DR LEVINE: Frightening people with this 'portent of doom'.

IRIS: Then spraying the clifftops with VX.

DR LEVINE: To make it look like the old nerve gas factory is leaking, that the air is poisoned, that the air is deadly.

DUSTY: What? Ha! Thass completely ridiculous! Why would I do that?

VIRGIL: I knaw why. To sell double glazin.

DUSTY wells up, wails and falls to his knees.

DUSTY: She made me do it, Virge! 'Twas yer muvver's idea. I ad no choice in the matter. She's strong, Virgil. Strong. She gotta power over me I kent resist. Like voodoo, ya knaw? Goddamn 'er! I'd do anythin for that woman. And she bleddy well knaws it! But we gotta keep quiet about this. Make it our little secret, eh?

IRIS: So… there is no proper Owlman?

DR LEVINE: Of course there isn't. The sinister force behind all of this is not the Ministry of Defence, or aliens, or mythological creatures. It's your mother, Virgil. Scare-mongering the village for financial gain. She is the heart of this conspiracy.

DUSTY: Oo the ell's this? Wycliffe?

DR LEVINE: Everett Levine. I'm Virgil's psychiatrist.

DUSTY: Dusty St. Day. I'm Virgil's dad.

VIRGIL: Stepdad.

DR LEVINE: He's the one who's married your mother?

VIRGIL: Yes, doctor.

DR LEVINE: I've heard your name mentioned before, Dusty.

DUSTY: Did I do your windows?

DR LEVINE: No. But if I remember rightly, you used to beat Virgil up at school…

DUSTY: No I never.

IRIS: Yes ya did.

DUSTY: Shut up, Iris.

DR LEVINE: I've just spent the last ten years unpicking the misery you put this boy through. A name like yours tends to stick.

VIRGIL: Doctor? It's fine. I'm over it now.

DR LEVINE: You're a bully, Dusty. You know that? A big fucking great bully! And I think you deserve a taste of your own medicine!

DR LEVINE attacks DUSTY.

IRIS: Kick 'is head in, doc!

VIRGIL breaks them up.

DUSTY: Bleddy lost it, you 'ave!

DR LEVINE: Come here and say that!

VIRGIL: Get a grip, doc.

DR LEVINE: *(Snaps out of it.)* Yes… Sorry, Virgil… I'm not setting a very good example.

DUSTY: No, pard. You ain't.

DR LEVINE: *(Squaring up again.)* Son of a –

IRIS halts DR LEVINE.

IRIS: 'ang on a minute. What about poor old Grace Pucky?

DUSTY: The Owlman scared 'er to death.

IRIS: *(To DUSTY.)* Right. Meaning you scared 'er to death!

DR LEVINE: You killed an innocent old woman?

DUSTY: Look, I'm just a pawn in all this! I just do what I'm told. She pulls the strings, Virge! You understand that, dun't ya, boy? She pulls the strings!

VIRGIL: When did this all start?

DUSTY: I'm sworn to secrecy.

DR LEVINE: Then we'll go to the authorities.

VIRGIL: And I'll tell mother.

DUSTY: O'right. I'll talk! Goddammit, I'll talk!

Beat.

Right after we was married she suddenly became all mysterious. Told me if I wanted to have me eyes opened I should come down ere. She never told me what I'd find. Let me discover that for meself. When I got back up, she suggested we put all this to good use. I agreed. And like that, the business took off. We ad it all sewn up. Our beautiful plan. But the truth is out. And now tis over.

DUSTY sobs. VIRGIL inspects the shaft mouth above him.

VIRGIL: It still dun't add up…

IRIS: I kent believe you did what she asked. This is lethal stuff.

DUSTY: I wear the proper gear. Loads of it strewed about the place.

VIRGIL finds a protective suit in the same place it was dumped 30 years ago – now decayed, covered in mould. He studies it and continues to look…

IRIS: The bastards oo dumped this stuff dumped everything.

DR LEVINE: Perhaps they just had to empty the factory in a hurry.

IRIS: Thass still no excuse!

DR LEVINE: It's no excuse. But it's also no great conspiracy.

IRIS: The more this day goes on, the more shaggin normal it gets.

VIRGIL: I wouldn't say that, Iris. Look at the name badge on these overcoat.

They all gather around VIRGIL and study the rotted overcoat.

IRIS: Oh, Virgil…

DR LEVINE: What does this mean?

VIRGIL: I dun't knaw, doctor. But I 'ave a small feelin my conspiracy-spreadin bully-marryin psychopathic Rastafarian mother might!

The Present. House. Night.

GERTRUDE is on the phone.

GERTRUDE: Dusty? Tis me again. Pick up yer phone willya, for God's sake! Virgil ain't in the house and it dun't take a genius to figure out why. Cus 'somebody' left me pissin keys lyin around! I warned you about 'im, didn't I? E may be mad but e ain't stoopid. Before you get back ere, scour Nancekuke. I dun't want that little shit stickin 'is nawse down holes e got no business to stick 'em. And whass takin so fuckin long at Phylis Perranzabuloe's? You scare 'er senseless then stop for a cuppa tea? Do not fail me, Dusty – you fuckin doughnut.

She hangs up.

GERTRUDE: *(To NANCY.)* Sorry for the foul language there, sweetheart. Mummy's pissed right off.

Enter DUSTY (still dressed as THE OWLMAN) and VIRGIL, followed by DR LEVINE and IRIS. DUSTY has his hands tied with rope. VIRGIL wears ALFRED PLOY's rotted old caretaker's coat he found in the mine.

GERTRUDE: Whass all this?

DR LEVINE: The game's up, Mrs Ploy!

IRIS: We've bin down there!

DR LEVINE: We've seen everything!

IRIS: We knaw exactly what you bin up to!

VIRGIL: O'right guys, 'hanks. If I could just –

GERTRUDE: Whass goin on, Dusty?

DUSTY: It weren't my fault. Honest. I just ran into 'em down there!

GERTRUDE: Down where?

DUSTY: Sally's Bottom.

VIRGIL produces an old canister of VX from the pocket of his coat and places it down. GERTRUDE barely gives anything away.

GERTRUDE: Thought I always told you never to play round there, boy.

DR LEVINE: And now we know why!

IRIS: How did you knaw those chemicals was dumped down that mine shaft?

GERTRUDE: What makes you think I did, girlie?

IRIS: Cus somebody ad to tell Dusty where to find this poison!

DUSTY: Iris!

GERTRUDE: Did ya spill yer guts, Dusty? Spill 'em that easy?

DUSTY: They ad to wrench it outta me, darlin.

IRIS: We didn't.

DR LEVINE: He was very forthcoming with his information.

GERTRUDE: *(To DUSTY.)* I shoulda knawn when push come to shove you'd squeal.

DUSTY: *(Squealing)* I didn't squeal!

DR LEVINE: A bully hates to be bullied.

GERTRUDE: Didn't I tell you to go back to Bodmin, doctor?

DR LEVINE: You did, Mrs Ploy. But I thought I'd take in some air before the long drive back. And I'm jolly glad I did.

IRIS: Because e met me!

DR LEVINE: Not only that, Iris.

IRIS: Because e saw the old chemical weapons factory and the entrance to the mine shaft.

DR LEVINE: Correct. All of which Virgil used to talk about. All of which I thought were just paranoid fantasies.

VIRGIL: Nope. They were real.

DR LEVINE: I know that now.

VIRGIL: I'm glad you've cleared a few things up for yerself, doctor.

DR LEVINE: You're going down, Mrs Ploy!

IRIS: Yeh! Not only did you drive Virgil mad all those year ago –

DR LEVINE: With your lies and manipulations!

IRIS: You spread fear and conspiracy through the village!

DR LEVINE: And people died, Mrs Ploy!

IRIS: Murderer!

VIRGIL: Iris, please!

IRIS: Sorry, Virge. It's just I was rather fond of Grace Pucky. She was a dear ole stick oo never did no one no 'arm.

DR LEVINE: These are serious crimes you've committed, Mrs Ploy. And they cannot go unpunished.

GERTRUDE: Grace Pucky? You kent pin 'er death on me. That was The Owlman. E's the one ya want. I just sell double glazin.

DUSTY: Eh?!

VIRGIL: Mother? I found 'is work clothes underground. They was old and rotted but I could still make out the name on 'em.

He peels back the lapel on his coat to reveal –

VIRGIL: Alfred Ploy.

GERTRUDE: Dun't you speak that name in ere! Take that thing off! Take it off!

VIRGIL: Those chemicals were dumped when the factory closed in 1976.

IRIS: Durin The Summer of Weirdness!

DR LEVINE: Right before Virgil was born!

VIRGIL: What happened, mother? Just tell me. I just wanna knaw the truth.

GERTRUDE: I… *(To IRIS.)* remember you. You're the Roscrow girl. You was sweet on my son ten year ago.

IRIS: I was.

VIRGIL: Mother?

GERTRUDE: And you was sweet on my husband one year ago.

DUSTY: We ad a ding-dong.

IRIS: Briefly.

GERTRUDE: You was broken-hearted. Dusty told me all about it.

IRIS: Oh, e did did e?

GERTRUDE: 'bout how you usta send 'im letters covered in stars and glitter and shit.

IRIS: *(To DUSTY.)* That was private correspondence, you knob-shank!

DR LEVINE: Sorry, Iris. But can Virgil keep on track with his thing for the moment?

IRIS: Huh? Oh. Yeh. Whatever.

VIRGIL: Thank you, doctor. Mother? You never told me nuthin as I was growin up. Not a dicky bird. The things I knaw about my dad, I dug up myself –

IRIS: Wi' my 'elp.

VIRGIL: With Iris's help, ten year ago. But I never got to the bottom of it. Dr Levine reckons if I was to hear what happened to the man I never knew, I might be able to lay some demons to rest.

DR LEVINE: Correct.

VIRGIL: It would 'elp me, Mother. Greatly 'elp me. If you just told me what became of 'im. I knaw you know, Mother. Please.

GERTRUDE: I… I…

Everyone hangs on her word.

GERTRUDE: Kent believe you would betray me like this, Dusty.

VIRGIL: Aw!

DUSTY: I didn't betray ya, baby one. 'Twas 'ard luck I got caught is all.

GERTRUDE: You got sloppy, Dusty. Again. This ain't no good.

DR LEVINE: Can we get back to Virgil, please?

DUSTY: Hang on a minute, Levine! This is important. *(To GERTRUDE.)* What do e mean "this ain't good"? Forgive me, eh?

GERTRUDE: No.

DUSTY: What? No? But if tis no then...where do we go from ere?

GERTRUDE: Thass it. Finito. There is no tomorra for us, Dusty.

DUSTY: Woah, babe! You serious?

She stares. DUSTY panics. He grabs the tape player and turns it on. Bob plays. DUSTY dances for her, desperate. GERTRUDE watches him, uninterested. GERTRUDE turns it off.

GERTRUDE: No, see... That cute li'l ass o' yours no longer holds my interest, Dusty.

DUSTY: It dun't work no more? *(Wiggling, weeping.)* Why dun't it work no more?

GERTRUDE: My fascination for it 'as waned.

DUSTY: No!

GERTRUDE: I've taken from it what I need.

DUSTY: But Gerty –

GERTRUDE: Now I dun't wanna see it no more.

DUSTY: Oh God! Why?

GERTRUDE: Cus you fucked up, Dusty. You fucked up cus yer stupid.

DUSTY: Oi.

GERTRUDE: Well, you are. I gave you this business on a plate and you squandered it all through downright stupidity.

DUSTY: Tis my business! These hands install the windas, woman! Not yours!

GERTRUDE: This again?

DUSTY: It's what we agreed!

GERTRUDE: We agreed to keep this thing a secret 'til the day we died!

DUSTY: So I made a mistake! I'm sorry!

GERTRUDE: You blew the whole fuckin thing, Dusty! Ruined everythin! Just like e did! *(Re: VIRGIL.)* And 'is father did before'n! I kent stand it! Yer all so weak of mind! Timid as rabbits! Blawn off course by the slightest fuckin breeze! 'orse piss for blood the lotta ya!

DUSTY: O'right. Thass enuff.

GERTRUDE: What?

DUSTY: Dun't you 'orse piss for blood me. Thass way outta line, lady. Thass one step too far!

GERTRUDE: 'orse piss for blood 'orse piss for blood 'orse piss for blood. Thass what pumps through your sorry heart. No iron. No fire. Whassa matter wi' ya? Pathetic!

DUSTY: You best stop now, Gertrude.

GERTRUDE: Dun't wanna look stupid in front of your son?

DUSTY: Stepson.

GERTRUDE: Stepson now, is it?

DUSTY: Yeh. It is. Virgil? *(Big revelation.)* I ain't your dad.

VIRGIL: I knaw.

DUSTY: I've never pretended to be.

VIRGIL: You did.

DUSTY: Well, I wun't any more! I put you through 'ell as a kid but I'm makin amends now. *(To GERTRUDE.)* Tell 'im what e needs to knaw.

GERTRUDE: Dun't you start!

DUSTY: You tell 'im or I will!

GERTRUDE: You dun't knaw what happened! You wadn't even born!

DUSTY: She's got me there, Virge.

VIRGIL: Tell me, mother.

GERTRUDE: I will not.

VIRGIL: I know you knaw what happened!

DR LEVINE: Tell him, Mrs Ploy!

IRIS: Go on! Tell 'im!

GERTRUDE: Why should I?

DUSTY: Cus e's yer son and you've kept'n in the dark all 'is life and e blatantly needs to know.

DR LEVINE: That's right, Dusty. Just tell him, Mrs Ploy!

IRIS: Please?

DR LEVINE: If not for him, then for us!

VIRGIL: Yer gonna tell me, mother, or so 'elp me, I'll pop this canister and gas us all!

He picks up canister and threatens to open it. Everyone recoils but GERTRUDE.

DR LEVINE: Virgil…?

DUSTY: That ain't a good idea.

VIRGIL: I'll do it! I will!

GERTRUDE: You wouldn't dare.

VIRGIL goes to open it.

DUSTY: Christ Almighty!

IRIS: Virgil, dun't!

DUSTY: Whass e got there? Tri-Oxine 432 or 0-ethyl S-2 di –

IRIS: VX! Tis VX!

DR LEVINE: Which one was the bad one?

IRIS: They're both not great, doc!

DUSTY: Put it down, Virge.

VIRGIL: No.

DUSTY: You'll flood the whole house.

IRIS: You'll kill us all!

VIRGIL: So be it! Whass the point in livin if you dunno oo you are?

DUSTY: Screw this!

DUSTY makes for the door. It's locked.

DUSTY: Shit.

DR LEVINE: Where's the key?

IRIS: She's got it.

GERTRUDE: No escape.

VIRGIL: And the whole house is airtight!

DUSTY: Bleddy double glazin!

GERTRUDE: Pull the pin. What do I care?

IRIS: We care!

DR LEVINE: Just tell him, Mrs Ploy!

DUSTY: Tell 'im!

VIRGIL: I'll do it, mother. I ain't jokin.

GERTRUDE: I knaw you aren't, boy. You got that same determined look in yer eye you ad ten year ago. But I ain't afraid to die and take some secrets wimme to my fuckin grave.

DR LEVINE: But it isn't just you that'll be dying!

GERTRUDE: There's no one in ere oo ain't too good for a gassin.

VIRGIL: What? Even Nancy?

GERTRUDE falters. She cradles NANCY.

VIRGIL: You know me, mother. I've never liked 'er.

GERTRUDE: I knaw you ab'm, you vicious shit.

VIRGIL: I'd gladly gas us all just to see that aberration laid to rest.

GERTRUDE: How could you say such things? She's yer sister!

VIRGIL: She ain't me sister. She's a cyst.

GERTRUDE: Oh! *(Covering NANCY's ears.)* Dun't listen to 'im Nancy!

VIRGIL: And quit callin that thing by name.

GERTRUDE: She is not a *thing*!

VIRGIL: Tis a foul disgustin lump.

GERTRUDE: She ain't no lump, fucker! Dusty! Fuckin do summin for fuck's sake! E's outta control! Like e was ten year ago! 'it 'im! Quick!

DUSTY shakes his head.

GERTRUDE: Dusty, you asshole!

VIRGIL: Tell me, mother.

GERTRUDE: Go to 'ell.

VIRGIL: Whatever you say, mother! We'll go to 'ell together!

VIRGIL goes to release the gas. Everyone cowers.

GERTRUDE: Wait.

He stops.

GERTRUDE: O'right, I'll tell ya goddammit. I shall speak what I 'ave never spoke of before. But knaw this, Virgil Ploy: yer gonna wish to God you'd never asked.

Pause.

Your father…was The Owlman of Mawnan Woods.

DR LEVINE: Oh Mrs Ploy –

GERTRUDE: All through that long hot summer, people saw things. The air was thick with strangeness. And it ad possessed yer father more than most… The last time I saw 'im alive, we went out in the boat. Up to Mawnan. 'Twas my decision. An attempt to talk. I was eight months pregnant, see? But e never spoke. We spent the day in silence. I left the pub early that night. And 'twas on my way back through Mawnan church yard, back to the beach where we'd pitched our tent, that I saw'n…

VIRGIL: You saw The Owlman?

GERTRUDE: Oh, I saw'n! Saw'n wimme own eyes! The beast from the stories! Great feathered devil! It flew outta the darkness of the wood, and it came for me! Wings spread wide. Eyes bright red. And 'issin it was. 'issin. I was so afraid. Afraid for my unborn child. Afraid that this demon would gaze into my eyes and I'd die before my baby was born…

(Whispers, remembering.)

Shut yer eyes, shut yer eyes
Keep 'em closed against the night
If the Owlman sees ya
Then yer sure to die of fright…

(To VIRGIL.) I tried to get outta the woods…but it ad me cornered… This thing came through the trees…this damn ghost story…as real as it could be…all I could see was its shape against the dark…all I could hear was the ungodly sounds it made… I fled through the trees but still it came. Closer. Closer. Like a

nightmare. In the end I could run no more. I fell to me knees, sobbin. Felt summin cold and 'ard under me hand. 'Twas a slab. A slab o' broken gravestone! And without even thinkin I –

GERTRUDE picks up the tape player and smashes it hard across DUSTY's head.

DUSTY: *(In shock.)* Some 'ot that August bank hol –

She brings it down on his head once, twice, three times. Bob plays 'Three Little Birds' and slowly winds down to a distorted stop. DUSTY is in a bloodied slump on the stairs. GERTRUDE continues as if nothing has happened.

GERTRUDE: I smashed 'is skull in. I ad killed the Owlman! But when I took a closer look, I saw 'twas a gas mask this thing wore. And beneath the gas mask, the face of yer father.

VIRGIL: You killed my father?

GERTRUDE: E was The Owlman, Virgil. E was insane. E was gonna kill me. And you. And Nancy. I was protectin ya.

VIRGIL: What did you do with him?

GERTRUDE: I went back to the tent and I got the small kindlin axe we took with us for campin and I chopped 'is body up into tiny pieces and loaded 'im bit by bit onto the boat. Once I got 'im back ere, I chucked each chunk ob'm down Sally's Bottom. But as the days went by, I couldn't believe what I'd done ad happened. So I climbed down to find 'im…and discovered what they'd dumped. Like you Virgil, I found his work clothes. And it dawned on me, down there in the darkness, what mighta transpired. Their secret. My secret. And Alfred's. All buried deep in the same black, endless pit. Strange thing was…when I searched for Alfred – for any ob'm – I could find not one piece… I emerged into the light. Gave birth. And ere we are. Now, I suggest we do the same wi' Dusty and sling'n down the shaft before people start askin questions. Give us a hand would ya?

Pause.

IRIS: *(Calmly, into her C.B.)* This is Iris Roscrow callin all extra-terrestrial beins – come in, over?

DR LEVINE: *(Musing to himself.)* How very interesting. Psychopathic behaviour triggered by severe shock…

IRIS: Sendin out a message to anyone in the area to come and pick me up at your nearest convenience, over?

DR LEVINE: Gertrude was compelled to psychologically re-orient herself –

IRIS: I'm beggin ya please, just somebody come and get me – quick as shaggin possible?

DR LEVINE: Becoming enmeshed in her own encrypted mythology, a mythology that was designed purely to obliterate the memory of her crime –

From IRIS's C.B. comes a strange and garbled 'message'.

IRIS: They've heard me. Contact is made!

VIRGIL: Iris? Dr Levine? I need a moment alone wimme mother.

DR LEVINE: Of course, Virgil. If you need me, I'll just be outside.

DR LEVINE exits and peers in through the window.

IRIS: I might not hang around, Virgil. They're comin to get me at last. It was nice seein you again.

IRIS exits and stands looking though the window for a while. VIRGIL closes the door. Locks it. He picks up the container.

GERTRUDE: Dusty could never keep a secret. But I reckon you could. Couldn't you, Virgil? You could keep a secret summin special. And I need someone to keep the business goin wimme. Someone with a good head. What e think, Virge? Dusty taught you the basics. You knaw the diff'rence between a bay and a bow. What e reckon? Ain't that what you've always wanted? A nice, normal, down-to-earth relationship with yer mother?

VIRGIL holds aloft the canister.

GERTRUDE: Virgil…?

VIRGIL: No more secrets, mother.

He pulls the pin. Lethal green gas emerges from the canister. DR LEVINE and IRIS watch through the glass as it fills the whole house.

GERTRUDE: *(A voice.)* 'Twas said it began as a bedtime story, to keep the children of the village sweet. 'You best be good as gold now, girl, or The Owlman of Mawnan will come for ya.'

THE OWLMAN appears in the darkness behind VIRGIL. It is ancient, indistinct, and all the more terrifying for it. Its wings slowly spread out, either side of VIRGIL. A strange, looming shape with red, red eyes.

GERTRUDE: *(A voice.)* 'Twas said that the mere sight of the fiend was a sign that terrible things were to befall the world. 'Twas said that when The Owlman came and cast 'is shadow over the land, you knew the end was near…

GERTRUDE: *(Whispers over and over.)*
Shut yer eyes, shut yer eyes
Keep 'em closed against the night
If The Owlman sees ya
Then yer sure to die of fright!

GERTRUDE falls to her knees before VIRGIL / OWLMAN.

GERTRUDE: *(A voice.)* But 'twas worse still if the monster looked you square in the eye. For Death would come to ya, swift and sure…

Blackout. THE OWLMAN's eyes burn in the darkness.

GERTRUDE: *(A voice.)* Thass what I believed anyway.

END.

49 DONKEYS HANGED

49 Donkeys Hanged was first performed at Theatre Royal Plymouth on Friday 23rd March 2018.

CAST

Randy Williams	Dom Coyote
Sally Tregersick	Buffy Davis
Stanley Bray	Ed Gaughan
Carl Grose	William Hartley
Joy Bray	Veronica Roberts
Solomon Singo	Joe Shire

CREATIVE TEAM

Director	Simon Stokes
Set & Costume Designer	Bob Bailey
Lighting Designer	Andy Purves
Sound Designer & Composition	Dom Coyote
Casting Director	Stephen Moore CDG
Assistant Director	Kay Michael
Costume Supervisor	Delia Lancaster
Fight Director	Alison De Burgh

PRODUCTION TEAM

Production Manager	Nick Soper
Stage Manager	Janet Gautrey
Deputy Stage Manager	Sarah Donaldson
Assistant Stage Manager	Sarah Marsland
Sound Programmer	Dan Mitcham
Drum Technician	Matt Hoyle
Assistant Electrician	John Barron
Set and costumes	Theatre Royal Plymouth
Props	Lizzie Props

CHARACTERS

STANLEY BRAY, a farmer

JOY BRAY, his wife

SALLY TREGERSICK, a local slaughter-woman

RANDY WILLIAMS, a local Country singer

CARL GROSE, a writer

SOLOMON SINGO, a South African farmer

DONKEYS, alive, hanged, ghostly and otherwise

Bosanko Farm. The outskirts of the village of Ventongimps, Cornwall. STANLEY BRAY, a farmer, stands before us.

BRAY: *(To us.)* So. You wanna knaw 'ow to 'ang a donkey?

Rumble of thunder.

BRAY: I seed the beast from 'cross the valley, stood there shiverin in Wheezer Jenkins' field. Bin there years e ad. Skin'n bone. 'alf dead and completely forgot. I nipped over, brung'n round and ere we are. Wheezer never cared fer'n. Wheezer wouldn' notice 'im gone. A cold-hearted basterd is Wheezer… I rigged the tree up earlier. Knotted the noose meself. Surprisingly easy 'twas. Me 'ands knew zackly what to do. God picked me, see? Gimme a sign and made us Donkey-hangin Expert. Best in Ventongimps, e said. I sank an iron spike inna the ground. Deep, like, so it could take the dead weight which is anythin but light. When I'd done wimme preparations, I led'n in all solemn from the barn to the rope…

A donkey hee-haws.

BRAY: I slung the noose round 'is neck and I took a good strong stance, swallered a dollop o' thick, dank air and with every ounce of strength I *'aaaaulled!*

BRAY hauls on the rope. The effort is immense. The donkey chokes.

BRAY: *(With each pull of the rope.)* G'won…! Geddup there…! C'mon ya basterd…! Gyahhh…!!!

Thunder crashes. Lightning flashes. Wind howls.

THE FIRST DONKEY IS HANGED.

BRAY: Thass one. Forty eight to go.

RANDY WILLIAMS sings a song as BRAY travels back to his farmhouse.

RANDY: *When yer sinkin in the mud*
And there's no iron in yer blood
And there's no one to hear yer sorrow and woes!

When nerves quit a-feelin'
And words lose all their meanin'
Well, buddy that's just how it goes!

When the Heavens open up

And there's no wine in yer cup
And yer feelin dead from yer head to your toes!

When the Lord God above
Says the world's run outta love
Might as well hang a donkey I s'poze!

Might as well hang a donkey
Might as well hang a donkey
Might as well hang a donkey I s'poze!

Farmhouse. Kitchen. Next morning.

There's a big ole armchair. Rayburn with a pan on top. Small table at the back. On it, a shrine for a lost child – a framed photo of a twelve-year-old boy on a tyre swing surrounded by trinkets, little toy cows, shoes, flowers.

There's a door which leads to the outside world and one to the rest of the house.

In the armchair sits JOY, BRAY's wife. She's seemingly an invalid. She stares out the window. BRAY prepares breakfast behind, boiling an egg. He turns, looks at her, looks to us…

BRAY: *(To us.)* Next day, I geddup, go 'bout me bizniz. I conjure a breakfast fer the wife. Joy. For the past thirty year since she bin sat in that chair starin out at the mist she's requested the exact same thing. Egg. Boiled. Two and a 'alf minutes precisely. Every mornin. Without fail. Egg. As sure as death. No variation. Joy. Chair. Egg. There.

He puts an egg in an egg cup before her. She moves it aside.

JOY: I dun't want egg today.

BRAY: Say that again, dear?

JOY: You heard.

BRAY: No egg? Thass a turn up for the books.

JOY: I dun't want it. Aren't eatin it.

BRAY: Egg? Boiled? Just the way ya like? Two and a 'alf minutes on the dot?

JOY: You let it boil fer three.

BRAY: No I never.

JOY: Yes you did.

BRAY: I never.

JOY: You did, Stanley. And I refuse to eat it.

BRAY: Dun't be daft, dear. Eat.

JOY: Take it away.

BRAY: For decades I bin immaculate –

JOY: Sloppy, Stanley.

BRAY: I bin good as gold.

JOY: Yer mind's not on the job.

Pause.

BRAY: 'ow 'bout I do you another?

JOY: G'won thun. Give it a go.

BRAY boils another. JOY stares out the window.

BRAY: Forgive me, wife. I gotta lot on me plate.

JOY: Lucky you. I got piss all.

BRAY: What I mean is, tis tough out there. Ya know?

JOY: This farm's overwhelmed you. My father said it would.

She stares at the window. BRAY watches her.

BRAY: Some storm last night.

JOY: ’ellish.

BRAY: You heard it?

JOY: How could I not? Almost took the roof off the place.

BRAY: Thass why I ad to geddout and check the barn. Assess the damage. I dunno if you heard. I hoped not to wake you.

JOY: I heard ya. Always do…

BRAY: I might hafto board up the windas later, ’case it storms again tonight. Joy? You listenin?

JOY: *(Staring, concerned.)* Where’s that donkey gone?

BRAY: Eh?

JOY: Li’l donkey ’cross the valley there. Ab’m seen’n today. You?

BRAY: Whassis? Donkey? What donkey? Eh?

JOY: Donkey over the valley there in Wheezer Jenkins’ field. I like to watch’n.

BRAY: Do ya? Since when?

JOY: Since I dunno. E bin stood there *years.*, e ’ave.

BRAY: What about’n?

JOY: I’m sayin e’s not there today.

BRAY: So?

JOY: I’m sayin I enjoyed ’is company. Liked to watch’n stand there in the mist. E’d eat or twitch ’is tail. Friendly l’il thing e was.

BRAY: How could you tell e was friendly from ’ere?

JOY: E *looked* friendly, Stanley.

BRAY: You dunno wi’ these animals, Joy. E could a bin a right asshole.

JOY: Where izze? Dear ob'm… e's always there.

BRAY: Didn't knaw you liked that donkey or ad even noticed a donkey was ever there cus you'd never once mentioned it before.

JOY: Aw ez. Dear little thing e is. Dear little lub'ly donkey. E makes my day e do. Lub'ly li'l fluffy thing, e is. Lub'ly li'l fluffy donkey. E's my best friend.

BRAY: Jesus.

He stares out the window too.

BRAY: Still, looks like e's gone now. Time to move on.

JOY: Gone? Gone where? I'm gettin concerned.

BRAY: Since when 'ave you cared 'bout a donkey?

JOY: I loved that poor, scraggy animal, Stanley!

BRAY: Loved?

JOY: E could be lost or trapped or injured somewhere! Best pop round Wheezer's and help look for 'em.

BRAY: I aren't doin that. I can't stand Wheezer Jenkins and Wheezer Jenkins kent stand me!

JOY: Well thun we should call the police.

BRAY: Police?! For a damned donkey?!

JOY: *(Hysterical.)* Summin must be done, Stanley!

BRAY: Joy, you're over-reactin!

JOY: *(Explodes.)* DUN'T YOU DARE TELL ME I'M OVER-REACTIN, STANLEY BRAY.

Pause.

BRAY: I'll pop round Wheezer's on me way to the village, o'right?

JOY: Whadde goin village for?

BRAY: I got some things to pick up.

JOY: Pick us up a couple Gristler's pasties, would ya?

BRAY: 'ell. Whass the occasion?

JOY: Don't screw wimme, Stanley.

BRAY: I'm not, am I?

JOY: You do know what tomorra is?

BRAY: Toozdee.

JOY: God in Heaven, Stanley Bray. Tis thirty years –

BRAY: 'course it is. Thirty years. I knaw.

JOY: Thirty year since our darlin boy vanished. Please tell me you remembered?

BRAY: 'course I did! No, no. I was keepin… quiet, to be truthful. I knew it was tomorra but… I didn't wanna… raise the issue for your sake.

JOY: Thirty year since I vowed never to step outside this house again!

BRAY: And you kept true to yer promise, dear, I'll give you that. For certain, we shall mark the moment. Wi' pasties.

JOY: Three.

BRAY: Three Gristler's pasties.

JOY: Lay the table and everythin. In case e…

BRAY: In case e comes 'ome. Ez.

JOY: Pass us 'is picture?

BRAY gets the framed photo and hands it to her. He watches her stare at it.

BRAY: Back soon, dear.

BRAY exits.

RANDY: *The dark is rising – oh lord!*
My sky is gone
The dirt's deciding – oh lord!

My skin and bone

In the house:

JOY: My beautiful Bobby… playin on the tyre swing… hangin from 'is fav'rite tree… the Blasted Oak… up the top field there… in his Dairy-land t-shirt…

(To photo.) Come 'ome, Bobby! Come 'ome…

RANDY: *And hell is calling – oh lord!*
My damned desire
And Heaven's falling – oh lord!
My world's on fire

BRAY stands out in the yard.

THE VOICE OF GOD: Ssssstanley Bray…
TIME TO HANG ANOTHER ONE, SSSTANLEY…

BRAY knows what he must do.

RANDY: *The white horse riding – oh lord!*
Your name in vain
And where you hiding – oh lord!
My soul's in chains

BRAY: *(To us.)* Unnerved as I was by Joy not eatin 'er first boiled egg in thirty year, I ad to forge on. I ad bizniz to attend to. I ad the farmhouse windas to board up so Joy wouldn't stare out no more, a clutch o' delicious Gristler's pasties to pick up, but most important of all, I ad donkeys to 'ang. But before I did that, I ad to find more of 'em.

RANDY: *My soul's in chains*
My soul's in chains…

BRAY: 'right, Randy?

RANDY: 'right, Stan? Whasson?

BRAY: Aw ya knaw.

RANDY: Same old, same old.

BRAY: Yeh. Yeh.

RANDY: Farm tickin over?

BRAY: Not really, no.

RANDY: No. No. How's Joy? She o'right?

BRAY: Right as she'll ever be, Rand.

RANDY: Dear of 'er.

BRAY: 'bout you? Still singin up the Bucket o' Blood?

RANDY: You know me, Stan. I aren't goin nowhere.

Awkward pause.

BRAY: 'ere Randy, you dunno no one oo ab'm got no donkey fer sale or no?

RANDY: Donkey?

BRAY: Small 'orse? Long ears? Often found on Christmas cards?

RANDY: Donkey. You tried up ole Wheezer Jenkins' place?

BRAY: Yeh no, I bin up there.

RANDY: *(Thinking.)* Donkey? Donkey? What e need a donkey for, Stan?

BRAY: 'elp out, round the farm, like... Joy's partial to a... donkey and ahh... Neb'm mind, Rand. Forget I ast.

BRAY makes to go.

RANDY: Wait. There is one place I know –

BRAY: Tell me.

RANDY: You wun't like it, Stan.

BRAY: I'm des'prate, Rand.

RANDY: Go ask me Auntie Sally up the abattoir. She 'as what you seek.

BRAY: Aw shit, no. Please. Anyone but 'er.

RANDY: Go.

RANDY sings:

Who knows what drives a man to madness?
Who knows what drives a man to love?
They say some men are born to gladness
Badness, it fits me like a glove

Tregersick Meat Packing, Inc. The boning floor.

A carcass of a cow swings in on chains. A butcher in plastic and masked noisily carves up the cow with a D-12 Chipley Deluxe bone-saw.

Enter BRAY.

BRAY: Sally… Sally! SALLLL-EEEEEE!!!!

The butcher stops sawing. She turns and sees BRAY. Removes her visor. This is SALLY TREGERSICK.

There is some distance between them and they have to shout over abattoir ambience.

SALLY: Fuck'er you doin ere?

BRAY: Nice to see you and all, Sal.

SALLY: Sling yer 'ook before you contaminate the whole f'kin floor!

BRAY: I shan't come any closer thun this.

SALLY: Smart move, slim. 'specially when I got a D12 Chipley Deluxe in me 'ands.

BRAY: Pretty sweet.

SALLY: Stanley f'kin Bray…

SALLY returns to the carcass and goes at it.

BRAY: *(To us.)* She whips out the dead cow's vitals with a surgeon's precision. What was inside is out in seconds flat. The heart is cut free and she squeezes the bugger dry… I kent 'elp but think she's tryin to make a point. Slaughterhouse Sally.

SALLY: You still ere?

BRAY: We need to talk. How can you stand it in ere? The bleddy noise!

She stops. She hits a button. An alarm bell rings through the factory. Everything stops.

SALLY: *(Into a CB radio which booms through the place.)* Possible contamination in Sector 3. Clear the bonin' floor until further notice! Thankin you.

The factory falls silent of machinery and squealing.

SALLY: The sawin and the squealin? Drowns out me thoughts. Me black and ragin thoughts.

BRAY: I knaw me comin ere is outta the blue –

SALLY: Whadda ya want, Bray? Speak before this meat spoils.

BRAY: Come for a favour, Sal.

SALLY: Favour? Are you outta your f'kin mind?

BRAY: Hear me out.

SALLY: After what happened? E wants a favour!

BRAY: Why? What happened?

SALLY: Oh, Stan. C'mon.

BRAY: Bobby disappeared.

SALLY: Dear God. How can you live with yerself?

BRAY: Life's tragic. But we find a way through.

SALLY: And Joy, did she "find a way through"?

BRAY: I didn't come ere for this.

SALLY: Aw, you just thought it'da be nice to pop in, eh? Pick up where we left off? Blow kisses through the bone-dusted blood-misted air?

BRAY: I'm after some donkeys, Sally.

She stares at him then lights a cigarette.

BRAY: That hygenic?

SALLY: All adds to the flavour. So. What e need donkeys for, Stan?

BRAY: One night last week, I saw God above me barn. Saw a light! Heard a voice what spoke to me. My whole bein felt seized by some unfathomable force. After that, I felt compelled to do 'is work.

SALLY: You bin sniffin too much sheep-dip, Bray.

BRAY: You got'ny or no?

SALLY: 'course I ab'm! This is a respectable slaughter-house. I dun't butcher barn-yard animals.

BRAY: Little dicky bird tole me got a whole shadowy sideline to the less reputable companies for the, shall we say, cheaper cuts.

SALLY: Oo told ya that?

BRAY: Your nephew, Randy.

SALLY: That boy. E got the voice of an angel and the tongue of a twat.

BRAY: 'ell, it dun't bother me what ya do! If you grind up donkeys to put in dog food thass your business.

SALLY: *(Smiles.)* That a Gristler's pasty in yer pocket or are you just pleased to-

BRAY: Yes. Tis a Gristler's pasty in me pocket. For me and Joy.

SALLY: Always a treat when you get in the Gristler's, eh Stan?

BRAY: Yes. Well, they're quality foodstuffs. They ain't cheap. And like the advert says: "There's summin special in every one."

SALLY: Oh yes there is. Hee…haw.

BRAY: Aw. God. Aw no. Aw shit God no. There's not… donkeys… in there… is there?

SALLY: What e think they put in there that makes 'em taste *so* good.

BRAY considers throwing the pasties away. But he stops.

BRAY: I kent turn up empty handed. She'll kill me…

SALLY: How is Joyful and Triumphant? O'right?

BRAY: Right as she'll ever be.

SALLY: Ain't seen 'er fer decades.

BRAY: She ab'm left the house in thirty year.

SALLY: Jesus. I should pop down there.

BRAY: Eh?

SALLY: To the farm. Clear the air.

BRAY: No need.

SALLY: I'd like to, fer me own peace o' mind.

THE VOICE OF GOD: Sssssssstannnleyyy…

BRAY: *(To SALLY.)* Look! I got shit to do. These donkeys –

SALLY: Donkeys. Funny…

BRAY: What is?

SALLY: You ain't the first to come in ere wi' the self-same strange request.

BRAY: Somebody bin ere wi' donkey queries before me?

SALLY: Yesterday.

BRAY: Oo?

SALLY: I dunno. Some chap. Freaky Keith spoke to 'em.

BRAY: Whaddid Freaky Keith say?

SALLY: Freaky Keith said this bloke turned up unannounced round the back askin about donkeys. Told Freaky Keith e was doin independent research for some classified project or some bollocks and reassured Freaky Keith e wadn't affiliated to any government body. Needless to say suspicion was greatly aroused in Freaky Keith and Freaky Keith ejected 'im from the property, but not before askin all sorts of odd questions. 'bout donkeys, like.

BRAY: Like what?

SALLY: Like got'ny donkeys for sale? Like, 'ow 'igh is a donkey in real life? Like, 'ow much a donkey weigh? Like, 'ow many donkeys d'you think I could get on the back of a flatbed truck?

BRAY: That *is* a good question…

SALLY: Freaky Keith said e gave off proper weird vibes which comin from Freaky Keith is sayin summin.

BRAY: What the 'ell would this chap want wi' donkeys?

SALLY: What the 'ell do *you* want with 'em?

BRAY: This bloke leave a name?

SALLY: One better. E left his business card…

She searches and finds it and hands it to him.

BRAY: Lives in Trura…

SALLY: Well that explains it. Pervert.

BRAY: Interestin.

SALLY: If you say so.

THE VOICE OF GOD: Sssssstanley…

BRAY: Sally, I need these animals and I knaw you got'm somewhere. You gonna givem me or no?

SALLY: O'right, I'll give ya the f'kin donkeys –

BRAY: Triffick.

SALLY: On one condition.

BRAY: 'ere we go.

SALLY: I wanna come down see Joy.

BRAY: She ain't forgiven neither of us.

SALLY: You're still alive!

BRAY: Barely! Looka me! I'm a bleddy 'usk!

SALLY: She never slung you out, though. She kept you under 'er roof. Thass big of 'er.

BRAY: She shunned the outside world. She ain't stood on 'er own two feet in three decades. Not without 'elp. Thass the only reason why I'm still there.

SALLY: Small price to pay. Tis time I did right by 'er.

BRAY: I dun't advise it. She's still bites.

SALLY: I can handle 'er.

BRAY: She'll crucify ya.

SALLY: Then thass what I deserve.

BRAY: Ain't gonna happen.

SALLY: Tis my conscience, Stanley Bray.

BRAY: Trust me on this. Stay away from my farm.

SALLY: Your farm?

BRAY: You knaw what I mean!

Pause.

SALLY: You said you loved me once. Do you remember?

BRAY: Yes, I do. Clear as day. Now, 'bout these donkeys.

A cacophony of braying donkeys.

RANDY sings:

RANDY: *Well I jumped the fence and escaped the farm*
I danced through fields running free from harm
But I ran into the butcher's arms
Now-hoo, I got the slaughter-house blues

Well I slipped the pan but fell in the fire
I told the truth and was called a lair
My future days are lookin' dire
Ohh-hoo, I got the slaughter-house blues

Well, the more I fight to clear my name
The more they tell me I'm a man insane
And the answer's like a bolt to the brain
Uh-ohhhh o-ho hoooo, I got the slaughter-house blues
Oh lord, I got the slaughter-house blues
So long, here come the slaughter-house –

Farmhouse. Night.

JOY sits in her chair. BRAY stands with pasties.

JOY: *(Furious.)* Where the 'ella you bin?

RANDY: *(Sings.) ... bluessssss.*

BRAY: Get the pasties.

JOY: Where'd e go to get 'em? Plymouth?

BRAY: They was 'ard to come by.

JOY: You try Mildred's?

BRAY: Mildred's closed last winter. I tried the post office in Perranzabuloe but they's only open Wednesday afternoons now. I tried Cakebread the baker's down St. Erme but she laffed in me face. I tried Tonkin's Garridge out on the Zelah bypass but tis a Costa now. Bolingey. Three

Burrows. St. Allen. I bin all over. Finally found a batch guess where?

JOY: I give up.

BRAY: Guess.

JOY: I dunno, Stanley.

BRAY: Callestick.

JOY: Aw.

BRAY: How weird's that? I get the pasties in the ice-cream capital o' the county! Of all places!

JOY: The world's gone mad.

BRAY: Thass what I thought. Anyhow, I got'n. I persisted. And I won the day. Ere.

JOY: Not 'ugely 'ungry actually.

BRAY stares.

JOY: I might pick at it later. Leave Bobby's out for'n though.

BRAY does the work. JOY waits for her moment.

JOY: So when on this elaborate pasty odyssey did you run into Sally Tregersick?

BRAY: *(Long pause.)* Eh?

JOY: You heard.

BRAY: Sally Tregersick? I dun't think I…

JOY: I can read your forehead like a damned book, man. The wrinkled brow speak volumes. And you got a look in yer eye and a spring in yer step that I ain't seen since you ad that dalliance with 'er way back when.

BRAY: It wadn't – we didn't –

JOY: Tis o'right. We ad our set-to. We made the necessary repairs to our marriage. Swore we'd be honest with one another from that moment forward. Did we not?

BRAY: And I thank my lucky stars every –

JOY: Where did you see 'er, Stanley?

BRAY: Oh! *Sally* Tregersick? Yes, I did see 'er. Christ. Yeh. Up the abattoir.

JOY: We got no livestock, Stanley. What e doin there?

BRAY: Don't get suspicious, my hen. 'Twas a last ditch attempt bar one at pasties. They gotta cafe there. I ran into 'er.

JOY: And what did that cow-carvin tart have to say for 'erself?

BRAY: Nuthin much. I barely reckernised 'er to be truthful. Christ, she looks some old now.

JOY: She was sweet on you once. She try 'er luck again?

BRAY: If she did I wadn't respondin. Not this time.

JOY: That was a doo, wannit? The Ventongimps Agricultural Christmas Ball. 'er drunk and 'er hands all over you.

BRAY: Embarrassin.

JOY: You didn't put up too much of a fight as I recall.

BRAY: Like you say, we worked it out.

JOY: You made it by the skin o' your teeth, pal.

BRAY: Don't I know it. She sent 'er regards.

JOY: Huh! Send 'em back.

BRAY: I shan't be seein 'er again, dear.

JOY: I've heard that before. I wanna go bed.

BRAY: 'bout yer Gristlers?

JOY: Ain't 'ungry.

BRAY: Prolly for the best.

JOY: Big day 'morra.

BRAY: Thirty years our boy's bin gone.

JOY: I want it to stop. This pain…

BRAY: Absolutely.

JOY: So I've decided that after three decades of self-imposed grief-stricken incarceration that perhaps tis time to let go.

BRAY: I see.

JOY: There's only so many tears a mother can shed.

BRAY: Whatever you need, I'm ere.

JOY: Gud cus tis time for me to step outside.

BRAY: Outside? Eh? Whass brought this on?

JOY: Thirty year sat indoors thass what.

BRAY: Wounds take longer to heal than you think, Joy.

JOY: Every hour of every day I've waited, hopin, prayin, that our Bobby would walk back in through that door. Thirty bleddy years…

BRAY: You kent give up 'ope.

JOY: 'ope 'urts, Stanley! 'ope's killin me. No. I'd do better to face facts bite the bullet and head up the top field –

BRAY: Tricky, Joy.

JOY: And give 'im a proper goodbye. Lay 'is pasty at the fut of 'is fav'rite tree. The blasted oak. You know the one?

BRAY: I know the one.

JOY: Where e usta swing.

BRAY: Aren't sure this is a good idea, Joy.

JOY: Too bad. I'm goin.

BRAY: Yard's a quagmire!

JOY: Then 'ose it down!

BRAY: Idn' as simple as that.

JOY: I've made up me mind, Stanley.

BRAY: I kent let you go out.

JOY: Tis my farm. I shall do what I like!

BRAY: And 'ow'd you plan on gettin up there? I kent carry ya!

JOY: I'll get there somehow!

BRAY: What e gonna do? Crawl? You ab'm walked in years! You kent even stand by yerself.

She stands.

BRAY: Shit.

Beat.

TIS A MIRACLE!

JOY: Miracle my fut. I just got me balls back!

BRAY: Aw fer godsake! Whass made you so damned determint all of a sudden?

JOY: Donkeys!

BRAY: What?

JOY: I's so fond o' that lub'ly li'l donkey out there. How come you only miss the things you love when they go? Dig out me wellies, Stanley. Tomorra, I shall bid farewell to our boy. Today, I shall drown in 'ope. But tomorra? Tomorra I shall take breath and start to live again!

Fields. Later that night.

RANDY: *(Sings.) Why me, oh Lord?*
Why force my sinner's hand?
All the thunder and light'nin
Won't help me understand
Why me, oh Lord?
Your mighty big finger
Points right down at me
Your eyes bright with Judgement
Are all that I see

Why me, oh Lord?

All the toil and heartache
Don't bring forth your good light
I'll be damned to walk the darkness
Of this long and endless night

5 DONKEYS HANGED.

BRAY has hanged three new donkeys and hangs a fourth –

He stumbles back, hands bleeding. He comes round from his fevered activity.

BRAY: *(To us.)* She wants to step outside? I kent allow it. I shall hafto board up the rest of the windas. Nail shut all the doors. She cannot see this. She wouldn't understand. On top o' that, there's the on-goin question of supply…

BRAY's hands hurt. He finds a handkerchief in his pocket and wraps it round his hand. He also finds the card that SALLY gave him.

BRAY: Donkey Pervert from Trura… Up to the same work as me. E might knaw where there's more donkeys…

THE VOICE OF GOD: Bray stands there. Not knowing what to do. Nothing happens.

BRAY: *(To himself.)* I knaw. I'll go Trura.

THE VOICE OF GOD: Bray doesn't move. Just tends to his bleeding hand…

BRAY: Nope. I'm off. Trura.

Beat.

I'm goin.

THE VOICE OF GOD: The lights start to fade…

BRAY: Eh?

The lights starts to fade.

BRAY: Oi!

THE VOICE OF GOD: Black out.

Black-out.

BRAY: fuck's goin on?!

Static. Feedback. Donkeys bray and voices echo as we tumble down a rabbit hole. Long pause. Then, the play judders into life again –

Farmhouse. Night.

BRAY stands there, breathless, looking over someone who's been dumped in the armchair. They have a sack on their head. Their hands are tied. BRAY whips the sack from their head.

Revealed is the writer, CARL GROSE (a sort of Cornish Jude Law.) He is groggy, sweaty, blinking in the light. Blood trickles from a wound on his head. His mouth is stuffed with a rag.

BRAY: Carl Gross?

He slaps GROSE. GROSE comes round, disoriented, and screams muffled screams. BRAY gestures to him that he's going to remove the rag. He does.

BRAY: Are you Carl Gross?

GROSE: Ahhhhhh!

BRAY: Shh! Are you Carl Gross?

GROSE: What? Y-yes. I am. That's me.

Beat.

Actually, it's pronounced *Grose.* G-R-O-S-E.

BRAY: So. Into donkeys then?

GROSE: Eh?

BRAY: Donkeys, pard. Where'd e get yours to?

GROSE: *(Taking in his surroundings.)* Where am I…?

BRAY: I ast you a question.

GROSE: My head… wait… you… you hit me!

BRAY: I'm gettin teasy now, Gross.

GROSE: Yeh, *Grose.* It's like "rose" but with a G in… front…

Beat.

You came to my home.

BRAY: Yep.

GROSE: You hit me and you've… kidnapped me!

BRAY: Yep. I needed to talk to ya.

GROSE: You could've talked to me there!

BRAY: You flew into a panic.

GROSE: Why am I tied to this chair? Untie me! Help! Help!

BRAY stuffs the rag in his mouth again.

BRAY: Shaddap! Now listen to me. I didn't wanna get these out but…

BRAY produces a strange device, heavy, rusty, like a giant nutcracker.

BRAY: Knaw what this is? Tis called a Burdizzo – after its Italian inventor. Common agricultural implement. Stainless steel. Retail for about 49.99. They go about the bullock's testicles. One good 'ard squeeze and – toot! – the cords are crushed. Once the blood supply is lost to that area necrosis sets in. The balls shrink, turn black, drop off. Now I ab'm used 'em in years… But you can bet yer sweet ass I ain't forgot 'ow.

GROSE weeps with terror.

BRAY: Sure, it might take me a couple goes to nail it, but I know they do the trick. Crush testicular gristle thick as yer thumb. Now, let's keep nice'n calm. And let's not scream. Cus if ya do… tis Burdizzo time. Got it?

GROSE nods emphatically. BRAY removes the gag. GROSE holds it in.

BRAY: Now, sounds like we both got an interest in donkeys. Whass your story? You hearin the Voice? Seen The Light? Mine was 'bove the barn. Compellin me to string 'em up! Where'd e get holda yours? Whass your method?

GROSE: For what?

BRAY: Hangin donkeys.

GROSE: Stanley Bray…?

BRAY: You know me?

GROSE: This can't be happening… I'm not… I don't… Oh, God, I'm not well…

BRAY: Thass why I tracked you down. Solidarity. I dunno whass goin on up 'ere… I got some sick notions. All put there b'God Almighty!

GROSE: I'm so sorry. I don't quite understand what's…

BRAY: Little bird tole me you bin snoopin round askin for donkeys to 'ang.

GROSE: What? No. I'm a writer.

BRAY: A what?

GROSE: All of this…? Is in my play…

BRAY: Play? What play? What e talkin about?

GROSE: The play I'm writing… you're in it.

BRAY: You ain't makin sense, boy. I'm talkin about donkey hangin! I'm talkin about a Mission from God!

GROSE: No. Yes. That's what you do. In the story.

BRAY: What story?

GROSE: I'm writing a play called "49 Donkeys Hanged". In it, you – Stanley Bray – a Cornish farmer at the end of his rope – starts hanging donkeys for some mysterious reason.

BRAY: Ah! So whass the reason?

GROSE: It's a mystery. In the play.

BRAY: Thass no good to me. I need answers. Now.

GROSE: Yes. I don't know.

BRAY: What?

GROSE: I don't… I don't know the answer.

BRAY: Right.

GROSE: I haven't written it yet.

BRAY: What?

GROSE: The play!

BRAY: What play?

GROSE: The play you – we! – are somehow – in – right now! It's not finished!

BRAY: O'right Gross –

GROSE: Grose.

BRAY: If you don't stop pissin about I shall lop a bollock off.

GROSE: It's true! I don't know! It's not done! *I'm* not supposed to be in it that's for certain!

BRAY: In it? In what?

GROSE: This… is a play, a story for the stage, that I haven't completed yet. Look, I know this must be hard but… you're not real. You are only a character.

BRAY: Oh, am I be fuck?

GROSE: Yes. I made you up. With my brain.

BRAY: Did you really? Well done you! Tell me more!

GROSE: This is Bosanko Farm. In the village of Ventongimps. Your wife Joy who hasn't left the house in thirty years is upstairs asleep in her bed. There's a picture in a frame behind me of a boy playing on a tyre swing. His name is Bobby.

BRAY: *(Shaken.)* Stop! How'd you knaw all this?

GROSE: Cus I made it up, Stanley.

BRAY: Go on thun. Tell me the story so far. From the beginning.

GROSE: O'right. It started with a newspaper headline I saw in Johannesberg.

BRAY: Johannesberg?

GROSE: I was performing in a theatre show out there. This was back in '99. We got invited by the British Council to play the Arts Alive Festival. We did a few shows in Jo'berg, and a few in this newly-built hall in Soweto. I remember seeing the townships – tin-roofed concrete block shacks. Housing families of six or seven or more. Animals everywhere. Dirt-tracks for roads. Extreme poverty. We did our shows to school kids. At the end, they stormed the stage. I felt like a rock star…

BRAY: Yeh, yeh. And the donkey hangin? Where does that fit in?

GROSE: I'm getting to that. I'm setting the scene. We were driving back from Soweto when I saw it… It was dusk. The sky was bright, bright orange. To the left of us, all along the motorway was this vast wasteland of wrecked cars and burning tyres. My head lent against the window. And I watched as these headlines flew by. Headlines from local papers I guess, pasted onto plywood and staked into the ground on posts. They flashed by hypnotically…

"PARTY ACCUSING OF VOTE RIGGING…"

"POOL CLEANER WINS LOTTERY…"

"NEW EDUCATION POLICY IMPLEMENTED…"

"49 DONKEYS HANGED…"

BRAY: Eh?

GROSE: That's what I said. "Did anyone see that headline?" I asked the others. They didn't. "49 Donkeys Hanged." What?! I had to know more! Back at our digs I found a paper with the story in it. Only small. But there is was. I hadn't imagined it. Turns out this farmer called Solomon Singo had gone and hung 49 donkeys from the trees on his farm. My mind exploded with questions. Why did he do that? *How* did he do that?

BRAY: And what did it say, this article?

GROSE: Very little. No more than I've just told you. Just that he did it. But for me, a writer, that was perfect. Because I had all I needed. The seed of an idea. You are based on Solomon Singo. You're part him, part my Uncle Trevor, part my imagination.

BRAY: The fuck're you talkin about?

GROSE: That's where you come from!

BRAY: I'm part South African farmer, part your imagination?

GROSE: And part my Uncle Trevor.

BRAY: You're off your f'kin head, mate!

GROSE: That's the Uncle Trevor talkin!

BRAY: I shall 'it you in a minute.

GROSE: Maybe too much Uncle Trev!

BRAY: Look, this idn't no game, Grouse.

GROSE: *Grose.*

BRAY: And I thought I was bleddy mad!

GROSE: Look, I'm sorry I can't help you. I really am. I just think we've exhausted all possibilities here and I really should be getting back.

BRAY: Back where?

GROSE: Home. I'd like you to take me home. Please. Perhaps when I finish the play you'll get your answer.

BRAY: Back to Trura? Back to your place? To yer study, right?

GROSE: Yes.

BRAY: That is a gud idea. Your first o' the night!

GROSE: Great. Let's go.

BRAY: You ain't comin.

GROSE: What?

BRAY: I'm off to investigate. See what you knaw and what you dun't, pard. I dun't trust you, see?

GROSE: I swear to you Stanley, I'm telling the truth!

BRAY stuffs the rag back into GROSE's mouth –

BRAY: Thass what I'm afraid of, Grossman!

And exits.

GROSE: *(With cloth in mouth.)* Grose! GROSE! It's GRROOSSSEEEE!!!!

GROSE looks about him.

GROSE: *(Voice-over.)* Fuck. Fuck. Fuck! Wait. What is this? Hello? I have a voice-over? This is great! I can actually hear myself think! This could be useful. OK, Grosey. Time to get out of here!

He strains against the ropes.

GROSE: *(Voice-over.)* Wait. Think. What are the facts? I am Carl Gross – Grose! Bastard! I live in Truro and I am a writer… This is all my doing. This is my play. I can control things from in here… Hell yeh, I can do what I want! In here, I am *God!*

Stares at ropes.

"The ropes around Grose's wrists magically disappear!"

They don't.

GROSE: *(Voice-over.)* 'kay. Breathe… "The knots happen to loosen around Grose's wrists of their own accord…?"

They don't.

GROSE: *(Voice-over.)* "Grose snaps the ropes with his own superhuman strength!"

He tries. Again, nothing.

GROSE: *(Voice-over.)* Shit. Wait. Let's think about this. I'm asking too much. Story… subplots… I just need a character with a genuinely good reason to come and get me out…

JOY: *(Off.)* Stanley? Zat you?

GROSE: *(Voice-over.)* And there's Joy…

Enter JOY, slowly, with walking stick.

JOY: Stanley, I heard a noise…

GROSE: Mmf! Mmff!

JOY: Oo're you? You're not Stanley! What're you doin in my kitchen?

GROSE tries to show his tied wrists.

JOY: Mate o' Stanley's are you? Tied you up 'as e? E 'as bin actin somewhat strange of late.

GROSE: Hmmm! Mmmfffff-hm!!

JOY: We ab'm ad visitors up 'ere for years. You'll hafto excuse the place. We've let ourselves go somewhat.

GROSE: Mmophh! Mmmoophh?!

JOY: I kent understand a word yer sayin!

GROSE desperately nods his head. She takes it out. GROSE gasps.

GROSE: Jesus…! Aw God… Aw christ! Thank you… Thank –

He looks at JOY, who stares at him, frozen, dish cloth in hand.

JOY: You.

GROSE: What?

JOY: Can it be?

GROSE: Sorry?

JOY: Bobby?

GROSE: Eh?

JOY: My son?

GROSE: Shit. No. No, no.

JOY: Bobby, tis you!

GROSE: Joy, listen to me –

JOY: You've come 'ome!

She embraces him. GROSE groans.

JOY: My Bobby! My boy! I kent believe it! Thirty long years I've waited! And on the very day I was about to give up 'ope, you come back!

GROSE: Joy, I'm not –

JOY: Mother. Call me mother.

GROSE: Uhhh –

JOY: Say it for god's sakes! All I wanted these past years was to hear my child utter that one sweet word. To know I was needed. To know I ad reason to exist! I heard it in dreams, Bobby, where I'd catch glimpses of ya, but dreams like that can drive a mother mad. Say it, my boy. Say it, do.

GROSE: Mmm…

JOY: Yeh!

GROSE: Mmmmmmm…

JOY: G'won!

GROSE: Mmmmmmmmotherrrrr.

JOY: The most beautiful sound in the world.

She whacks him.

GROSE: Ahh!

JOY: I thought you was dead! We all did! Where the hella you bin?

GROSE: Please –

JOY: I forgive you.

GROSE: I am not the person you think I am.

JOY: I understand. Thirty years is a long time. You've changed. Become a man I see. Stand. Lemme get a good look at you.

GROSE: You'll hafto undo these ropes. Mother.

JOY: Oh. Oh, yes I see. 'course, my boy.

She starts to attack the knots then stops.

JOY: Father found you did e? Brought you 'ome? No wonder e bin actin all shifty of late. Where did e find you?

GROSE: Truro.

JOY: Trura? Thass where you bin fer thirty years? Why'd you run away Bobby? Why'd you stay away for so long?

She stops.

JOY: You aren't gonna run away again, are ya?

GROSE shakes his head.

JOY: You promise never to run away again? Cus I couldn't bare to lose you a second time. You promise?

GROSE: I promise.

She unties his ropes.

JOY: Now how 'bout a nice cuppa coffee?

GROSE: Please, mother.

JOY slowly turns and heads for the counter. GROSE jumps up but his legs fail him. He scrabbles for the door. Tries it.

GROSE: Of course. Locked from the outside. And the windows? All boarded up!

JOY: You know Bobby, today I was plannin on biddin farewell to your memory. Leavin the house fer the first time in years. But now yer 'ome, I don't need to. Pasty there, if yer hungry.

GROSE: This is a nightmare.

BRAY appears on the far side of the farm.

BRAY: *(Howls.)* Basterd!

JOY: Oh! Father's 'ome.

GROSE: *(Realizes he's free.)* Shit. Do up these knots, would ya?

JOY: Eh?

GROSE: Re-do the ropes! Where's that manky dishcloth? Joy? Joy! Tie me up!

JOY: Tie you up? Whass wrong wi' you Bobby? I just undid ya!

GROSE stuffs the dish cloth back in his mouth and concentrates.

GROSE: *(Voice-over.)* JOY!

JOY: *(Looking about her.)* Ahhh! Oo's there?

GROSE: *(Voice-over.)* This is your mind talking to you, Joy.

JOY: Aw. Righto.

GROSE: *(Voiceover.)* Tie up Bobby, quick!

JOY: You must be jokin. Wi' my arthritis?

GROSE: *(Voice-over.)* Quick march, Joy! Go! Go! Go!

JOY moves with almost disconcerting speed as if possessed. She ties the ropes.

GROSE: *(Voice-over.)* Nice and tight! Nice and tight! That's it. Jolly good. Around we go... And you're feeling sleepy, Joy... very sleepy...

JOY: I'm not, I ad a solid night's kip.

GROSE: *(Voice-over.)* Exit Joy! Exit Joy! Exit Joy!

JOY exits super-fast.

Enter BRAY, furious, with a script in his hand.

BRAY: How did you knaw, Grouse?

GROSE: Mmf?

BRAY: 'ow'd you knaw what happened? Oo you bin talkin to? Just oo the 'ell are you?

GROSE: Moowhob?

BRAY swipes the cloth from GROSE's mouth.

GROSE: I don't understand.

BRAY: *(Wafting the script.)* Says 'ere I killed Bobby.

GROSE: Yes. You did.

BRAY: By accident, mind! I wouldna killed me own son on purpose!

GROSE: Of course not. But it works, right? The missing son. Gone thirty years. Is he alive? No! Why not? Cus the father killed him! *Whaaat?!*

BRAY: The most terrible secret a man could have, a secret that only I knew...

GROSE: Good twist. Sadly gone for nothing now.

BRAY: Yet you knaw the whole damn story!

GROSE: Bobby caught you and Sally Tregersick together...

BRAY: I'd sworn never to see 'er again...

GROSE: Cus Joy'd kick you out if you did and you'd have nothing...

BRAY: But we met up one last time, at my behest, on the edge o'the farm, down by the pond…

GROSE: Cus no one goes down by the pond…

BRAY: Not in winter, but sod's law there was the boy, ticklin' trout… We saw each other from across the water. I called 'is name. E ran. I gived chase. Back up the lane to the farm. I ad to catch'n 'fore e got to Joy otherwise all was lost.

GROSE: You cut him off at the yard, stopped him from reaching the house –

BRAY: I'm wild. E's terrified. I dunno what I'll do to'n if I catch 'em.

GROSE: E tears off up to the top field –

BRAY: Clambers up 'is fav'rite tree –

GROSE: The Blasted Oak –

BRAY: I'm howlin mad, spittin feathers –

GROSE: E's ragin too. Threatens to tell Joy everything!

BRAY: "Dun't you dare, boy!"

GROSE: "I'm gonna tell 'er!"

BRAY: "You'll regret it if ya do!"

GROSE: "And you'll lose everythin! She'll see you off! Like she shoulda done years ago!"

BRAY: Come 'ere, ya little –

GROSE: And he slips.

BRAY: And e falls.

GROSE: And 'is skull splits.

BRAY: I dun't understand. No one knew this but me.

GROSE: Stanley, it's a story.

BRAY: Whatever tis, whass done is done. The secret's bin buried long enuff. I just hafto keep it that way.

GROSE: And how are you going to do that?

BRAY: Destroy the evidence.

BRAY slings the script into the Rayburn.

GROSE: My play!

BRAY: Not so clever now, eh Carol?

GROSE: Carl! I've made copious notes.

BRAY: So I saw. Every notebook you filled, every scrap of paper, every word you wrote on the subject? I burned it all.

GROSE: What?!

BRAY: And yer li'l computer? I smashed the shit out of it. Whadde think o' that, Mr Writer Man?

GROSE: I should've backed-up.

BRAY: All of it's gone, pard. All ash in the wind.

GROSE: This is insane!

BRAY: Only one last piece to do away with.

GROSE: What?

BRAY: You. I'm gonna crack open that skull o' yours and let it all drain out. The secret o' what I done will stay safe wimme.

GROSE: Hey man, let's be cool, yeh? You don't need to do this. And I'll tell you why. It's OK, see? Cus Joy thinks I'm Bob –

BRAY: Yatter, yatter, yatter. Dun't you Trura lot ever shut up?

BRAY stuffs GROSE's mouth with the rag again. GROSE suddenly panics and strains against his bonds. He tries to look behind him as BRAY sorts through various kitchen implements (knife, oven-gloves, carving fork, rolling pin)… BRAY finally settles on an heavy old frying pan.

BRAY: Easy now, Groggs. The more you struggle, the messier it'll be…

BRAY takes a good strong stance and prepares to swing. GROSE squeezes his eyes tight shut as we go to –

SALLY's porch.

SALLY drinks a beer and watches the sun come up. RANDY is with her. They sing.

RANDY / SALLY: *My hope is like the setting sun*
My heart's a fallin' star
My road ahead is nearly done
Who knew I'd come this far

Oh my word, oh! My days!
How fast the river flows
How short the time on God's good earth
How long the shadows grow

I'll bid goodbye to you, my friend
I'll travel on alone
I'm lettin' go my selfish ways
Oh lord, I'm comin' home…

SALLY: I'm dyin, Rand. Dyin of too much f'kin rage. Tis eatin me up inside. I'm bad meat, Rand, and it's got me gud. I ain't long for this world. I need to sort me shit out. Put me affairs into order. Bid farewell to my loved ones. Beg forgiveness from those I done wrong by. Grace those in the dark with a spark o' Truth, p'raps? Thass the least I could do 'fore I go, right? A last chance of Absolution. Before my last sun sets. Nice 'armonizin wi' ya, boy.

She drinks up and exits. RANDY watches her go.

Back to the farmhouse –

BRAY goes to swing the pan when –

THE VOICE OF GOD/GROSE: *(Voice-over.)* Stanleyyy!!!

BRAY: Eh?

THE VOICE OF GOD/GROSE: Hang more donkeys, Stan! Hang more donkeys!

BRAY: No! Not now!

THE VOICE OF GOD/GROSE: *(Voice-over.)* THERE IS STILL WORK TO BE DONE!!!

BRAY: Jus' lemme killum, I'll be right wi' you!

THE VOICE OF GOD/GROSE: BUT THIS IS GOD, STANLEY! HEED MY VOICE!

BRAY: I do, oh Lord. I do! But Christ, I gotta whack this prick first!

BRAY tries to swing the pan at GROSE but is halted by an invisible force. It is a battle of wills. The pan trembles back and forth, back and forth…

THE VOICE OF GOD/GROSE: Exit Bray!

BRAY: Die, ya basterd!

THE VOICE OF GOD/GROSE: Exit Bray!

BRAY: Gonna kill yooouuuu!

THE VOICE OF GOD/GROSE: Exit Bray! Exit Bray! Exit Bray!

BRAY relaxes, drops the pan.

BRAY: *(To GOD.)* O'right. You win. I'll do it.

THE VOICE OF GOD/GROSE: Thank fuck for that.

BRAY: But when I'm done hangin that last donkey, I'm comin back for this one!

BRAY whacks GROSE across the head with the pan. He knocks him out cold.

Field. Dawn.

BRAY charges for the field. RANDY sings.

RANDY: *And I was born with nuthin to me*
And I will die with nuthin more
And I will do what good God tells me
And I will strive forever more

And I will sing my pilgrim's heart out
And I will run til spirit flags
And I will climb your holy mountain
And I will walk your road in rags

And will I ever see the light, Lord?
And find home in Kingdom Come?
And will I ever be set free, Lord?
And oh my God, what have I done?

BRAY nooses a donkey, spits in his hands and hangs it. He emits a primal howl as he hangs another. And another. Until –

<u>24 Donkeys Hanged</u>

This continues, meanwhile, back in the –

Farmhouse.

JOY brings GROSE round. She undoes the ropes. We see she's put GROSE in a yellow yellow Dairy-land T-shirt with a big cow on it. It's many sizes too small.

JOY: Bobby.

She removes the rag from his mouth.

GROSE: Mother?

JOY: Yes, child. I'm 'ere. Yer free now. No more ropes.

GROSE: *(Re: the T-shirt.)* Whassis?

JOY: Been laid out on yer bed all ironed waitin for your return.

GROSE: Bit tight. Cuts into the neck.

JOY: Your fav'rite t-shirt, Bobby. From Dairy-land. My God, you loved animals. Pigs. 'orses. Sheeps. You wanted to marry a cow, 'member that?

GROSE: No. Wait. Yeh.

JOY: My little boy… Stand up.

She helps him up.

JOY: There e is. There's my Bobby. I still kent believe yer back. Tis almost too much to bare to see your face again.

GROSE: Where's father?

JOY: Out.

GROSE: Mother, we hafto get off the farm.

JOY: What? Why?

GROSE: E wants to kill me.

JOY: Oo do?

GROSE: Father.

JOY: Bobby…

GROSE: When e comes back e's gonna do me in.

JOY: Nonsense!

GROSE: E tied me up. You saw. Cracked me over the head with a fryin pan, look. E said when e gets back e's gonna finish me off.

JOY: No! E's just got ya back, sweetheart. I know e can be a cumudgeon at times –

GROSE: You dun't know what e's capable of!

JOY: E is my husband. I know'n well enuff.

GROSE: You bin out there?

JOY: Eh?

GROSE: You seen what e's done?

JOY: Done? Done?

GROSE: E's keepin summin from you.

JOY: What sorta summin?

GROSE: You'd know it if you took a step outside.

JOY: Ab'm done that in thirty year!

GROSE: E's hangin donkeys, mother.

JOY: Oh!

Beat.

Say that again, Bobby?

GROSE: Donkeys. 'angin 'em. Father is.

JOY: 'angin d–? Now Bobby, why on earth would e do such a thing?

GROSE: Cus God told 'im to!

JOY: Yer pullin my leg!

GROSE: I'm not! Wheezer Jenkins' mule?

JOY: Not lub'ly li'l fluffy li'l donkey?

GROSE: Wheezer's was the first! E bin stringin up one after the other on my fav'rite tree –

JOY: The Blasted Oak!

GROSE: Ain't no tyre swing there now, ma. Just the fly-blown corpses of a herd of poor sweet innocent mules. And they hang from other trees, too, and from the beams in the barns and any place e can throw up a rope!

JOY: I think I woulda noticed if a donkey or two was strung up round Bosanka, boy.

GROSE: Not when e's boarded up they windas, you wouldn't! Locked shut the doors!

JOY: E said 'twas for the storm…

GROSE: E dun't want ya to see the 'orrors e's created out there! E's outta control. E's lost the plot! And e said e's gonna 'ang me next! Said it as e walked out that door. I'm scared, mother. *Scared.*

JOY: O'right, boy. Let's figure out a way to get outta 'ere.

There's a hammering on the front door. GROSE jumps.

VOICE: Joy? Joy!

JOY: Oo's there?

VOICE: Sally Tregersick!

JOY: Slaughter-house Sally? What you doin ere?

SALLY: Joy, open up! I gotta talk to ya!

JOY: You ain't comin into my house, ya bitch!

Pause.

That shut 'er up.

SALLY rips her Chipley D-12 into life and cuts through the front door. SALLY bursts in.

SALLY: Fuck me Reg, you seen it out there?!

JOY: Seen what?

SALLY: What e's done to yer farm! Transformed it into the Ventongimps Jackass Massacre!

GROSE: See, mother?

SALLY: Now I knaw why e came to me needing donkeys! Sick f'ker!

JOY: Whadda you want, Tregersick?

SALLY: Joy. Before you kick off, I came to say I'm sorry!

JOY: Thirty years too late fer that!

SALLY: And beg for forgiveness!

JOY: Then you come to the wrong place!

SALLY: And to tell ya the truth. Listen, your Stanley –

JOY: What about my Stanley?

SALLY: E's bin lyin to ya all these years and my conscience kent take it no more. Joy, your boy, Bobby, is –

JOY: Right 'ere.

SALLY: Eh?

JOY: This is Bobby. E's come 'ome. Look at'n! Look at the man e's become!

SALLY: You ain't Bobby…

GROSE: Yes, I am.

SALLY: How can you be? Joy, Bobby's… e's…

(To GROSE.) Wait, I know you… I seen you before… at the abattoir!

GROSE: I remember 'er now, mother! This is the old bag I caught canoodlin wi' father that day by the pond! The day I ran away!

JOY: That was the reason you ran, Bobby? You saw them two… kissin?

GROSE: 'Twas more than kissin, mother!

SALLY: 'ang on a minute. This dun't make sense.

(To GROSE.)

You're dead.

JOY: *(Rounding on SALLY.)* No, Tregersick. You are. Outside. I'm gonna kick your ass from 'ere to St. Erme!

GROSE: 'it 'er, mum!

JOY charges for SALLY. They end up in –

The Yard.

JOY: I'm gonna rip yer head off and shit down yer neck!

SALLY: Jesus, Joy! I only came up ere for forgiveness!

JOY: Huh!

SALLY: I need to right me wrongs. I need Absolution! I'm dyin see?

JOY: Dyin? Really? Let me 'elp you along wi' that!

They have a big fight around the yard. Epic punches are thrown. RANDY plays banjo, yodels and goads them on. Finally JOY knocks SALLY out cold.

JOY: And stay down!

Field.

BRAY hangs donkey after donkey.

<u>31 DONKEYS HANGED.</u>

He hangs another one…

BRAY: *(To us.)* Now, I knaw what yer thinkin. Where did e get all these donkeys from? This is just pushin the limits of credibility, right? I poached from all over. Ransacked the donkey sanctuary. Newquay zoo. Dairy-land. 'ands are shredded. Runnin outta strength. And rope. But I kent stop. I'm in The Flow. I got this donkey hangin lark down to a fine art… Hyaaaa!

He hauls on rope again. **<u>33.</u>**

BRAY: All I gotta do is put me back into it. See it through. When the last donkey is 'anged, thass the end of it. Gotta be.

He hangs another. He moves on to another donkey, nooses it and makes to haul when he hears a solitary voice singing (an African song) from the mist of the fields.

BRAY: Oo's there?

Enter SOLOMON SINGO, a South African farmer, from the audience.

SINGO: Good day, friend.

BRAY: Come far 'ave we?

SINGO: Oh yes. Most definitely.

BRAY: Solomon Singo.

SINGO: My reputation precedes me.

BRAY: Stanley Bray.

SINGO: I see you've been doing all the donkey work, Stanley Bray.

BRAY: I got very little option, Solomon. It has to be done.

SINGO: Hah. I know your pain. Impressive work.

BRAY: I 'ear you was a bit of an expert yerself?

SINGO: I have dabbled. What made you do this, may I ask?

BRAY: Heard a voice one night. Saw this light. Felt a divine purpose come over me. I ad no choice. God made me do this. Lord knaws why.

SINGO says nothing.

BRAY: 'bout you, Sol? why'd *you* 'ang 'em?

SINGO: Ah! The very expensive question!

As SINGO tells his story, BRAY continues to hang donkeys…

SINGO: I did because, like you, I had no choice. I did it because my wife was dying… It all started when a herd of wild donkeys swarmed the farm!

Donkeys hee-haw.

SINGO: Hey! Hey! Hey! Where did you all come from? Back! H'up! Mother of God! This is Bad.

(To BRAY.) There were donkeys everywhere. Wild ones. They broke through the fences and trampled the crops. This is my livelihood. If they're too damaged –

BRAY: You get nuthin.

SINGO: I just need them rounded up. Please, I ask the authorities. *Alright, Singo. You want help? I'll send one o'the boys round in a buccy. But you'll hafto cull them yourself.* Will you leave me a gun? You see, I have no gun. *Gun? Listen to Singo. He wants a gun! You'll get no gun. Gun's too easy. You might get ideas. We'd have an insurrection on our hands. No. We'll leave you rope, Singo. Lots and lots of rope!*

BRAY hangs another.

SINGO: I tell them that hanging these creatures is impossible. There are too many! They remind me to do as I'm told. If I lose my job, how will I afford to pay for all that medication for my poor, sick wife? I will do my best, I tell them, with the rope they leave…

BRAY hangs another donkey.

42 DONKEYS HANGED.

BRAY: And you did it?

SINGO: I had nothing. No tools. No gun. I was a tenant farmer. I worked for the corporation. I was powerless. Of course I did it, Stanley. And oh, how I paid the price. First, I was a laughing stock from the other farmers for doing such a thing. Then the papers caught wind of it and turned me into a cruel and crazy donkey-hanging monster! People came to my home, in mobs, to pelt me with stones. I defended myself. My home. My family. I fought back. I had to. The authorities arrested me. I went to jail. I only did six months. But it was long enough. My wife died in the second month of my imprisonment. She died because I wasn't there to take care of her…

BRAY: What became of you?

SINGO: I faded away. Came to dust on the warm evening breeze… I became the only thing I had left… a story.

BRAY: And then that basterd went and stole it.

SINGO: Ah yes, this… what's his name?

BRAY: Thass the one. Writer Feller. Saw your story in the headlines. Took it 'ome with him. Changed it completely. Based me on you and a bit of 'is Uncle Trevor and ere we are!

Beat.

Huh. Basterd was tellin the truth, mind.

SINGO: I should very much like to meet with our Writer Friend.

BRAY: And you shall. I got the bugger trussed-up and knocked-out cold in me kitchen. Gyahhh!

BRAY HANGS THE 49TH DONKEY.

BRAY: There! Thass the lot ob'm. All 49. Jesus… looka that. Helluva thing.

SINGO: You've created a masterpiece, Stanley.

BRAY: But I feel no diff'rent. I was expectin… an answer.

SINGO: The truth is never that simple. It always has a greater price than you think.

BRAY: A price more'n this?

SINGO: We are at the mercy of strange and terrible forces, Stanley. Perhaps the hanging of these donkeys is simply a sign that, like me, you now have no other option but to confront those who seek to exploit you.

BRAY: 'hank you, Sol. Yer an inspiration. And you 'ave remembered me to my true purpose in life. Let's go kill Charles Growth.

They make for the farmhouse and stumble into –

JOY, who bars their way.

JOY: 'usband!

BRAY: Jesus, Joy. How'd you get out?

JOY: What 'ave you done?

BRAY: I can explain!

JOY: The boy's told me everythin.

BRAY: *(Sees GROSE watching from a distance.)* Whatever e's told ya, tis a lie.

JOY: Dun't look like much of a lie from where I'm standin, Stanley. Dear li'l donkeys… Bosanko is sullied! You need to go.

BRAY: Eh?

JOY: Get off my farm and never come back.

BRAY: Now Joy –

JOY: Cut down all these lub'ly strung-up li'l donkeys and sod off.

BRAY: Listen to me –

JOY: We've heard enuff from you! Ab'm we, Bobby?

GROSE: Yeh.

BRAY: Bobby?

JOY: Yes. E's alive, Stan! Our boy is alive! As if you didn't knaw!

BRAY: That ain't our son, dear.

JOY: 'course tis. Look at'n. E 'adn' changed one bit.

BRAY: E's an imposter, Joy. E needs stringin up!

GROSE: See, mother?

JOY: You touch one 'air on 'is head I will turn you inside out, man!

SINGO: *(To BRAY, quiet.)* Is this the writer?

BRAY: Thass 'im, Sol.

JOY: *(Re: SINGO.)* Oo the 'ell's this with ya now?

BRAY: This 'ere's Farmer Sol from Johannesberg. 'member 'im, Gross?

JOY: Johannesberg?!

SINGO: Hallo, Mr. Writer! It's Solomon. Solomon Singo.

GROSE stares in disbelief.

JOY: Oo's Solomon Singo when e's at 'ome?

GROSE: Ain't got a clue, mother.

BRAY: What you doin, Gross? Surely even you kent stoop this low?

GROSE: She wants you out, father! Sling yer 'ook!

JOY: Well said, Bobby.

GROSE: 'hanks, mum.

BRAY: Gyah, you f'kin –

Beat.

E's pulled the wool over yer eyes, wife. Just hand'n over to me, now.

JOY: Never! I just got'n back. I shan't lose'n again.

BRAY: This is cruel, Gross. Damned cruel.

GROSE: Same old shit from father, eh ma? The excuses, the endless stories. "Just poppin out, dear. Won't be long. No, you stay put, dear. Bring you 'ome a nice tasty pasty!" All the while e's hangin donkeys behind yer back.

JOY: That and worse, Bobby boy!

BRAY: 'is name is *Gross.*

JOY: Tis Bobby.

BRAY: Gross!

JOY: Tell'n, Bobby.

GROSE: *(To BRAY.)* Bobby. I'm Bobby.

SALLY: *(From out of nowhere.)* Gross!

They all turn. SALLY stands, with a face splattered with blood.

SALLY: E's f'kin Gross.

BRAY: Sally?

JOY: Thought I put ya down, Tregersick!

BRAY: What the 'ell are you doin ere?

SALLY: I knaw oo this chap is!

BRAY: I told ya to stay away!

SALLY: *(To GROSE.)* You're the donkey pervert from Trura!

JOY: Eh?

BRAY: Yes e is!

GROSE: No I'm not!

SALLY: Stanley's right, Joy. E ain't your boy. And I can prove it. Cus I saw what happened thirty year ago –

BRAY: Keep yer mouth shut, Sally.

SALLY: She needs to knaw the truth!

BRAY: Dun't you dare!

JOY: Truth? What truth?

SALLY: Joy, Bobby, yer boy, is –

BRAY: Alive and well! Our long-lost son is back. Right, Bobby?

GROSE: Ummm… Yep?

JOY: Thass what I bin tellin ya, Stanley! *(To GROSE.)* All this gross this and gross that from they lot. Why dun't they believe ya?

GROSE: They'm mad, mother.

SALLY: Stanley. Dun't do this. You gotta tell 'er the truth!

JOY: Slaughter-house Sally 'ccusin you a donkey bizniz sayin she knaws you –

GROSE: Never seen 'er before in me life!

BRAY: Get back to yer bonin floor, Sal.

GROSE: Not til she came through the front door with a Chipley Deluxe!

BRAY: Or I'll drown ya in the slurry pit!

SALLY: O, I give up!

JOY: What e mean you never seen 'er before?

GROSE: I ab'm. S'true, mother.

JOY: Then 'ow come you told me you saw 'em thirty year ago canoodlin down by the pond?

GROSE: Oh. Yeh. Well, I… I *did* see 'er *then*. When they was canoodlin. Down by the…pond.

JOY: So why say you never seen 'er before?

BRAY: Cus e was never there, Joy! Bobby was!

GROSE: It was a long time ago, mother. I was… a child.

BRAY: Bobby was ten.

GROSE: Thass it. I was ten. Ten years old.

JOY: No… You was *twelve*.

GROSE: I was… Was I? Yes, I think yer right, mother. I was twelve. Yep.

JOY studies GROSE intently.

GROSE: We must cast 'im out, mother! Look at this place! Bosanko Farm, once beautiful, now blighted. E brought this farm to ruin. Poisoned the land with buried secrets. E's a no-good basterd liar! Always was. Just like your father usta say.

JOY: Bobby? Look me square in the eye and tell me. Tell me you are Bobby.

GROSE: Oo else would I be, ma?

BRAY: E's a pryin donkey-obsessed –

SALLY: Pervert.

BRAY: Writer from Trura by the name of Carl Grose.

GROSE: Oh so NOW he gets it fucking right!

BOOM. Everyone stops. Stares. GROSE realizes his error.

GROSE: I mean… shit.

JOY: So you're *not* Bobby…?

GROSE: 'course I am. Don't be so –

Beat.

No, Joy. I'm not Bobby.

JOY: This was all lie?

GROSE: I don't belong here Joy. I'm sorry. I hafto go back.

JOY: So… e's gone? E's gone again? Just like that?

SALLY: *(To GROSE.)* How could you do such a thing?

GROSE: I hafto go.

GROSE starts to make his exit, and almost leaves when –

BRAY: "Grose finds himself pinned to the spot."

GROSE can't move.

GROSE: *(Unable to walk.)* What's going on? You can't do this!

BRAY: It appears I can. "Grose approaches the noose Bray has prepared for 'im."

GROSE: *(Against his will, GROSE starts to walk toward BRAY.)* No. No!

BRAY: You made me do such terrible things.

SALLY: You broke my heart and tried to kill me off.

JOY: You made me believe that my long-lost beloved son ad come back to me.

RANDY: You made me sing in a terrifically limited musical genre!

GROSE: I had to find a way out. Please! Forgive me? Joy?

GROSE is put in the noose.

JOY: 'ang 'im, Stanley.

GROSE: Oh god!

BRAY: This is the endin you ad in mind, Grose?

BRAY goes to hang him.

GROSE: Wait!

BRAY stops.

I wouldn't if I were you. This is my work and it's unfinished. Hang me and your whole world falls apart.

BRAY: We'll take our chances.

GROSE: I created you. I give you purpose.

BRAY: Once yer dead, we'll do what we like.

SINGO: Oh, yes. This is very true.

BRAY: It was nice for us to meet our maker.

SINGO: *(Into GROSE's ear.)* Now tis time to meet yours!

BRAY goes to hang GROSE.

GROSE: Stop! Let me live and I'll fix all this!

SALLY: Too late for that! I'm nearly dead!

BRAY goes to hang GROSE.

GROSE: Let me live and I'll write you all a happy ending… I can fix it! I swear!

JOY: 'ow?

GROSE: Bobby could come back, Joy! For real. Sally, you could have a successful operation and make a miraculous recovery! Randy, I could get you into rap! I could reverse it all!

BRAY: Sounds like a bollocks endin to me!

BRAY goes to hang GROSE.

GROSE: I'll tell her, Bray!

BRAY stops.

GROSE: I'll tell her everything. If I'm not Bobby, I can tell her the truth. I can tell her what happened that tragic day –

BRAY: Not if I 'ang you first, bud!

BRAY goes to hang GROSE.

SINGO: Stanley Bray.

BRAY: What is it, Sol?

SINGO: I really shouldn't intervene like this but… This is not the answer. This is not how it should end.

BRAY: Think we all agree tis the perfect endin!

He goes to hang GROSE.

SINGO: Hanging him will bring no peace. Look at him. Who is he? He is the one who has taken our stories, changed the facts, exploited our hearts – and for what? A few cheap laughs?

BRAY: E asta pay for what e's done!

SINGO: And he will. But there are other ways to pay.

BRAY: I got no choice in this!

SINGO: Today, you do. Trust me. Your task is done. The voice is gone. 49 donkeys hanged.

BRAY: And nuthin 'as changed!

SINGO: No, Stanley. Everything has! Look to where this journey has led you. You wanted illumination? Truth? This is the moment, Stanley Bray. Make. Your. Choice.

BRAY looks to JOY.

BRAY: Joy, I killed Bobby. Killed the boy by accident. E caught me and Sally together and I chase'n to stop 'im from tellin ya and e climbed the Blasted Oak and e fell. I kept the truth from ya cus I knew it'd kill you and I'd lose everythin. Each day I thought about tellin ya, but then, time went on and… I let it be. And I lived the lie.

Devastated, JOY walks off, back to the house.

BRAY: Thass the end o' that. The end of all things.

SINGO: What better place to begin than at the end?

BRAY: There's no comin back from that, Sol.

SINGO: Time will tell, Stanley Bray. Go to her.

BRAY makes his way back to the house.

SINGO: Sally, you must come with me now.

SALLY: Aw. Where we goin?

SINGO: We will let the wind take us. We will fade like thought into the light. We will become a sweet song in someone's dream…

SALLY: Okeedoke.

She stands with him. RANDY joins them.

SINGO: *(To GROSE.)* And you… what becomes of you?

GROSE: I go home?

SINGO: Home? You are home, Kenneth Grolsch.

GROSE: It's Carl… oh fuck it. Solomon, if I could just –

SINGO: You don't have a choice, brah. Go. Redeem yourself.

RANDY starts to play as GROSE makes his way to the farmhouse.

GROSE enters.

GROSE: Mother? Father? I'm back.

They stare at him.

GROSE: It's me. It's really me. I bin gone a long ole time, but I'm 'ome now. And I'm… 'ell, I'm 'ere to stay.

JOY: Bobby.

He is ushered in and made to sit. JOY talks to him continuously (with GROSE nodding or shaking his head at the various questions) throughout the following.

BRAY: *(To us.)* Turned out Solomon Singo was bang-on the munny. This was the endin we was after. And all it took was hangin a few donkeys. Our son Bobby was back. For real, this time. And with 'im properly alive, Joy could 'ardly 'ate me ad infinitum. Oh, it would take time, but time was summin we did 'ave. 'Twas a small wonder to see 'er smile again. Bobby was back. And so was Joy.

JOY: Stanley? Breakfast. We're wastin away ere.

BRAY: What'll it be today, dear?

JOY: Today I think I shall 'ave… egg.

BRAY: A fine choice. And you Bobby?

GROSE goes to speak but –

JOY: Egg. E'll have egg, wun't you, boy? Need summin in yer stomach if e's to work that farm. 220 acres is not to be sniffed at.

BRAY: Egg all round.

JOY: You mind you cook they eggs to perfection, Stanley Bray!

BRAY: Two'n 'alf minutes on the nail.

JOY: *(Looking out the window.)* What a view. I never tire of it. The valley and the fields and that. I could stare at it all day. Couldn't you Bobby? Aw yeh. I could stare and stare at this view forever…

GROSE lets this sink in. He stares at the view. His eyes fill with terror. Somewhere across the valley, a lone donkey brays.

RANDY sings us out.

RANDY: *When yer sinkin in the mud*
And there's no iron in yer blood
And there's no one to hear yer sorrow and woes!

When nerves quit a-feelin'
And words lose all their meanin'
Well, buddy that's just how it goes!

When the Heavens open up
And there's no wine in yer cup
And yer feelin dead from yer head to your toes!

When the Lord God above
Says the world's run outta love
Might as well hang a donkey I s'poze!

Might as well hang a donkey
Might as well hang a donkey
Might as well hang a donkey I s'poze!

THE END

THE KNEEBONE CADILLAC

The Kneebone Cadillac was performed at Theatre Royal Plymouth on Thursday 15 November 2018.

CAST *(in alphabetical order)*

Ennis Munroe	Shaun Jenkinson
Slick Kneebone	Callum Mcintyre
Jed Kneebone/Hooper Munroe/ Duke Longhorn	Glyn Pritchard
Phylis Vanloo/Loretta Kneebone	Emily Raymond
Maddy Kneebone	Hannah Traylen
Dwight Kneebone	Joe Wiltshire Smith

CREATIVE TEAM

Writer	*Carl Grose*
Director	*Simon Stokes*
Set & Costume Designer	*Bob Bailey*
Lighting Designer	*Andy Purves*
Sound Designer & Composition	*Dom Coyote*
asting Director	*Marc Frankum CDG*
Costume Supervisor	*Delia Lancaster*
Assistant Director	*Freddie Crossley*

PRODUCTION

Production Manager	*Hugh Borthwick*
Stage Manager	*Emily Bagshaw*
Deputy Stage Manager	*Claire Litton*
Assistant Stage Manager	*Mason Walter Cooper*
Sound Programmer	*Dan Mitcham*
Production Assistant	*Lauren Walsh*
Set & Costumes	*Theatre Royal Plymouth*
Cadillac & Chevrolet	*Russell Beck Studios*

In darkness, an air-horn blares. Epic cheering erupts and music pounds.

TANNOY: **Okee-dokee, is every bugger ready? Buckle up, bucket-heads! Tis time to eat dirt, taste blud and spit oil! We'm on a collision course for chaos! So let's put the pedal to the metal and git this show on the road! Drivers? Start yer engines!**

Many engines roar to life –

TANNOY: **ON YER MARKS… GET SET…** ***GOOOOO!!!***

The deafening howl of thirty cars tearing across the start line, then fade to –

Kneebone Scrap Metal and Haulage. A scrap yard half a mile outside United Downs, a post-industrial wasteland in the mid-Cornwall rust-belt.

Amongst the detritus we find the last surviving members of the Kneebone clan. SLICK (the eldest), DWIGHT (the middle child) and MADELINE (or MADDY – the youngest).

SLICK, breathless, pats down a mound of dirt before them and leans on his shovel.

MADDY: And you reckon this a good idea, Slick?

SLICK: Eh?

MADDY: Buryin Father in the f'kin scrap yard?

SLICK: To take 'is final rest in earth what remembers 'im. Like the 'ard rock miners of old. Tis want e wanted, Maddy.

DWIGHT: Tis what e wanted, Maddy.

MADDY: Coulda stuck 'im somewhere li'l bit nicer.

SLICK: Like where?

MADDY: Up on the ridge by the old mine stacks where Granddaddy 'eck's buried.

DWIGHT: Thass where the new Waitrose is goin.

MADDY: But did we hafta puddem in vertical?

SLICK: 'Bury me facin True West', e said. 'True West. Wimme boots on. Wimme 'ank Willams records. And put me in *straight* so I keep a beady eye on you buggers!' 'Twas 'is dyin wish, Baby Sister.

DWIGHT: There's no better restin place than this, Slick. S'lub'ly.

SLICK: Thass it, Dwight. E's in the ground now and 'appy.

DWIGHT: Ideal. We all done? Cus I got shit to do.

SLICK: No Dwight, we ain't 'done'. I gotta few words to impart…

(Solemn.) Daddy? You did things yer own way. You operated above the law and you bowed to no one. You built this mighty empire from the ground up with yer bare 'ands. Kneebone Scrap Metal and Haulage. Today, United Downs loses 'er fav'rite son. Jedidiah Kneebone. Father. Hero. Legend.

MADDY: E wadn't Clint f'kin Eastwood, Slick.

DWIGHT: No but e was close friends wi' the man, Maddy, so shut yer trap.

MADDY: Balls, bro. E never knew Clint Eastwood.

DWIGHT: E did too. Clint come round ere couple times when e was filmin up Charleston –

MADDY: 'Where Eagles Dare'.

DWIGHT: 'Where Eagles Dare' back in '68. Then e came ere again. Twenty odd years back. I was born. You wadn't.

MADDY: So you remember 'im do ya?

DWIGHT: Yeh. No. But Daddy tole me all about it.

MADDY: Aw well, it must be true!

SLICK: Christ! This is some solemn shit I'm doin right ere!

DWIGHT: Sorry Slick.

SLICK: *(Back to solemn.)* Like the long line of Kneebones before 'im, Daddy stood firm in the face of adversity –

MADDY: Clint Eastwood my ass.

SLICK: E… Aw, you pricks made me lose me thread now!

DWIGHT: Think you said some lub'ly shit, Slick. We done?

SLICK: No! Now let us honour 'is memory in song…

SLICK sings 'Rawhide'. He gives it everything.

SLICK: 'Keep rollin rollin rollin
Though the streams are swollen
Keep them dogies rollin, rawhide!
Through rain and wind and weather
'ell bent for leather
Wishin my gal was by my side
All the things I'm missin
Good vittles, love and kissin
Are waitin at the end of my ride – '

(To siblings, spoken.) As rehearsed!

DWIGHT and MADDY join in on the responses (in brackets).

ALL: 'Move 'em on! (head 'em up!)
Head 'em up! (move 'em on!)
Move 'em on! (head 'em up!)
RAWHIDE!
Cut 'em out! (ride 'em in!)
Ride 'em in! (cut 'em out!)
Cut 'em out! (ride 'em in!)
RAWHIDE!'

SLICK produces a whip and attempts to crack it.

SLICK: Hyaa! Hyaaa!

He falls before the grave.

SLICK: LOVE YOU, DADDY! F'KIN LOVE YOU!!!

DWIGHT: Jesus…

MADDY: *(To us.)* Sorry 'bout this. Fuck it. No I ain't. This is what it's like ere in United Downs, on the Kneebone ranch, wimme daft-as-assholes brothers. It's what tis always bin like. Although I must admit, things 'ave bin comin to an 'ead of late, what wi' Dad dyin and brother Slick's missis Carol leavin and takin li'l Kelly with 'er. Carol told me e was just too angry to be around.

SLICK pounds a tyre with an iron bar repeatedly.

SLICK: Why? Why? Why? Why? Why?! WHY?!!

MADDY: *(To us.)* Kent see it meself, can you? E was arrested up the pub last week for handin Nigel Lame 'is giblets.

SLICK bites the iron bar with rage.

MADDY: It does not go unnoticed round these parts that Slick is close to breakin…

SLICK: *(Finally calm.)* Be at peace, old man. Be at peace.

DWIGHT's mobile goes off to the tune of 'Who Let The Dogs Out'.

DWIGHT: Shit. Sorry.

(Answers, tries to be quiet.) O'right Ennis?

ENNIS: O'right Dwight? Can you talk or no?

DWIGHT: I kent, bud, no. I'm at me dad's funeral.

ENNIS: Aw right. You locate that missin package?

DWIGHT: I ain't ad a minute to look, bud. I'll get to it once we're done ere.

ENNIS: You gotta find it, Dwight. We're gonna die else. They're gonna kill us dead.

DWIGHT: Chillax, Ennis. I'll figure it out. Now just lay low and wait for me to call.

He hangs up.

SLICK: Oo was that?

DWIGHT: Wrong number.

MADDY: *(To us.)* That was Dwight's dipstick mate Ennis Munroe. Dwight kept this quiet from Slick cus the Munroe clan are sworn enemies o' the Kneebones and Slick would 'it the roof if e knew oo Dwight was hangin with. E'd also rip Dwight a new asshole if e knew the shit e and Ennis ad got into last week…

Last week, in moonlight –

DWIGHT: Evenin gentlemen. Thank you for comin.

Two MANCUNIAN DRUG LORDS enter.

MADDY: *(To us.)* The daft planks ad the bright idea to make their fortune at drug dealin-

MANCUNIAN DRUG LORD 1: What's with the scrap yard rendezvous in the dead of night, lads?

DWIGHT: We thought you'd appreciate the moody environs in which to do biznizz.

ENNIS: Tis like in the movies, eh?

MANCUNIAN DRUG LORD 1: We usually do biznizz in broad daylight –

MANCUNIAN DRUG LORD2: In Caffe Nero's.

MANCUNIAN DRUG LORD1: Draws less attention, ya know?

DWIGHT & ENNIS: Aw.

MADDY: *(To us.)* These were top Mancunian drug lords what ad come down, see? They'd sent down the merch for sellin. Now they'd come for their munny.

MANCUNIAN DRUG LORD 1: We've come for our munny.

MANCUNIAN DRUG LORD 2: You have got our munny, haven't you boys?

DWIGHT and ENNIS look to each other.

MADDY: *(To us.)* 'course they hadn't got their munny. They ad failed to sell a single speck of it. I wouldn't buy nice quality drugs off these two f'kin pebbles, would you?

MANCUNIAN DRUG LORD 1: You said you'd done this before.

DWIGHT: Totally, pard. Totally.

ENNIS: Sell drugs to anyone we can.

DWIGHT: Yeh. Small kids. Old… women.

ENNIS: Animals.

MANCUNIAN DRUG LORD 1: You sell drugs to animals?

DWIGHT: Usually. Usually this stuff's flyin off the shelves.

MANCUNIAN DRUG LORD 2: How much did you manage to sell?

DWIGHT: Not much of it.

ENNIS: Not none of it.

DWIGHT: So we'd like to give the whole lot back!

DWIGHT holds up the package of drugs.

MANCUNIAN DRUG LORD 1: Give it back? Ya can't do that.

MANCUNIAN DRUG LORD 2: I knew it. Big Drug Cheeses my arse!

ENNIS: *(Suddenly wide-eyed and strange.)* Whaddid you call me?

DWIGHT: E called you a Big Cheese, bud.

ENNIS: Am I?

He starts to look about him, terrified.

DWIGHT: You o'right, mate?

MADDY: *(To us.)* Turns out they was so terrified about handin the drugs back unsold they decided to chug back whatever dregs o' drugs they ad left over from Trevithick Day revels –

ENNIS: *(Coming up.)* I'm a BIG CHEESE…?!!

MADDY: *(To us.)* Dutch courage was the thinkin. Daft twats.

ENNIS: I 'ate cheese, Dwight! I kent stand it! I kent be cheese!

VOICE: Oi! Oo's there!

An Alsatian barks, off. Torchlight sweeps.

MANCUNIAN DRUG LORD 2: What the fook's going on?

MANCUNIAN DRUG LORD 1: Oo's this now?

DWIGHT: Shit! Coppers!

ENNIS: Chuck the drugs, Dwight!

In his drug-addled confusion, DWIGHT hurls the package into darkness.

MANCUNIAN DRUG LORD 2: What ya doin, ya bluddy amateurs?!

DWIGHT: Ad to ditch it, mate! They'll arrest us!

MANCUNIAN DRUG LORD 1: Ya prize knob! That's our merchandise!

Dog barks closer –

MANCUNIAN DRUG LORD 2: We'll be back for you two!

They run off.

ENNIS: F'kin *cheeeeeseeee!!!*

ENNIS and DWIGHT howl as they collapse into their bad trips.

Back to the funeral –

MADDY: *(To us.)* It wadn't the police at all but good ole Taffy, the yard 'and, doin a rare security check with 'is Alsatian dog, Samantha. The night, though, was a total calamity.

(To DWIGHT.) Found they drugs, bro?

DWIGHT: *(Whispering.)* I kent find 'em anywhere. And if I kent find 'em, I gotta re-pay the munny. And if I kent re-pay the munny the Manchester Crew'll 'and me and Ennis our bodger'n balls!

MADDY: How much was it worth?

DWIGHT: 'leb'm.

MADDY: 'undred?

DWIGHT: No.

MADDY: Thousand?! Dwight, you dob-head!

DWIGHT: Dun't tell Slick will ya, Baby Sister?

MADDY: *(To us.)* So thass me brothers. Hangin by their fingernails, the pair ob'm. And me? I'm about to make it a whole lot worse.

SLICK: Gather round, family. As you know, before Daddy died, e summoned all of us to 'is bedside one be one so e could make 'is peace. You should knaw now that in 'is final moments e entrusted to me 'is Winchester rifle –

DWIGHT: Not the one off the kitchen wall?!

SLICK: Yes. That gun is a symbol –

DWIGHT: I ad me eye on that.

SLICK: Tuff. E gave it to me. Tis a symbol –

MADDY: Fake anyway, innit? Dun't actually work.

SLICK: Yes it do. Daddy usta shoot adders up the field with it. She was passed down from Great Great Granddaddy Tobias to Grandpa Heck to Daddy to me and tis a symbol –

DWIGHT: Thass bullshit. All e gave me was this! 'is crappy ring.

MADDY: 'is Masonic Ring.

SLICK: Tis a symbol o' Kneebone strength –

DWIGHT: Dad wadn't even in the Masons!

MADDY: So? It'll get ya free parkin up Trura.

DWIGHT: F'kin lame-ass ring.

SLICK: Will you quit goin on about yer damned ring and be thankful to Daddy for bequeathin anything at all!

DWIGHT: Thass o'right for you to say. You gotta cool bleddy gun!

SLICK: And that gun is a *symbol* of Kneebone strength and say-so which'd mean I am now in charge! OK? This yard's mine. 'ouse. Biznizz too.

MADDY: 'ang on a minute-

SLICK: What I say goes! *I* am now head o' the family!

MADDY: Dick-head o' the family.

DWIGHT: Ha.

SLICK goes to deck DWIGHT.

She said it!

MADDY: Ha.

DWIGHT: What e leave you thun?

MADDY: Eh?

DWIGHT: Daddy bestow you anythin?

SLICK: 'er? I doubt it.

MADDY: What e mean? Yeh! 'course e did! I was 'is fav'rite.

SLICK: No you wadn't!

DWIGHT: What e leave ya?

MADDY: Guess.

DWIGHT: If tis bigger'n this ring I shall go f'kin bananas!

SLICK: She's pullin yer leg, bro. It wun't be much. What e give ya? 'is John Wayne belt-buckle? The Graceland shoe-horn? 'is Texan tooth-picks?

DWIGHT: C'on thun, spit it out!

MADDY: You ain't gonna like it, boys.

SLICK: Tell us!

MADDY: The Cadillac, dear brothers. Daddy left me the Cadillac!

SLICK & DWIGHT: *WHAT?!*

VVVVVVRRRRR-RRRROOOOMMMMMMMMMMMMMMM!!!!!!

TANNOY: ***Annnnnd* they're off! The shit's flyin and the loser is buyin! The question on all of our lips is: oo will survive and what will be left ob'm?**

The Kneebone lock-up.

Before MADDY is the shape of something magnificent covered by an old tarpaulin. She throws it back, reveals a car, and climbs into the driving seat of –

The Kneebone Cadillac.

She puts her hands on the wheel, closes her eyes and inhales deeply-

MADDY: And it's Madeline Kneebone in 'er father's exquisite 1958 Cadillac Eldorado. The infamous vehicle known throughout United Downs to be 'is pride and joy. A car e fawned and fussed over more'n 'is damned family! Now ere she is, shreddin up the Race-Way with 'is only daughter at the wheel! Born to burn rubber, yes, Kneebone has taken the f'kin curve! She's in the f'kin lead! She's headed for the f'kin finish line and –

A match is struck and a cigar is lit. Someone's there. In the shadows. A man in a cowboy hat. The GHOST OF JED KNEEBONE.

MADDY: I dun't believe in ghosts.

JED: Neither do I, but ere we are.

MADDY: 'hanks for the car, Dad.

JED: I aren't usin it no more.

MADDY: Brothers 'it the roof when I told 'em. Slick said I wadn't worthy.

JED: You aren't. Not yet.

MADDY: Time to prove 'em wrong. Time to enter The Boneshaker.

JED: I give you my beloved car and yer big plan is to smash it to smithereens?

MADDY: Stipulation for entry, pops.

JED: Right. Gotta be vintage. Gotta be American. Ker-rist.

MADDY: You took me to they races. Tis your fault I'm a fanatic.

JED: If yer gunna do this you'll need to fix 'er up proper.

MADDY: I'm a kipper wi' cars. Learnt from the best.

JED: She need more care and attention than you can provide.

MADDY: Any suggestions?

JED: Just one. 'ooper Munroe.

MADDY: Munroe? I thought you couldn't stand 'im?

JED: I 'ate 'is basterd guts. But e's the only sonofagun I trust in the whole damn Duchy whass skilled enuff to treat my baby girl the way she deserve.

MADDY: Thanks Dad...

JED: The car, I'm talkin about.

MADDY: 'ooper's sought after. Three month waitin list. Why'd e stoop to help a Kneebone?

JED: Cus e owes me one. You tell'n from me, the rage-riddled spirit o' Jedidiah Kneebone, that slimy no gud basterd owes me BIG TIME!!!

MADDY: What're the chances, you reckon? Of me? Winnin The Boneshaker? And 'ooper Munroe agreein to fix 'er up? And gettin one over on my two twatty brothers? And of this car whass bin sat ere for years ever even startin at all?

JED: Only one way to find out.

She turns the key. Nothing. But then – a splutter. It catches, splutters, rattles and roars into life!

MADDY: For Death or Glory, eh Dad?

She looks around but, of course, he isn't there.

MADDY: *(To us.)* Tis a trick tryin to maintain a low profile in a vintage Cadillac Eldorado but I take 'er through the back gates and out over the Badlands so me brothers wouldn't catch me. After the funeral Slick tasked me wi' sortin the spread for Father's wake that night. With any luck I'd be back from 'ooper Munroe's in time so as not to arouse any suspicion… Ha. Best laid plans… But what could I do? I ad destiny callin. *Destiny.*

The sound of the Caddy rattling into –

Munroe's Motors, out Blackwater.

Enter HOOPER MUNROE, wiping his hands with an oily rag.

MADDY: Howdy, mister. Beautiful day.

HOOPER: Answer's no.

MADDY: I ab'm asked a question yet.

HOOPER: I knaw what yer gonna ask. I'm too busy.

MADDY: But this ere's no ordinary car.

HOOPER: I knaw zackly what kinda car it is. I reckernise it of old. I also knaw oo it belong to, too. Which is why, despite sendin oo I presume is 'is daughter round to do 'is dirty work, I shan't be acceptin any biznizz off you today, 'hanks all the same.

MADDY: E's dead. We buried'm today. In the yard.

HOOPER: You shoulda put the basterd through the crusher, just to be sure.

MADDY: I heard tell you two didn't see eye to eye.

HOOPER: Ain't that the Understatement o' the Year. Look, I'm sorry for yer loss but I got work to do.

MADDY: Car's mine. E left it me.

HOOPER: Helluva legacy.

MADDY: I'm gonna enter the race with it.

HOOPER: What race?

MADDY: Boneshaker.

HOOPER: Hah.

MADDY: Summin funny, bud?

HOOPER: That race ain't for beginners, girl.

MADDY: I bin drivin since I was six.

HOOPER: What I mean is, it ain't for the faint of heart.

MADDY: I'm Jed Kneebone's girl. Father dragged me to every ear-bleedin contest when I was a tacker. I seen car carnage on the Race-Way up close and full-throttle. Every lung-full o' burnin petrol, every tyre-shriek and blow-out, every chassis-crunchin collision I bore witness to made me love this circus of chaos more! I studied every gear-grindin psycho on the track…

HOOPER: You see the masters at work? 'ank Carlyon? Barry Polmassick? Jonnie 'T-Bird' Hawkins? Then you'll knaw it's no picnic.

MADDY: I'd have that lot fer breakfast and shit 'em out be noon.

HOOPER: Bold words.

MADDY: That silky lot never did much for me. My hero and the true star of the Race-Way was always Phylis Vanloo.

HOOPER: Vanloo? Christ. Thass goin back.

MADDY: She's prolly retired now. Or in traction.

HOOPER: Or dead.

MADDY: I remember the first time I seen 'er. 'Twas the day o' The Great Boneshaker 30 Car Pile-up…

PHYLIS VANLOO enters in her prime, all black leather and yellow and white lightning bolts.

MADDY: She strode out from the pit to 'er car. I was 'angin off the wall, eyes agog at 'er banger. Though you could hardly call it that. She drove a vintage hearse, immaculate oil-black Chevrolet, wi' jags o' steel teeth for the fender. She called it The Banshee…

PHYLIS: *(To MADDY.)* Some f'kin car, eh? 740 'orse power'd throb under that bonnet. You 'it the gas, she 'ollers like all 'ell's at yer 'eels.

MADDY: She's beautiful. Can I –

PHYLIS: You keep yer greasy mits off! She just bin waxed. Whass yer name, maid?

MADDY: Maddy.

PHYLIS: Kneebone spawn ain't ya?

MADDY: Yes I am.

PHYLIS: And whadda you wanna be when you grow up?

MADDY: Gonna be a stock car racer. Like you.

PHYLIS: You'll never be like me, girlie. There can be only one queen o' the Race-Way.

MADDY: How'd you knaw yer gonna win?

PHYLIS: I fear nuthin. Knaw why? Cus God 'erself blessed me wi' zero imagination. I cannot picture pain, therefore I do not concern meself with it. In that respect, I am free.

MADDY: To do what?

PHYLIS: To become one wi' the car. Blud and metal. Dashboard and bone. And in that one sweet moment I am free from the endless toil o' this shit-ass life. Death or

Glory! I got no time for the mamby-pamby in betweens. *Kill me or crown me queen!* See what I'm sayin?

MADDY nods.

PHYLIS: Enjoy the race, kid.

She exits.

HOOPER: She did become one with the car that day. One o' the most horrific collisions I've ever seen.

MADDY: But she won.

HOOPER: She paid the price.

MADDY: Death or Glory.

HOOPER: Yer as mad as 'er.

MADDY: I take that as a compliment. So will ya?

HOOPER: Will I what?

MADDY: Fix 'er up?

HOOPER: I repeat. Answer's no.

MADDY: But e told me to come to you.

HOOPER: Yeh. To piss me off!

MADDY: E said you owed 'im one.

HOOPER: I dun't owe that awful basterd one goddamn thing!

MADDY: What e ever do to you?

HOOPER: It's what e did to everyone in United Downs! Yer father was a thief. A cheat. A bare-faced liar. All excuses when e ad to cough up. All spit'n fisticuffs when someone crossed'n. Always played it like e was better'n the rest of us. And cruel! I've never knawn anyone so cruel. Cruel to the bone e was. Cruel to everyone. And cruellest of all to yer poor mother, God rest 'er soul!

MADDY: Did you know 'er?

HOOPER: I knew 'er. Everyone came to the Race-Way back then.

MADDY: What was she like?

HOOPER: She was a sweet-pea in a sea o' sewage!

MADDY: We never speak of 'er at 'ome.

HOOPER: I kent imagine yer brothers havin a good word to say 'bout anyone.

MADDY: They ain't so bad.

Enter ENNIS from the garridge with phone.

ENNIS: Dad, tis 'ank Carlyon. E wants to knaw if 'is axle's –

He sees MADDY and stares.

MADDY: 'right Ennis?

He stares.

ENNIS: Hi Maddy.

HOOPER: *(Takes phone, to DWIGHT.)* Piss off thun.

ENNIS: Bye Maddy.

Exit ENNIS.

HOOPER: E ain't biologically mine. I wanna make that quite clear. Nice lad but ultimately a waste o' bleddy space.

(To phone.) Be right with you, 'ank.

(To MADDY.) I gotta go.

MADDY: This car ain't gonna fix itself!

HOOPER: Listen. As pleasant as you seem to be, there's nuthin in this world would make me wanna 'elp that nasty shit out – even if e is dead! Which, by the way, I'm glad e is! Now do me a favour, take yer car and never come back!

MADDY: Yer undecided. I'll pop back later, shall I?

HOOPER: Fuck off, Kneebone!

TANNOY: **Boom! Thass a punch to the gut that'll cost 'er precious time. She'll hafto think fast if she's to crawl out this one!**

Kneebone home. Night.

SLICK is drunk and in mid-flow. He's in his daddy's Stetson. He swigs from a can of beer. The Winchester rifle is nearby. MADDY sits at a table with a pile of old ledgers and mouldy shoe-boxes full of receipts and invoices. She adds things up on an old calculator. DWIGHT glumly sits eating a tray of cocktail pasties.

SLICK: Not one basterd came! Not one! Oo do they think they are? To not turn up to Daddy's wake? After the spread we laid on? Free cocktail pasties! Eh? Man of 'is stature? Rude! Where's the sense of whassiscalled? Spus to be a celebration of 'is life, ya knaw?

MADDY: Nice of Carol to show 'er face.

SLICK: Carol? She was the one person I *didn't* want comin!

MADDY: She thought the world o' Dad.

SLICK: She wun't welcome! Not in this house!

DWIGHT: She made 'er choice when she dumped you, Slick.

SLICK: She didn't dump me, Dwight. She walked out, OK? And good riddance say I!

MADDY: 'Twas a peace offerin, Slick. She wants you to see yer daughter. Sendin yer off, like that? Shootin yerself in the fut!

Drains a beer, crushes a can, chucks it.

SLICK: For generations we Kneebones 'ave stood firm in the face of adversity, ya knaw? Ya knaw? Once, we was men! Borne from the earth! Hewn from granite! Shaped be the 'ands o' Nature! We looked like Clint, for godsake. Not now, mind. Now we look like f'kin Dwight!

DWIGHT: 'anks very much.

The GHOST OF JED enters besides SLICK. MADDY sees him. The others don't.

SLICK: True! Fled at the first sign o' trouble this afternoon, ya yella-bellied coward! Thank God I was ere to see'n off. You woulda bin proud, Daddy! Debtors ad the place surrounded. Small army ob'm. Ad us under siege. Some fight.

(Mimes pot-shots.) Pow! Chtt-Chtt! Pow! Chtt-Chtt! Turns out this wadn't a replica after all, eh Madeline? Took that basterd bailiff's earlobe clean off. Helluva shot. I sent 'em packin, Daddy.

MADDY: For the meantime.

SLICK: They wun't risk comin back ere. Not now they've tasted Kneebone fire.

MADDY: Slick? This final tax demand? It all adds up.

(Showing countless letters.) There's decades o' back-dated unpaid fines ere. Father never paid a penny o' tax in 'is life!

SLICK: E was above all that shit.

(To heaven.) Wadn't you, Daddy?

JED: I'm over ere, ya prick.

MADDY: Eighty-nine thousand pound and forty-nine pee!

DWIGHT: We're so screwed.

SLICK: No we ain't! We fight the basterds!

MADDY: *(Holding it up and waving it.)* They gived us a Notice of Eviction, Slick!

SLICK: They can go to 'ell.

MADDY: We got seb'm days 'fore they send in the bulldozers and level this place flat.

DWIGHT: Then what?

MADDY: They'll sell this land to pay off Dad's enormous f'kin debt and we'll be homeless, brother!

DWIGHT stuffs another pasty in his gob.

SLICK: They kent take our 'ome! This is Kneebone territory! I'd head 'em off at the pass! Take 'em all out! We'm outlaws now, my bewties! Jus' like Daddy! Yeeee-hoooo!

MADDY: This is f'kin serious, Slick! We're gonna lose everythin! All thanks to 'im!

SLICK: Hey!

MADDY: Keep defendin 'im, Slick, but yer the one liable for this debt.

SLICK: Me?!

MADDY: Yer head o' the family now, remember?

SLICK: Shit.

MADDY: Thass sobered 'im up!

DWIGHT: So all this is Slick's problem? Thank God.

MADDY: It's all our problem, Dwight. We need to put our heads together and figure out just what the fuck we're gonna do about it.

SLICK: If they're comin back, we'll need more ammo.

MADDY: No. Dun't need ammo, Slick. We *need* to pay this debt off. Thass the reality of it.

SLICK: We need a bleddy bright idea.

DWIGHT: We need a munny-makin scheme.

MADDY: We need a f'kin miracle.

DWIGHT: I got summin.

MADDY: What is it, Dwight?

DWIGHT: Kidnap Prince Charles.

MADDY: Aw God.

SLICK: Wait. Let's 'ear 'im out. Keep talkin, bro.

DWIGHT: Well, we… we uhh… yeh, we kidnap Prince Charles.

SLICK: 'ow?

DWIGHT: Umm. Well. Thass as far as I got re: any elaboration of a plan. But e's always down on royal visits inne?

MADDY: E does own 'alf the f'kin place.

DWIGHT: Zackly. Plenty of chances to nab 'im. Shouldn't be too tricky to infiltrate one of 'is ribbon-cuttin Duchy Biscuit affairs or whatever. We lie in wait. In disguise. We catch the bugger. Hold'n hostage. Charge eighty-nine grand forty-nine pee for his release. Job done.

SLICK: 'bout Camilla?

MADDY: Ere, get double for Camilla.

DWIGHT: Now yer talkin.

SLICK: Not a bad idea that, bro.

DWIGHT: Yeh?

MADDY: No. It ain't a bad idea. It's the worst idea I ever heard!

DWIGHT: O'right Maddy. I dun't see you bringin any offers to the table.

SLICK: 'old 'ard. I got it. I know zackly what to do. Arizona.

MADDY: What about it?

SLICK: We go there.

MADDY: Why?

SLICK: Cus thass where the gold is.

DWIGHT: What gold?

SLICK: Daddy's gold what e always spoke of in stories. That lost fortune out in the Americas wi' the family name on it. The uhh…

MADDY: The Kneebone Bonanza.

SLICK: Thass it.

MADDY: Damme Slick, that dun't exist! Tis one of 'is made up stories!

SLICK: You say that sister, but I bin rootin through Daddy's possessions –

JED: Nosey li'l shit.

SLICK: And I found this…

He clumsily produces a small wooden chest and shares the contents.

SLICK: This ere's a well-old photo o' Great-Great-Granddaddy Tobias. Emigrated from St. Day in eighteen 'undred and summin for the mines and fell in wi' a 'ard rock crowd oo 'it the mother-lode out in the Arizona mountains. Gold.

DWIGHT: Yes!

SLICK: Daddy said the venture ended in betrayal and bloodshed and all were killed –

MADDY: Funny that.

SLICK: The whereabouts o' the shaft was lost to all but for the fact that Tobias's missis oo's name is now long forgot –

MADDY: Jenny Retallack.

SLICK: Wrote down the exact location in a letter which Daddy said she sent back 'ome ere right before she died. Daddy tole me 'is father kept these secret dreck'shuns in a small book of 'is, a crappy ole diary, which Daddy said mysteriously vanished after 'eck's untimely death.

DWIGHT: But you found it?

SLICK: Well. Ere's the thing. No. But this photo is of Granddaddy standin outside the actual mine.

MADDY: E's standin outside *a* mine, Slick.

SLICK: And if ya need any more convincin there's this.

He produces a rusty old tobacco tin. He shakes it. Something rattles inside. He opens it.

SLICK: Behold!

They all look into the tin.

DWIGHT: Holy shit. What is it?

SLICK: Gold! A sweet, sweet nugget sent 'ome from the Kneebone mother-lode!

SLICK holds it up.

MADDY: It's a speck!

SLICK: It's a taster! There's more where that came from! And we're gonna find it!

DWIGHT: F'kin YES!

MADDY: With Great Great Grannie Retallack's ancient treasure map whass in Granddaddy 'eck's secret diary that you kent find?

SLICK: Zackly! Daddy's showin us the way. All we gotta do is get out there and take it!

JED: Yup. Thass all you gotta do, boy.

SLICK: Arizona! Oo's wimme?

DWIGHT: I'll go. Sounds brilliant.

MADDY: This is f'kin nuts.

JED: Ha!

MADDY: Havin fun, pops?

JED: Tis better'n bleddy telly!

MADDY: This is all your fault!

DWIGHT: Oo she talkin to?

MADDY: I aren't goin Arizona just cus Father fucked it up!

SLICK: You take that back.

MADDY: C'mon Slick! You knaw e's to blame for the shit we're in!

SLICK: How dare you say that 'bout Daddy! The legacy e left us!

MADDY: What legacy? E left us piss all but a yard fulla junk and a mountain o' debt and a huge heap o' hate from the good people of United Downs.

SLICK: Basterds!

MADDY: They ain't basterds, Slick, they kent stand us. Knaw why? Cus father was such a monumental asshole!

DWIGHT: 'least e left you a Caddy, Maddy!

MADDY: Yeh and I kent do nuthin with it cus no bugger'll fix 'er up cus Jed was such a shit in life!

SLICK: Fix 'er up? Oo's fixin 'er up?

JED: Uh-oh.

MADDY: No one.

SLICK: You ab'm better o' taken that car out, girl.

MADDY: 'course I ab'm. She dun't even go anyhow.

SLICK: So you've tried to start 'er up?

MADDY: Yeh. No. Bin sat in the shed for years annit?

SLICK: If yer lyin to me I'll f'kin-

MADDY: I aren't. Anyhow, it's my car.

SLICK: It ain't your car! Dun't touch it. Dun't even look at it. Daddy's Caddy. Got it?

Enter ENNIS, breathless.

ENNIS: 'right, Dwight?

DWIGHT: Dude, what you doin ere?

SLICK: Munroe's boy?!

MADDY: Aw shit.

SLICK: Whass all this thun? 'ooper send you over did e? Come to rub our nawses in it 'ave ya? Come to gloat, now that Daddy's dead?

ENNIS: Actually I just needed a quick word wi' Dwight.

(To DWIGHT.) You found they drugs yet?

DWIGHT: Shhh –

SLICK: Drugs? What drugs? Whass e talkin about?

DWIGHT: I 'ave absolutely no idea whatsoever.

ENNIS: Yes you do. Our big drug deal what went wrong in your scrap yard, remember?

DWIGHT: Rings a bell, yeh.

SLICK: You did dodgy dealins in Daddy's yard?

ENNIS: And now the Manchester Crew wanna kill us.

SLICK: *(With gun.)* They'll hafto get in line. We dun't like Munroes on our land. Never 'ave done.

MADDY: Slick, put the gun down. Dwight, get 'im out of ere 'fore there's bloodshed.

DWIGHT: We're goin.

He's just about to exit when –

ENNIS: (*To MADDY.*) Good to see you at me dad's earlier, Maddy.

SLICK: Wait. Whaddid you say?

MADDY: Go on, you two. Fuck off.

SLICK: *(Aims gun.)* Stop right there. Siddown Ennis. Chillax. Cocktail pasty? Cheese on a stick?

ENNIS: *(Quiet, wide-eyed horror.)* Cheese…

MADDY: Slick-

SLICK: You said you see Maddy earlier?

ENNIS: Umm…

SLICK: At yer dad's garridge?

ENNIS: Well…

SLICK: What was she doin there, Ennis Munroe?

MADDY: I was gettin diesel for the –

SLICK: Ennis Munroe I'm talkin to!

(To ENNIS.) Well? What was Maddy doin there? Talkin to yer dad? Talkin to… 'ooper Munroe? What about, Ennis? What was the topic o' conversation?

ENNIS starts to trip-out again under the pressure.

ENNIS: They was… I dun't… aw God! They was talkin about fixin up a car! The car she bought in! An old, beat-up Cadillac!

MADDY: Slick, I can explain.

SLICK: You went to 'ooper wi' that car?

MADDY: I'm gonna enter The Boneshaker with it.

SLICK: Yer gonna do what?

MADDY: I'm gonna win the big prize!

SLICK: Oh no you're not, maid.

MADDY: Ten grand, Slick!

SLICK: Thass a piss in the ocean next to Arizona. Forget The Boneshaker.

MADDY: Do what I like. Tis my car.

SLICK: It's Daddy's.

MADDY: E gave it to me on 'is damn death bed.

DWIGHT: Why the 'ell Daddy give 'er the Caddy?

SLICK: E was between worlds, Dwight. E didn't know what e was doin.

DWIGHT: All I got was this shitty ring.

SLICK: You kent 'ave it. She's too precious. She's priceless!

MADDY: Priceless my ass!

SLICK: That car usta belong to Elvis!

MADDY: Did it bollocks!

SLICK: Plus it 'as great sentimental value. I was conceived in that car!

DWIGHT: So was I!

SLICK: You was Redruth Cinema!

ENNIS: Slick's right, Dwight. Me dad said the car was prolly worth a bob or two.

MADDY: Nobody's askin you, Ennis.

ENNIS: I'm just sayin, you could 'awk the vehicle and pay off the Manchester Crew easy.

DWIGHT: Really? And the debtors too? What about it, Slick?

SLICK: We ain't sellin the Caddy!

MADDY: No f'kin way. I need that car!

SLICK: You dun't get a say in the matter!

DWIGHT: Be better off sellin it than seein it get trashed in a stock car race!

SLICK: Over my dead body do we sell that car to some rich wanker on eBay and over my dead body again does that car go in The Boneshaker!

MADDY: You dunno what this means to me! I bin gearin up to this moment me whole life!

SLICK: I dun't give two shits what it means! I've solved the damned problem! We are goin to Arizona! All of us!

ENNIS: What me and all?

ALL: NO!

MADDY: Arizona's a damned fairy tale, Slick! There is no gold!

SLICK: Get this through yer thick head! I'm in charge! You do as I say! I'm daddy now! O'right? I got the 'at, the boots and I got the Winchester! And anyone oo dares cross me gets peppered wi' lead!

SLICK has the rifle and aims it at them all.

ENNIS: E's bleddy lost it.

SLICK: Damn right I 'ave, Ennis Munroe! I gotta keep this family together, 'ave I? Thass my job izzit? I ask for this, did I? No I bleddy never! I jus' wanna ride the plains, ya knaw? Instead I gotta deal wi' prick-asses like 'ooper Munroe and son! Ex-wives stickin their nawses in! Whole villages oo diss my daddy by not turnin up to pay their *respects!* (thass the word!) And to cap it all, my idiot family do the f'kin reverse o' what I tell'n to! Well, knaw what? I've… ad e-*f'kin… NUFFFFFFFF!*

SLICK emits a primordial howl and runs outside with the Winchester. We hear the gun go off several times. BLAMM! BLAMM!

ENNIS: Bleddy 'ell! Oo's e shootin at?

BLAMM!

MADDY: You boys better scram. I'll take care o' Captain Insanity out there.

DWIGHT puts his thumbs up and he and ENNIS run off.

(To us.) I followed the sound o' Winchester gun-shot into the thick black night and out into the Badlands – that skull-littered, burnt-out car-scarred arsenic-drenched waste-ground behind the yard…

In the dark –

MADDY: Slick?

BLAMM! BLAMM!!! BLAMMM!!! She finds him.

Put it down, brother!

SLICK: If I wanna shoot the shit outta shit then thass what I shall do!

MADDY: Look, I'm sorry I went to 'ooper but Father's ghost told me to go there.

SLICK: Dun't take the piss outta me, girl.

MADDY: I aren't! I swear, Slick, I bin seein 'im ever since e died. Smellin 'is cigars, ya knaw?

SLICK: Seein 'im? Why you seein' 'im? Why kent I see'n? Why kent I smell'n? Why you?!

MADDY: Dun't ask me how it works, bro. Dead can do what they like, it seems. Tis only us alive ones oo kent fart without the sky crashin down.

Beat.

'ooper refused to fix 'er up.

SLICK: Thass some gud news.

MADDY: Why dun't we work on 'er together?

SLICK: So you can go smash the shit out of it?

MADDY: I'll do ya proud, Slick. You and Daddy. You'll see.

SLICK: The Eldorado is a Kneebone family heirloom. It does not belong to you.

MADDY: I'm Kneebone! I'm family! Why kent it be mine?

SLICK: No, see… no.

MADDY: Look, I kent 'elp it if I was 'is fav'rite.

SLICK: Fav'rite? How could you possibly be 'is fav'rite?

MADDY: P'raps cus, I dunno, I'm 'is only daughter?

SLICK: Yeh but yer not, though, are ya?

MADDY: Ha ha.

SLICK: Yeh but… you *aren't* Jed's child, Maddy. You do knaw that, dun't ya?

MADDY: Dick.

SLICK: Deep down, Baby Sister, you knaw it to be true.

MADDY: Yer fulla shit, Slick.

SLICK: Dun't you feel it? Yer diff'rent to the rest of us.

MADDY: Yeh, I got a brain.

SLICK: You know what I mean.

MADDY: Yer lyin. Jed's my dad.

SLICK: No Maddy. E's not.

MADDY: I think e'd a told me after all these years.

SLICK: P'raps e couldn't bring 'imself to after mother died. P'raps e just likes to keep a gud story spinnin.

MADDY: If e idn' me dad then oo is?

SLICK: Take a punt, why dun't ya?

MADDY: Tell me!

SLICK: Oo'd ya think? Oo's the screamin bleddy obvious? C'mon Madeline. Oo did Daddy's ghost send ya to accidentally on purpose?

MADDY: 'ooper?

SLICK: Why'd ya think Daddy despised Munroe so much? Munroe ad an ding-dong wi' mother. A ding-dong down at the Race-Way. A ding-dong that dumped you into this caper. Thass why the Caddy ain't yours Maddy – cus you ain't pure Kneebone. Never 'ave bin.

Blue flashing lights and police sirens approach through the darkness.

SLICK: Look oo it idn! Debtor wi' the shot-off earlobe musta dobbed me in!

(Shouting.) C'mon thun, ya basterds! You'll never take me alive! Weee-hooooo!

He fires the gun again – BLAMM! – and he exits into darkness.

MADDY: Slick! Wait!

(To us.) But e lost 'imself to the darkness wi' the law 'ot on 'is 'eels.

DWIGHT: *(Off.)* 'elp! 'elp! Christ. Now what?

MADDY: *(To us.)* I ran back to the yard, followin Dwight's cries for 'elp –

DWIGHT and ENNIS sit screaming inside the Caddy whilst one of the TWO MANCUNIAN DRUG LORDS glugs petrol from a canister over the hood.

MADDY: *(Arriving.)* Oi! Whass goin on!

ENNIS: Thank God! It's yer little sister!

DWIGHT: Maddy! Get Slick!

MADDY: E's gone.

MANCUNIAN DRUG LORD: Back off, love. This dun't concern you.

MADDY: Actually it does, love, cus thass my Caddy you're pourin petrol on. You two the Manchunian Drug Lords, I take it?

MANCUNIAN DRUG LORD: Aye, love. That's us.

MANCUNIAN DRUG LORD 2: These clowns owe us munny. They can't pay. So they're gonna hafto die.

He chucks the empty canister away.

MADDY: I knaw. They bin unprofessional. They're outta their depth. And p'raps they do deserve punishment.

One MANCUNIAN strikes a match. MADDY instantly blows it out.

MADDY: Me brother and 'is mate 'ave scoured the scrap for the drugs. E kent find it for love nor munny.

MANCUNIAN DRUG LORD 2: Thass their hard cheese.

ENNIS: Cheeeeese…

A match is struck. She blows it out.

MADDY: Yeh but wait. What if I can get yer munny?

ENNIS: Can ya?

MANCUNIAN DRUG LORD DWIGHT: Can ya?

DWIGHT: Can ya?

MADDY: I can. All leb'm grand. But you'll hafto wait til Bank 'oliday Munday. And I'm gonna need my car to do it.

The MANCUNIANS study her, give each other a look, and go.

DWIGHT: But Maddy, what you gonna do?

MADDY: What I always do, bro. What I do best.

R R R R R R R O O O O O R R R R R R R R R R R R - VVVOOOOOOMMMMMMMMM!!!!!!!!!

TANNOY: **Smashin stuff from Kneebone there! And it looks like she might 'ave summin else up 'er sleeve! Right on!**

MADDY: *(To us.)* Me head was a wasp nest o' questions. I was Jed's fav'rite and I wadn't even 'is? Slick knew all these years and never told? And most important of all, does 'ooper even know? If e didn't, well then, 'twas time for the goddamn truth…

MUNROE's garridge.

MADDY arrives. HOOPER emerges with his oily rag.

MADDY: Howdy stranger!

HOOPER: Goddammit. Why you back?

MADDY: Just double-checkin to see if you'd changed yer mind on matters of motors?

HOOPER: I 'ave not.

MADDY: Cus you never knaw, you mighta slept on it and when you woke this mornin you realized that shit, I was that rare kinda bird – a rabid underdog, a symbol of 'ope in a dyin world or a lost soul in dire need – and you thought, to 'ell with it! I'll let go the old grudges, chuck that bad blood down the drain and propel the girl onward to victory! Am I right?

HOOPER: Nope.

MADDY: Please, 'ooper? You must 'ave some weakness!

HOOPER: Too busy. Too pissy. Aren't budgin.

MADDY: *(To us.)* In light o' new information, I try a new tactic.

(To HOOPER.) What if I asked ya to see me less as me father's daughter, and more me mother's?

HOOPER: What e mean?

MADDY: I aren't all Jed, am I? I'm 'alf me mother. And you liked 'er. Right?

HOOPER is silent.

MADDY: Come on, 'oop. I knaw you 'ated Jed, but I bet you always dreamed o' gettin yer 'ands on this bewty.

HOOPER: Damn yer gud.

MADDY: So you'll do it?

HOOPER: I'll take a squint. Assess the damage.

MADDY: Ideal.

HOOPER: She might be too far gone. Aren't makin no promises.

He lays down on a creeper and rolls himself under the Caddy.

MADDY: You go for it, mate. She'll go. You'll see. You gotta give Jed one thing. E did take gud care of 'er.

HOOPER: *(From underneath.)* Took care o' the wrong thing if you ask me.

MADDY: 'oop? Am I like 'er? Me mother, I mean?

HOOPER: You share some similarities. Yer more like 'im.

MADDY: Shit. Really?

HOOPER: Well, you lack 'is vile nature. But you got 'is way wi' words. E'd spin stories like webs.

MADDY: F'kin stories. All bollocks, mind.

HOOPER: E tell ya the one 'bout the gold mine in Arizona?

MADDY: Only every day. And 'ow Elvis usta own this Cadillac.

HOOPER: Thass right. And 'ow 'is Father 'eck used to use a hypnotised rattlesnake as a walkin stick.

MADDY: And 'ow Clint Eastwood popped round the house for tea one time.

HOOPER: *(Slides out from under the car.)* Now that one was true.

MADDY: Eh? Fuck off.

HOOPER: Yeh, you definitely sound like 'im o'right. Write this down: 5862060349.

MADDY scrabbles to catch-up, writes it on a piece of paper.

MADDY: 58620603…

HOOPER: 49.

MADDY: 49.

HOOPER: So we can cross-check the make and model number.

MADDY: Whass she like?

HOOPER: Worse'n I thought. Suspension's gone. We gotta re-fit that, and thass a big job, otherwise you'll drag. Need new gear-box. New clutch. Shocks. S'all gotta come out and be replaced. You kent stick any ole crap in there.

MADDY: Dun't sound too bad.

HOOPER: Then you got yer comp modifications. Requirements for racin. Reinforce the chassis. Thass a massive job. Put a roll-cage in. Take the glass out. Yer lookin at a lotta munny ere.

MADDY: I hafto pay?!

HOOPER: I aren't a charity, maid.

MADDY: Shit. I'm skint as a basterd.

HOOPER: Well. You'll hafto reimburse me with yer winnings thun, wun't ya?

MADDY: You'd do that?

HOOPER: Why not? All I knaw is cars. Ennis couldn't give a crap about'n. Tis nice to 'elp out.

MADDY: 'ooper?

HOOPER: Listen, I knaw you got plenty questions.

MADDY: You do?

HOOPER: But we got less'n three days to get this hunk o' junk ship-shape. If we do this, I suggest we focus, keep the chit-chat to a minimum and knuckle down to a wordless state o' deep concentration. OK?

MADDY: Yep.

HOOPER: Tis damn near impossible in the time we got to get 'er road-worthy. So I'm gonna hafto pull in some favours wi' this.

He takes the scrap of paper with the number on it.

HOOPER: I'm gonna call my mate Dave Speltzer. E's General Motors in Detroit. Cadillac Man. Best in 'is field. I'll run these numbers through 'im, see if e can advise on the fix-up.

MADDY: What the 'ell can e do from Detroit?

HOOPER: I got a risky plan to use Waber carburettors from a Jag engine seein as we ain't got an actual Caddy twin set.

MADDY: Will that work? She's pretty specific.

HOOPER: If anyone'll know, it'll be Dave.

He makes to go.

MADDY: 'ooper? I got summin I need to say…

HOOPER: You'n thank me when we're done. Meantime, get the bleddy kettle on.

He exits.

MADDY: *(To us.)* All I gotta do is say the words 'you are my dad' and tis all 'appy family hugs'n and sparkles and f'kin rainbows!

Golsithney Special Unit – a low security mental institution just off the A30. SLICK stands before us in asylum scrubs.

SLICK: Let me out! I shouldn't be in ere! I ain't mad! I was just teasy thass all! 'ot-'eaded! I wadn't gonna 'urt no one! Oi! You kent keep me in ere! I got shit to do! The bulldozers're comin! I got gold to find! Arizona gold! Kneebone gold!

LORETTA, a wild, white-haired woman, patient of Golsithney, turns. She holds a lump of glittering granite in her hand.

LORETTA: Kneebone? Oo dares speak of Kneebone in ere?

SLICK: Wadn't talkin to you, ole girl. Oi! Guard! I gotta call me family!

LORETTA: I knew I'd 'ave a visitor today. The stones told me. The stones knaw all…

SLICK: I aren't visitin, bird. I'm an inmate. But not for long cus unlike you I aren't stark ravin mad, see?

LORETTA: No one's mad in Golsithney Special Unit, Slick.

SLICK: How'd you know my name?

LORETTA: You dun't remember me do ya? I remember you. Six years old and shittin the bath.

SLICK: 'ow the fuck d'you knaw that?

LORETTA: We'm kin, boy. We'm blud. We'm family. Tis me. Tis yer Auntie Loretta.

SLICK: Auntie 'etta? I ain't seen you fer –

LORETTA: Twenty years I bin in ere! Twenty years of blissful incarceration!

SLICK: 'member Daddy said you went off yer rocker and got sent to Golsithney.

LORETTA: I was never 'sent' anywhere, boy. I committed meself.

SLICK: How come?

LORETTA: Get away from the family. They was drivin me nuts. Awful people they were. How was Jed ever allowed to breed? 'ow many are you now? The Kneebone brood?

SLICK: There's three of us. Me. Dwight. Maddy.

LORETTA: Three?! Christ. Like a damned virus!

SLICK: Auntie? There's summin you should knaw. Our daddy, yer brother, Jed's –

LORETTA: I knaw. Dead. Stones told me. I am sorry for yer loss, boy. But tis also a blessed relief, I'm sure. E was a dreadful asshole.

SLICK: E was a great man!

LORETTA: Asshole. And I tell you this wi' some authority. I was 'is sister. Heck was my father. I saw the poison seep down from generation to generation.

SLICK: Daddy could be 'ard. But that was 'is way. E made me the man I am now.

LORETTA: And what kinda man is that, Slick? I only ask cus me eyes, me eyes are dim, and I cannot see too well these days. Me sense o' smell, however, is still purdy keen. I can tell from ere e left you in deep, deep shit.

SLICK: Nuthin that I kent solve.

LORETTA: And whass e left ya to take upon yer shoulders, boy?

SLICK: I just gotta find eighty-nine grand in unpaid tax to save the Kneebone Ranch from the bulldozers.

LORETTA: See? Asshole.

SLICK: But I got a plan.

LORETTA: Right. Arizona. You think there's gold in them there 'ills?

SLICK: I'm goin after the lost mine Daddy always told me about.

LORETTA: The one Great-Great-Grandfather Tobias found back in 1849? The Kneebone Bonanza?

SLICK: Thass the one!

LORETTA: Great idea Slick, except –

SLICK: What?

LORETTA: It dun't exist!

SLICK: Dun't f'kin tell me that! *Really?!*

LORETTA: Total bullshit. Every word. Good story though, eh?

SLICK: But 'ang on! I found a tobacca tin in Daddy's chest with a nugget o' gold in it! Proof of the family's 'ard rock days!

LORETTA: Oh, that fragment did come from Tobias's Arizona dig o'right.

SLICK: So there *was* a mine!

LORETTA: Riddled wi' rich veins of Iron Pyrites. Fool's Gold. Close to the rich stuff in compound but missin one special property. Any value whatsoever.

SLICK: Fuck! Fuck a f'kin – *duck!* Why would e…? Thass our only 'ope of… What a f'kin – !

LORETTA: Say it. Call the basterd for what e is! Knock'n off 'is pedestal! Cut 'em down to size, leave 'em in the dirt and ride on!

SLICK: Asshole.

LORETTA: Kent hear ya.

SLICK: E's an asshole.

LORETTA: Oo's an asshole?

SLICK: Jed Kneebone is! An asshole!

LORETTA: A dreadful one! Your daddy!

SLICK: My daddy's a DREADFUL ASSHOLE!!!

(To the heavens.) Hear that? Asshole?

LORETTA: Ahhhh! The stones whisper to me! Quartz crystal vibrates ancient truth and 'ums –

SLICK: F'kin stones. Guard!

LORETTA: 'ums from the deep down darkness! You've denounced the bugger. You stand tall like Trethevy quoit, and able to 'ear the voice of truth what emanates from the ancient rock!

(Voices the stone, strangely.) Slick my boy, the curse is lifted! Become the man that nature gifted!

SLICK: Could do. I'm still f'kin buggered though, aren't I?

LORETTA: Yes you are. But I 'ave summin that might 'elp ya.

LORETTA looks around then produces a small leather-bound diary from her jacket.

SLICK: *(In awe.)* No way… The Kneebone Diary?

LORETTA: You got it.

SLICK: Daddy said 'twas lost!

LORETTA: I stole it from 'im right before I put meself in ere. For twenty years I've 'eld safe the contents o' this diary from Jed's grubby 'ands.

SLICK: Whass in it thass so special?

LORETTA: 'North of nuthin, says the stones,
Walk the line then find the bones…'

SLICK: Fuck's that mean?

LORETTA: Dreck'shuns. Clues. Written down by Granddaddy 'eck. To find the treasure!

SLICK: 'ang on a mo. You just told me there was no treasure.

LORETTA: I said 'twas no Arizona Gold. But there *was* a Kneebone Bonanza.

SLICK: Tell me!

LORETTA: There's a vast stash of copper.

SLICK: Copper?

LORETTA: Tons of it. Communications cable. Laid by British Forces in World War Two. Illegally dug up out the ground by Jed and my father. Sold off for profit piece by piece. For a time, we was rich! The munny we made was enuff to set up the Kneebone Scrap Metal Empire. But the good folk of United Downs got suspicious. Caught wind of our thievery and turned on us. 'eck was forced to 'ide what metal was left. One night, e went out and buried it on Kneebone territory. Somewhere out in the Badlands. Wrote down a series of clues that only e could decipher. Then promptly dropped dead. Thass when I nabbed the diary and came ere. But I reckon tis time to hand this over… to you.

SLICK: Copper's worth a fortune, Auntie! How many tons is there? Do you remember?

LORETTA: There was crates of the stuff. Thick as yer arm. And heavy, too.

SLICK: Yeeehoo! I gotta find me that copper!

LORETTA: Find it and put it to good use! Follow the clues, dig that shit up, save the family. Easy. Ere.

She hands him the diary.

SLICK: Cheers for this, Auntie. I'm sorry we all took you for mad as shit. I woulda come visit if I'd knawn you were *this* sane!

LORETTA: G'luck, Slick.

(Voices stone.) G'luck, Slick.

SLICK: *(Hollering.)* Let me out! I shouldn't be in ere! I ain't mad, ya knaw! Oi! Guard!

Scrap yard.

DWIGHT, dressed as a lion, drags ENNIS in. ENNIS has a bag on his head.

DWIGHT: Bundle 'im bundle 'im bundle 'im and –

DWIGHT whips the bag off to reveal… Prince Charles. Or a mask of him.

DWIGHT: We got you, Prince Charles! Now cough up 'undred grand or I'll chuck ya down a mine shaft!

ENNIS takes the mask off.

ENNIS: Is this gonna work, Dwight?

DWIGHT takes his lion head off.

DWIGHT: What e talkin about, bud? We just walked through it. It's fool-proof! We kidnap Prince Charles –

ENNIS: Dressed as a lion?

DWIGHT: It's the Royal Cornwall Show, Ennis! They're all dressed as lions!

ENNIS: And yer sure e'll be there?

DWIGHT: Kenny Mudd got a cousin in Special Branch oo divulged Charlie Boy's gonna chopper in on the Sunday to judge the dog show. We got the intel. Tis a dead cert.

ENNIS: I dunno, mate. I sense disaster.

DWIGHT: I need you, Ennis, I kent kidnap the bugger on me own.

ENNIS: But Maddy said she was gonna win The Boneshaker and pay off the Manchester Crew for us.

DWIGHT: She ain't gonna win, bud. I can tell ya that fer nuthin. Slick'll never let 'er get away with it.

ENNIS: E kent stop 'er. E's locked up in Golsithney inne?

DWIGHT: Look, Maddy got us out the Mank shit and found us some more time, but she ain't gonna solve our shit. That'll be us. We're the boys, Enn. We're the *Boys.*

ENNIS: *(Walking off.)* Sorry Dwight. There's summin funny in my tummy tells me this ain't gonna work.

DWIGHT: Ennis mate, where e goin?

ENNIS: To 'ide. From the gangsters. And try not to get killed. You knaw, me dad said you Kneebones were nuthin but ass-pain and trouble. With a capital T!

DWIGHT: Aw yeh? Well you're Ennis with a silent P!

Exit ENNIS, hurt.

DWIGHT: Sorry, Enn, I didn't mean that. O'right look, we'll keep lookin for the merchandise! It's gotta be round ere somewhere, eh? Ennis? Ennis!

He searches through piles of scrap –

DWIGHT: Shit… shit… shit…

But it's useless. DWIGHT sinks to his knees before JED's grave.

DWIGHT: Daddy, I knaw you was never that keen on me, but like it or no I am your son. Please. Tell me what I gotta do to get outta this mess. Show yerself, Daddy, and 'elp *me.* If this shitty ring does anythin at all let it reveal your spirit to me… now!

He closes his eyes tightly and kisses the ring. As he does so, a man enters before him. This is DUKE LONGHORNE, a strange, rich American.

DUKE: Are you alright, son?

DWIGHT opens his eyes and sees DUKE.

DWIGHT: Daddy? Izzit you?

DWIGHT embraces DUKE.

DUKE: I ain't yer daddy. Now unhand me and step away.

DWIGHT: Sorry, ole chap. I kissed me ring and 'oped for a ghost but uhh… what can I help ya with?

DUKE: I'm lookin' for Jed Kneebone.

DWIGHT: Yer standin on 'im.

DUKE: Say what?

DWIGHT: We buried 'im right where you stand.

DUKE: Ho! He's dead?

DWIGHT: As a donut.

DUKE: Ain't you brutes heard of gravestones round these parts?

DWIGHT: Yeh. They'm pricy. We'm skint.

DUKE: You his boy?

DWIGHT: One ob'm. There's Baby Sister (she's a girl) and then me and me brother Slick.

DUKE: Slick. Shit. And you must be…

DWIGHT: Dwight.

DUKE: Dwight. Right. Jed. Dead. Damn. I knew the Old World was goin', but now it's truly gone. Jed was the last of his kind. Sheee-it.

DWIGHT: There's folk singin hallelujah round the village. You a mate of 'is?

DUKE: Name's Longhorne. Duke Lornhorne. I've travelled all the way from Phoenix, Arizona to see the S.O.B. but ahh, too late. Too late…

DWIGHT: You knew 'im?

DUKE: Oh, I knew him. I came here once, as a young man, in search of my ancestors. Built pumps. For mines. I met your daddy at the Race-Way and we got to talkin'. It was like we were long lost family members. Hell, p'raps we were wayback in the tangle of time! He invited me to stay in that very house yonder.

DWIGHT: Thass our house!

DUKE: Right. And where is your mother, that exquisite white rose, who held all us love-struck fools in the palm of her hand?

DWIGHT: Oh. Mum. She…

DUKE: When?

DWIGHT: Dunno. I was three. Twenty-odd years ago now.

DUKE: Damn. She was…

DWIGHT: Yeh. She was. Sorry you come all this way, Duke, and that they're both, ya knaw, dead. But thass life, I spus?

DUKE: It does seem that my comin' over has somewhat been in vain. Unless *you* can answer one question for me?

DWIGHT: Shoot.

DUKE: Did Jed keep a hold of 'is cars?

DWIGHT: Eh?

DUKE: Strange question, I know. I'm talking about one car in particular. A 1958 Cadillac Eldorado?

DWIGHT: Maybe…

DUKE: Reason I ask, and the reason I'm here, is that was my Cadillac, see? I lost 'er to Jed in a idjit drunken goddamn card game! ('scuse my French.) Jed was loaded. He coulda bought his own damn car. But he wanted mine. It killed me to hand 'er over. For years I've had his words rollin' round my skull –

JED: *(A voice.)* If you ever land on yer feet, Longhorne, and if ever I'm stony-broke, come on over and buy 'er back off me!

DUKE: So here I am. Hopin' somewhat uncharitably that times is now hard for you Kneebones and that Jed kept my precious vehicle in mint condition and may wanna sell it. For a sweet price.

DWIGHT: Wait. You wanna buy back the Caddy?

DUKE: I've made a lotta munny in the intervening years. I've tried to fill my empty life with the finer things. But I never felt complete without my beloved Caddy. Yes, I want it back son. And I am willing to pay whatever the hell it takes!

DWIGHT smiles.

The sound of roaring engines hurtling past – RAAAAA-RAAAHHHHHOOOWW!!!!

TANNOY: **And they're comin round the bend at full throttle! Tis only a matter o' time now before the first collision, ladies and gents!**

HOOPER's garridge.

MADDY alone. The sound of a purring, powerful car pulling in…

MADDY: *(To us.)* A car glides into the forecourt, creepin like a shadow. Its engine purs, deep and crisp and evil. Before us, a battered black hearse. Patched-up but magnificent. The driver emerges bent and broken, and hobbles t'ward me. It kent be. But it is… My childhood hero. Ex-queen of The Boneshaker. Phylis Vanloo.

Enter PHYLIS VANLOO. She is a completely different person now. She's stiff, bent, broken. She has a black cane with a silver skull on it. Her whole body creaks with the braces on her limbs.

PHYLIS: Munroe about?

MADDY: On the phone.

PHYLIS: Be long, will e?

MADDY: I shouldn't think so. E's just placing a call to – *(Blurts.)* I'm your biggest fan, Ms. Vanloo!

PHYLIS: Are ya now?

MADDY: 'Twas you made me wanna become a stock car racer.

PHYLIS: Is that what you are?

MADDY: I will be. Soon. Come Munday. You gave me some advice when I was six years old.

PHYLIS: Oh yeh? What did I say?

MADDY: Fear nuthin. Become one wi' the car. For Death or Glory.

PHYLIS: Nuggets all. You keep at it, girl. And ya knaw, if you try 'ard and do yer best, one day you could grow up to look just… like… me…

MADDY's smile fades as HOOPER enters.

HOOPER: I left Dave a message but e'll get back to us quick.

PHYLIS: Howzit hangin, 'oop?

HOOPER: Christ! Phylis? Long time no see. Yer lookin… well.

PHYLIS: No need for sweet-talk, 'oop. I knaw what I look like. A vengeful spirit resurrected. Give the Banshee a toon-up wouldya?

HOOPER: No can do, Phylis. I'm proper stacked.

PHYLIS: C'mon Munroe. After all I bin through?

HOOPER: I didn't think you survived that terrible day.

PHYLIS: Nearly didn't. I used me prize munny to 'ave meself put back together by the finest surgeons in Treliske. My body is a mass o' scars and crooked from all they broken bones set bad. Two 'undred steel pins holdin me spine in place.

HOOPER: I saw you stretchered-out. Yer damn 'elmet was cracked in two. Yer head was –

PHYLIS: Obliterated. Pulverised. Smashed to atoms. I gotta titanium skull now.

HOOPER: You sure paid the price for winnin that race.

PHYLIS: I'd do it all again. In fact –

HOOPER: God, no!

PHYLIS: I'm makin me big comeback. This is Bank 'oliday Munday, the Banshee shall ride the raceway once more! Gonna reclaim my title.

MADDY: What?!

PHYLIS: You dun't rate the idea, miss?

MADDY: No! I mean, I do! It's just…

HOOPER: She's enterin too.

PHYLIS: So I heard. You dun't look like Boneshaker material to me, bird. Gotta car?

HOOPER: Oh, she's gotta car.

PHYLIS: Is that what I think it is?

MADDY: The Kneebone Cadillac.

PHYLIS: 'ow thrillin! Long 'ave I dreamt of decimatin this magnificent mow-sheen on the Race-Way. How'd e prise it out of Jed's sweaty grip?

MADDY: E gave it me on 'is deathbed.

PHYLIS: Well! The Kneebones and the Munroes all snuggled up together. This is a turn-up for the books.
Poor Jed'd be spinnin in 'is grave! 'specially if e knew 'is beloved car was about to be taken apart by yours truly.

MADDY: Well. Maybe you'll take it apart. Maybe you wun't.

PHYLIS: I gave you advice back along. Now lemme give you some more, my darlin. Beware The Boneshaker. You might not come out of it as pretty as I did.

MADDY: I'm gonna win.

PHYLIS: Whassat?

MADDY: Said I'm gonna win.

PHYLIS: There's a fire in you. I like it. Tis a rare quality these days. Where'd e acquire that to, I wonder? This *rage.* Cultivated by yer complicated upbringing, I'll wager. Jed wadn't the most loving of fathers eh? And then of course there's yer poor mother's untimely death. Yesss. That'd put a tiger in yer tank!

HOOPER: O'right, Phylis –

PHYLIS: And then there's the whole sordid question over oo your daddy really is.

HOOPER: Thass enuff, Vanloo!

PHYLIS: What? The child oughta knaw! I bet they Kneebones just swept it under the carpet. 'nother skeleton in the closet!

HOOPER: We dun't 'ave time for this.

MADDY: Thing is Phylis, I know oo my real father is.

PHYLIS: Oh ya do, do ya?

MADDY: I do.

PHYLIS: Yer up to speed. More power to yer elbow. Good fer you. Question what niggles me is oo told Jed that yer daddy was Duke Longhorne?

MADDY: Eh?

PHYLIS: Cus I remember yer mother tellin me in the strickest o' confidence that she'd ad a ding-dong wi' some Yank oo'd come over. That was the last time I saw 'er before she, ya knaw, died givin birth to you.

HOOPER: Jesus, Vanloo.

MADDY: *(To HOOPER.)* But I thought you loved 'er…

HOOPER: *(Taken aback.)* Loved your mother? I ad feelins for 'er but… she never ad eyes for me.

MADDY: I dun't understand.

PHYLIS: Oh, Maddy dear, you… you thought that… you did, you thought that 'ooper was daddy!

MADDY: What? No I never! I just… Longhorne. Yes. E's my… uhh.

(Changes tack.) Know what? I just remembered I gotta pick up me brother from the asylum. Sorry to dash.

MADDY gets in the Caddy –

PHYLIS: Shame. She looked like a worthy opponent.

MADDY drives. The sound of her mobile ringing. It goes to answer machine.

HOOPER: *(Voice only.)* Maddy, it's 'ooper. I'm not sure what just happened there. Look, that woman's awful wicked. She'll do anythin to win. Come back and let's get on wi' the repairs. Call me if ya get this.

Scrap yard.

MADDY enters. SLICK is already there, standing over the grave.

MADDY: I's gonna come pick you up.

SLICK: They called next of kin. Carol came. She vouched for me.

MADDY: Thass good.

SLICK: Didn't feel good. Li'l Kelly seein me shuffle out a mental 'ospital. But I got to see 'er for the first time in ages.

MADDY: I'm glad, Slick.

SLICK: I shouldna told you 'bout Daddy like that. In that way. Pissed up on the Badlands and bearin arms.

MADDY: When was you gonna tell me? When was any bugger?

SLICK: I dunno. I just thought Daddy woulda got round to it 'ventually.

MADDY: Tis all by the by now, anyways.

SLICK: Better off without'n. Daddy's fulla shit. I's too blind to see it. You wadn't. You was bang on the munny.

MADDY: Christ, what happened to you up Golsithney?

SLICK: Met Auntie Loretta.

MADDY: Loopy Loretta?! Thought she died!

SLICK: She ain't dead and she ain't loopy. She talks to stones but besides that she's pretty straight. She put me right on a couple things. Plus, she gave me this! The Kneebone Diary!

He shows her the diary.

MADDY: No f'kin way!

SLICK: Yes f'kin way! This diary 'olds the key to our salvation, Mads. And tis right under our nawses!

Enter DWIGHT, breathless. He has a heavy sports bag with him.

DWIGHT: There you are! Now dun't go mad. I done summin radical. Brilliant. But radical. Ready? Dun't go mad –

He opens up a bag full of money.

SLICK: Where'd e git that sorta cash?

DWIGHT: Sold the Caddy.

SLICK: You what?!

DWIGHT: You said you wouldn't go mad!

SLICK: No I never!

DWIGHT: Guess how much?

SLICK: Didn't I tell ya not to do that?

DWIGHT: Guess how much?

SLICK: How much?

DWIGHT: 100K. 100K. 100 sweet-ass K! We can pay the debtors off *and* the Manchester Crew. Thass f'kin gud innit? C'mon, Kneebones! You gotta admit, thass Dwight on fire, thass is! I knaw I do fuck most things up but this is the first scheme I pulled off whass ever worked, innit? You gotta gimme some credit for this!

SLICK inspects the money.

SLICK: Dwight, brother… You are a bleddy genius!

DWIGHT: Am I?

SLICK: You should've asked me first!

DWIGHT: I knaw. I woulda. But I ad to strike quick, Slick! Like Daddy always taught us.

SLICK: Daddy be damned! This is you, brother. You turned this family's fortunes around!

DWIGHT: Yeehoo!

SLICK: And I got the Kneebone Diary ere. There's a wealth o' copper cable buried somewhere on this land and this book will lead right us to it.

DWIGHT: Say that again.

SLICK: We're f'kin rich, bro!

They dance in celebration.

MADDY: I was gonna race that car Bank 'oliday Munday, Dwight.

DWIGHT: Yeh well. Ten pissy grand 'gainst my 'undred ain't no contest at all, Mads.

MADDY: That car wadn't yours to sell, bro.

SLICK: Not strickly true now, girl, given the light shed on your murky origins.

DWIGHT: Eh?

SLICK: Daddy ain't 'er daddy. 'ooper is.

DWIGHT: Aw.

MADDY: Oo'd you sell 'er to, Dwight?

DWIGHT: Well. Weird story. I was out ere earlier when this freaky 'merican dude turns up out the f'kin blue claimin e'd pay through 'is teef for the Eldorado. Said e was the one brung the Caddy to Daddy in the first place. Went be the name of Duke Longhorne.

MADDY: Ha! 'course e did!

DWIGHT: Duke Longhorne?

MADDY: Oo else would it be, on this day o' days?!

DWIGHT: I went for broke and e delivered. One 'undred thou'. In the bag.

SLICK: Good goin, bro.

MADDY: *Great* goin, bro.

DWIGHT: I knaw you ad yer heart set on this race, Mads. I knaw 'twas yer 'big dream' or whatever. But let's face it, you'da never won.

SLICK: No. Never. E's right. Now get on the accounts and make sure we dun't hafto pay no tax for this cash! I gotta call Carol.

DWIGHT: I gotta phone Ennis.

They both get their mobiles out and dial. MADDY goes to the accounts.

SLICK: Carol. It's me –

DWIGHT: 'right Enn? Tis Dwightastic ere.

SLICK: Listen, 'twas gud to see you yesterday –

DWIGHT: Dude, our problems are over.

SLICK: No, I knaw. But it was a start and I –

DWIGHT: Ole Dwighty boy's sorted it out.

SLICK: I wanted to tell ya: no more cash troubles.

SLICK & DWIGHT: I got the munny.

DWIGHT: Sold the damned Caddy din I mate.

SLICK: Sold the Cadillac. Dwight did.

DWIGHT: What e mean: your idea? Was it fuck!

SLICK: *(Weighing a wodge of bank notes.)* No, it's ere. It's right in front o' me.

DWIGHT: One 'undred K, baby. 89 to the stop the bulldozers –

SLICK: And leb'm to pay off Dwight's drug lords.

DWIGHT: Which I'll do tomorra.

SLICK: Meantime, I'm goin pub. Fancy it?

DWIGHT: Toast my goddamn genius. Drinks on me. See ya there…

They exit leaving MADDY alone to work on the accounts. JED speaks to her from Beyond.

JED: Thass that thun. Order's bin restored. Brothers'll pay off the debts. Everythin's wrapped up nicely. Job done. Except –

MADDY: Except they sold me car and did not give two shits. I've lost. I've no 'ope of racin. I've no damned car. What else am I to do?

JED: Talk to yer daddy.

MADDY: I am.

JED: Yer new daddy.

MADDY: 'ooper?

HOOPER: Yer *other* new daddy.

MADDY: Longhorne!

Brakes squeal. MADDY stands before the Caddy. LONGHORNE sits at the wheel.

DUKE: You're my what?!

MADDY: Yer goddamn daughter, Duke!

DUKE: How is that even possible?

MADDY: You ad a ding-dong wi' me mother eighteen-odd year ago, remember?

DUKE: Oh, sweet Lord!

MADDY: You believe me?

DUKE: I've always had this empty place in my heart. I thought wealth and riches would fill it. It did not. I hoped the Caddy would, too. Yet I found a treasure of a wholly different kind.

MADDY: Me!

DUKE: I have a lot to make up for.

MADDY: Yes indeed, pops.

DUKE: What can I do? You name it, it's yours.

MADDY: Can I borrow yer car?

DUKE: Borrow?

MADDY: For The Boneshaker?

DUKE: Might get trashed.

MADDY: There is that chance.

DUKE: So to borrow it is –

MADDY: Yer right. Best just gimme it.

DUKE: But then you wouldn't appreciate its value.

MADDY: Oh, I appreciate its value o'right.

DUKE: Tell ya what. You can have it.

MADDY: Cheers, daddio!

DUKE: But you gotta buy it back off me.

MADDY: Thass 100k! Where the fuck am I gonna find –

(PING! – a lightbulb moment.) 'undred grand comin right up, pops!

(To us.) As me brothers drank the pub dry, I took the Caddy round to 'ooper and demanded e got to work immediately. Duke came. And Jed was there too, in spectral form! It was kinda sweet! The three ob'm there, tappin their feet to Johnny Cash as the transmission got replaced and new shocks went in and by God, by the time they were done I swear that car looked factory-new! The time ad come. And I was ready.

RAAWWWWWWWWWWWW-NNNNNNNNNNNNNNNNN!!!!!!!

The United Downs Race-Way.

It's night. There's smoke and roar, pounding music and cheering. MADDY and PHYLIS ceremoniously don their helmets, give each other the eye and get in their cars as –

TANNOY: **And it's a pit-stop for the last drivers remainin. Time to draw breath one last time before we speed full-tilt into the grand finale! There's everythin to play for and everythin to lose!**

Next day, the Kneebone House –

Enter SLICK and DWIGHT, hungover.

SLICK: O'right bro?

DWIGHT: O'right bro?

SLICK: Beautiful Bank 'oliday Monday.

DWIGHT: Even me 'angover feels pleasant today.

SLICK: I knaw what you mean, bro. I feel wildly optimistic about literally everythin.

DWIGHT: I knaw what you mean, bro. Right. I'm off to pay the Manchester crew their leb'm grand.

SLICK: And I'm off to pay the Revenue eighty-nine K and call they basterd bailiffs off. Let's divvy it up.

They open the bag and freeze –

DWIGHT: Whass all this?

SLICK: Whass all what?

(He inspects the contents of the bag.) Old receipts? Ledgers?

DWIGHT: This ain't right, Slick! We bin robbed!

SLICK: No, brother. We bin stitched up!

DWIGHT & SLICK: *Maddy!*

RUUUUUUUU-RRRRRROOOOOOARRRRRRRRRRRRRRRRR RR!!!!!!!

TANNOY: ***Annnnnd* they're off on the final leg of this extraordinary contest!**

MADDY drives the Caddy. PHYLIS is in the Banshee. They tear around the track.

TANNOY: **Truly, this 'as bin a Boneshaker for the ages! Ere comes veteran o' the Race-Way Phylis Vanloo –**

PHYLIS: Outta my way, dipstick!

PHYLIS jerks her wheel – KERR-RASSHHH!

TANNOY: **She just wheel-slammed 'ank Carlyon into the wall! E'll feel that in the mornin! First-timer Maddy Kneebone swoops in –**

MADDY: Take no prisoners!

MADDY spins her wheel – SSSCRREEEEE-DOFFF!!!

TANNOY: **Side-swipes current title-holder Barry Polmassick and flips 'im like a burger!**

MADDY: Kiss my chassis, Barry!

TANNOY: **Kneebone takes the lead –**

The GHOST OF JED appears in the Caddy beside MADDY.

MADDY: What the fuck you doin ere?! Tryin to f'kin concentrate!

The roar of the cars cuts out dead –

Kneebone Territory – the Badlands.

SLICK has the Diary held out before him and reads.

SLICK: 'North of nuthin, says the stones,
Walk the line then find the bones…'

(He stops.) Walk the line?' Johnnie Cash lyric innit? Walk. Walk where? What line? Shit. I'm close, Auntie Loretta! I can almost smell that f'kin copper!

Elsewhere, DWIGHT and ENNIS dig with shovels. A shadowy MANCUNIAN DRUG LORD holds a torch on them both.

MANCHUNIAN DRUG LORD: Keep diggin, boys. Nice'n deep, yeh?

ENNIS: Why they got us diggin, Dwight?

DWIGHT: To hide the bodies, Ennis.

ENNIS: What bodies, Dwight?

DWIGHT: *Our* bodies, Ennis…

They dig.

SLICK: *(Reads the diary again.)*
'Where treasure 'ides, time 'as forgot
But Daddy 'eck 'as marked the spot!'
'eck marked the spot? *'eck's marked the spot!* But *where?!*
Auntie Loretta! These clues make no sense whatsofuckinever!

Back to the roar of the race –

TANNOY: **Ere's Johnnie 'T-Bird' 'awkins caught in a Banshee-Cadillac samwich! E kent go nowhere! Ere comes the Fender-bender! Ouch! Thass Johnnie out the race!**

MADDY: You still ere, old man?

TANNOY: **Only two vehicles remain. It's Kneebone and Vanloo, neck n' neck and at each other's throats! There can be only one queen o' the raceway!**

PHYLIS spins the wheel. KER-RUNCH!!!

TANNOY: **Vanloo's taken a chunk outta the Caddy! Kneebone's all over the shop –**

MADDY spins the wheel. BOOMMM!!!

TANNOY: **Kneebone retaliates with a vicious nudge! Vanloo's in a spin! Can she recover?**

Breaks squeal. MADDY's stopped. VANLOO's stopped. Both are breathless. Engines idle.

TANNOY: **The two opponents, now face to face. Two titans of the stock car. The air is absolutely electric!**

PHYLIS: *(Shouting to MADDY.)* I 'ope you like 'ospital food Kneebone, cus thass what you'll be eatin from now on!

MADDY stares.

PHYLIS: *(Shouting.)* I shall use your sweet young blud to paint my wings! You hear me?

MADDY stares.

PHYLIS: *(Shouting.)*

Yer daddy must be so proud, girl! Oh wait – which one?

MADDY: Let's quit the chat Vanloo and finish this!

MADDY revs. Stares. PHYLIS's grin falters.

TANNOY: **It appears our champions are about to enter into a deadly game of Chicken…**

MADDY: I'd get the fuck outta this car if I were you, Dad!

JED leaps out the Caddy and watches on.

TANNOY: **In a battle of nerves, no one swerves!**

PHYLIS: I made you, Maddy Kneebone!

MADDY: I am one wi' the car!

PHYLIS: I can destroy you!

MADDY: I fear nuthin. I need no one!

PHYLIS: For Death –

MADDY: Or Glory!

MADDY floors it. So does PHYLIS. They careen towards each other screaming and – KERRRRRRRRRRRRRRRRRRRRR-RASSSSHHHHHHHHHHHHHHHH!!!!!!!!!

TANNOY: **That was Absolute Carmageddon! Surely no bugger coulda survived that... But wait... there's someone in the smoke... emergin from the flamin wreckage...**

From the flames, MADDY emerges dazed with the steering wheel in one hand, crash helmet in the other.

TANNOY: **And the winner o' this year's United Downs Boneshaker Stock Car race in 'er 1958 Cadillac Eldorado is... Maddy Kneebone!**

Wild cheering as she holds the steering wheel aloft in triumph. She sees JED. JED doffs his hat and disappears into the smoke.

The Kneebone Yard –

MADDY: *(To us.)* Remarkably, me brothers didn't kill me for stealin the 100K. Turns out they was so relieved wi' how it all came out in the wash –

DWIGHT: The Manks got us diggin our own graves –

ENNIS: Just like in the movies.

DWIGHT: We was shittin it big-time, wadn't we Enn?

ENNIS: We thought this was curtains for Ennis and Dwight.

DWIGHT: But then one o' the Manks stopped and said –

ENNIS: *(Mank accent.)* 'What's the ring on your finger, son?'

DWIGHT: Masonic Ring, I says. And the Manky drug lord says –

ENNIS: *(Mank accent.)* 'You're not in the Masons, are ya?'

DWIGHT: Ennis smashes the accent, dunne Mads? Anyways, I think fast and say: Ummmmmmm… yeh? I *am* in the Masons. So's Ennis. We're 'igh-rankin members o' the Grand Lodge or whatever the fuck I said.

ENNIS: And the Manks give each other a look and then –

DWIGHT: Gone! They peg it back to Manky-land. If Daddy adn't bestowed me this ring, mine and Ennis's ass would be grass.

ENNIS: But then this is when it gets really weird!

DWIGHT: Cus in the grave we dug, out on the Badlands there, we 'it summin, down in the dirt –

SLICK enters with a length of thick gleaming copper cable.

SLICK: Copper! They'd found it! Crates o' the stuff! Damn near ten ton of it! The Kneebone Bonanza!

DWIGHT: Ten ton? Whass that in real munny?

MADDY: *(To us.)* Copper's four forty-five a pound on the market. Thass eight thousand nine 'undred quid a ton. Which d'bring ten ton to the value of… eighty-nine K.

SLICK: Perfect! Pay them basterd bailiffs off to the penny once we sell it!

MADDY: Thass a job for you two innit?

DWIGHT: Dwight and Ennis? Copper merchants? What e think Enn?

ENNIS: Long as there's no cheese involved, Dwight, I'm up for it.

MADDY: *(To us.)* Gotta letter from Auntie Loretta.

She reads it as –

LORETTA: Dearest Maddy, Congrats on the race. I'm glad that dreadful car was finally put to gud use. Now that me brother's passed I can at long last put some family matters straight wi' ya. See, there was always some confusion 'bout oo yer daddy actually was. I'm sure by now you knaw t'wadn't Jed. Despite what you may've heard, it idn't 'ooper Munroe. And t'idn some Yank named Duke Longhorne either. Now that Jed's dead I can *finally* tell you the truth about oo yer father *really* is –

MADDY: Christ. Not another one?!

LORETTA: Yer mother told me in strickest o' confidence that the chap she'd a big ding-dong with was –

Pause.

Clint Eastwood.

MADDY: Clint Eastwood?!

LORETTA: Yes. Clint's daddy. True.

MADDY: *(To us.)* And it could well be. Legend 'as it that e came to visit several times.

LORETTA: Christ, e loved yer mother. 'Twas all very tricky. Anyhow, I thought you should knaw. Yours, Auntie Loretta.

Enter CLINT, spurs a-jangling.

MADDY: Howdy Clint. Nice to meet ya. Name's Maddy. I'm yer illegitimate daughter from United Downs near St. Day what you never knew you ad. You OK wi' that?

CLINT: Yup.

Exit CLINT, spurs a-jangling.

MADDY: *(To us.)* I ad a whole welter o' Daddies to chose from! I didn't need to pick one! After checkin out Clint, I could head for Arizona, get to knaw Duke some more. Or I could stay ere and ask Munroe for a job at 'is garridge. The opportunities are endless. But first, I think I'm gonna use my prize munny to buy a nice lump o'granite. There's an old cowboy in dire need of a headstone. E deserves that, at the very least... The debt e left us would get paid off in copper. But we was still skint and prayin for f'kin miracles.

SLICK: Ere Maddy, you sure you wanna put the Caddy through the crusher?

MADDY: I got a steerin wheel and some bruises to boot. Thass momentos enuff for me, Slick. Time to say goodbye to the ole thing.

(To us.) I saw no sense in keepin it. She'd served 'er purpose. In more ways'n one.

SLICK: Last chance!

MADDY: Scrap the fucker!

The sound of a slow hydraulic hiss as the Cadillac is crushed. Then, a claw is slowly lowered in. The claw opens and a block of crushed metal is dumped with an almighty WHUMP! at MADDY's feet.

MADDY: Thanks for the car, Jed.

MADDY's mobile rings.

MADDY: 'right 'oop?

HOOPER: Maddy! You ain't still got that Cadillac steering wheel to 'and, 'ave ya?

MADDY: I 'ave indeed, 'oop.

HOOPER: Can you check summin for me? See if the centre of the wheel itself, the 'ub of it, comes loose or lifts off…?

MADDY: *(Checking.)* It comes off, yeh.

HOOPER: OK. Maddy, is there anythin written inside?

MADDY: There is but tis 'ard to read…

HOOPER: Can ya clean it up?

MADDY: There's an inscription of some kind…

HOOPER: Tell me what it says.

MADDY: It says… 'Dear Elvis. 'appy birthday. Yours, Johnnie Cash.'

HOOPER: My God. It's true! Dave Speltzer called me back from Detroit, *ravin.* E cross-checked the model number. E couldn't believe what e found. Maddy, you are the owner of a one-off purpose-built car that Cadillac themselves thought was lost. Jed wadn't makin this up! It did belong to Elvis Presley! And ere's the news – it's worth MILLIONS! (*MADDY looks at the crushed cube beside her.*) Now, I knaw the car's in bad shape. But I think I could fix 'er up. Whadda ya reckon? Maddy? Maddy? You there?

MADDY: 'oop, I'm gonna hafto call ya back.

SLICK and DWIGHT join her.

SLICK: What did 'ooper want?

MADDY: Oh you know 'ooper. Nuthin really. You wouldn't be interested.

SLICK: Look, Maddy. E's yer daddy. And tis true, we did 'ate 'is guts. But all that shit's behind us now.

DWIGHT: Yeh, all that shit's behind us now.

SLICK: No more secrets, eh?

MADDY: Right, brother. No more secrets.

The End.

Thank you...

To my mum and dad for the endless inspiration, to my sister Natalie, who knows more than anyone what's made up in these plays and what isn't. Love you all.

To Si, Dan, Brett – the Harvey brothers who become the Gunwallow brothers literally ten years ago to the day! Thank you, boys. You rocked. Time for a sequel?

To the brilliant producer Claire Grove who commissioned an early version of *49 Donkeys Hanged* and the *Kneebone* clan for BBC radio. Thanks Claire. Miss you. Hell yeh.

To the brilliant casts and production teams on all of these plays at The Drum Theatre, Plymouth – and in particular to Louise Schumann, David Prescott and Simon Stokes, who commissioned and directed all but one of these plays. Simon's passion for new writing knows no bounds – and I thank him for his endless wisdom, endless support and his (sort of) endless patience. Thanks Simon. Always exciting!

To my amazing partner Mandy and our beautiful boy, Arthur. Thank you for everything. I love you both so much. These are for you.

And finally to Nick Darke… who encouraged, understood, laughed, raged, took the piss, forewarned, forbade, challenged and advised in all the right places, and whose incredible words still echo daily.

Thanks, Nick.

(PS I'm still working on that "one-roomer".)

Carl Grose
August, 2019

Carl Grose was born in Cornwall in 1975. His plays include *Quick Silver, Superstition Mountain, Grand Guignol, The 13 Midnight Challenges of Angelus Diablo, Stay Brave Brian Gravy, Gargantua, Wormy Close, Horse Piss For Blood, 49 Donkeys Hanged, The Kneebone Cadillac* and *The No-Brainer.* Other writing includes *Beauty & The Beast, The Dark Philosophers* and *Never Try This at Home* (Told By An Idiot), *Oedipussy* (Spymonkey), *Alaska* (Black Fish), *The Hartlepool Monkey* (Gyre & Gimble) and the musical *The Grinning Man* (Bristol Old Vic / Trafalgar Studios). Carl also works with the internationally acclaimed theatre company Kneehigh for the past 25 years. He has appeared in numerous shows including Nick Darke's *The King of Prussia* and *The Riot, Nights at The Circus, Cymbeline, Blast!* and *Hansel & Gretel.* Writing for Kneehigh includes *Tristan & Yseult, The Bacchae* (both with Anna Maria Murphy), *Wagstaffe the Wind-up Boy, Cymbeline, Hansel & Gretel, The Wild Bride, Dead Dog in a Suitcase,* and most recently *The Tin Drum.*

A NOTE ON THE COVER ART

The cover illustration to this collection is by Daryl Waller, my favourite living artist in the whole world. Incredibly we grew up within the self-same square mile in the fine cathedral city of Truro. The moment I laid eyes on his picture 'Yeti', I fell in love with it, and knew it should be a book cover. It is such a thrill to have it as my book cover.

For me, the picture throws up so many feelings, so many meanings, tells so many stories. Like all of Daryl's work it inspires me to work. But I also wanted it for my cover because, to me, it perfectly personifies the playwriting process. The Yeti, caught, exposed, nowhere to run. The solitary log cabin. The baying mob complete with flaming torches. The innocent, collapsed, perhaps dead. And, of course, a watermelon.

When you can encapsulate a state of mind and a creative process and a way of life with a simple image like this, who needs words?

Daryl's work can be seen and purchased at Darylwaller.com

By the same author

Hansel & Gretel
ISBN: 9781849430579

The Dark Philosophers
ISBN: 9781849431460

Dead Dog in a Suitcase (and other love songs)
ISBN: 9781783191567

www.ingramcontent.com/pod-product-compliance
Ingram Content Group UK Ltd.
Pitfield, Milton Keynes, MK11 3LW, UK
UKHW020719280225
455688UK00012B/419

9 781786 825674